The Sociological Interpretation
of Religion

The Sociological Interpretation
of Religion

ROLAND ROBERTSON

Associate Professor of Sociology, University of Pittsburgh

OXFORD
BASIL BLACKWELL
1970

631 09870 4 Cloth bound edition
631 09860 7 Paper bound edition

Library of Congress Catalog
Card Number: 69–20430

Printed in Great Britain by
Western Printing Services Ltd Bristol,
and bound by The Kemp Hall Bindery, Oxford

In memory of my father

Contents

Acknowledgments

This book has been written as one of a series of introductions to major topics in the field of sociology. The editor of the series has, however, been indulgent enough to allow me to attempt also to break new ground in the sociology of religion. The effort to accomplish both of these goals has required much more moral support than I envisaged at the outset and thus my primary acknowledgment must be to Jenny Robertson. Her encouragement and assistance have ranged from the mundane and practical to the purely intellectual. I cannot thank her enough for tolerating, and facilitating the production of, 'the religion book'.

My profuse thanks go to Bryan Wilson, who helped to crystallize my interest in the sociology of religion when I was a graduate student at the University of Leeds (1961–2) and who has continued to stimulate this interest ever since that period. He has been so kind and generous with his time as to read the entire manuscript, offering detailed suggestions and criticisms. Without him this book would have been significantly the poorer; although, of course, he bears no responsibility for the contents.

Friends who have helped me in numerous discussions include Joseph Seldin, Andrew Tudor, Burkart Holzner and Bob Towler. I am specially grateful to Peter Nettl and Herminio Martins for having demonstrated to me the intellectual rewards to be gained from taking 'the larger view' of sociological problems and for stimulating many of my current interests. I also wish to acknowledge the help of Stuart Mews and Edmund Johnson.

On the secretarial side, I am extremely grateful for the conscientious assistance of Josephine Stagno at the University of Pittsburgh and Sue Best and Marion Pocock at the University of Essex.

1

Introduction

As is the case in most branches of sociology, the sociology of
religion has been introduced and outlined in books and monographs
on many occasions during the last ten years or so. Numerous books
of readings and selections from the field have also appeared. My
purpose in writing this book has been different from most others—
which is not to say that there is no need for introductory texts and
sets of readings. Whether this difference of approach is worthwhile
will, of course, be for others to judge. All the same, my reasons for
both trying to make it different and concluding that it is so at the
stage of publication should be specified.

With but a few exceptions, recent offerings in the field of the
sociology of religion as a whole have failed to question the boundaries and assumptions of the sub-discipline.[1]* Perhaps the term
'sub-discipline' pinpoints part of the problem. It seems that many
sociologists believe the area of inquiry has been adequately staked-
out and to this extent they are willing to accept what has been
available at the time of writing as an appropriate demarcation of the
relevant from the irrelevant. This point is, in the case of the sociology
of religion, bound up closely with certain accumulated 'neuroses'
about the alleged dangers of getting too involved in religious as
opposed to sociological questions—so avoiding the undeniable
proposition that religious commitment is nothing if not primarily
a cultural phenomenon and that the same is true of sociology.
Recently there has also been an ethnocentric type of parochialism
in the field, which has led to sociologists ignoring much of the
highly significant literature on non-Western societies to be found in
the work of anthropologists and students of comparative religion. It
must be readily conceded in reference to this last point that the

* Notes for this chapter begin on page 6.

B

present book is not by any means as adventurous as the author would ideally have wished it to be. But the compelling concern to do something to offset professional and sub-disciplinary parochialism has, at least in terms of effort, been followed through from the original programming of this book. It is for these reasons that the title of the book should be taken as literally as possible. It *has* been conceived of as a discussion of the sociological interpretation of religion—being therefore primarily concerned with assumptions, perspectives, ways of analysing religious phenomena and so on. This statement does *not* mean, however, that I am solely concerned with the adumbration of a new paradigmatic or analytic framework. Much more is at issue than this. Bearing in mind that the book is, for extra-intellectual reasons, intended to introduce the reader to the field it does contain what might be called cross-summaries of important works in the sociology of religion. By 'cross-summary' I mean a sustained attempt to bring together comparable propositions on similar themes from different contributors to the sociology of religion—trying, in other words, to get at the basic preoccupations of the sociological study of religion in a more satisfactory manner than the well-tried (and badly wanting) *ad hoc* procedure. In more substantive, intellectual-scientific terms, the reader will discover fairly extensive discussions of what the author regards as the most salient contributions to the field. Salience in this connection does not necessarily mean intellectually outstanding. More often than not the latter *is* the criterion of salience—but other contributions are discussed where they assist in the illustration and elaboration of a particular theme.

On the basis of these comments it should be obvious that the reader is not going to be presented with much in the way of empirical data either of a quantitative or qualitative kind, although frequent indirect allusions are made to empirical data. (Moreover most of the chapters incorporate, pay respect to and are partly based upon empirical data.) There are plenty of data in the existing body of work in the field, many of them having been made available in a form which bears on another characteristic of the present contribution: the analysis in the following chapters is only in part concerned with what is frequently called institutional religion—that is visible religious commitment and practice as these are discoverable in terms of formal organizations and culturally well-accepted conceptions.[2] Rather, the analysis tries to get behind and reconstruct some of the usual categories.

Three major preoccupations mark this essay. First there is an overriding concern with theoretical problems, which sometimes shade into philosophical, theological or methodological areas. In speaking of theory I use this term rather loosely. Although much of the analysis is geared towards facilitating the explanation of religious phenomena and the ascertainment of causal relationships, the reader should not be led to anticipate a theory or a set of theories organized along the ideal lines of philosophies of science. Nor should he or she anticipate formally or statistically presented generalizations or theorems. In one sense theory here means what Dahrendorf has called para-theory or what König terms 'theory of society'.[3] As Dahrendorf notes, much is to be gained in reflecting on 'the nature and course of human society'. This is what para-theory partially involves. It is also concerned with the understanding of the wider context of a particular set of problems and the implications of the conventional wisdom in dealing with these. Although much has been done by a small group of American sociologists of religion to make the sub-discipline more respectable in the strict sense of the word 'theory', the fact remains that much of what is of interest to the sociologist of religion remains unamenable to highly rigorous and exact analytic treatment—mainly because of the cultural variability and richness of religion. Many sociologists of religion regard this richness as central to their studies. Another aspect of this point is that there is a very prominent historical dimension which is taken by sociologists to be central to the study of religion. In *this* particular respect there remains an unashamed conservative disciplinary bias in the chapters which follow.

It would not be putting the matter too strongly to say that this book is dedicated to the idea of religion as culture. Religious beliefs, symbols and values comprise the departure point. That type of work which authors locate as belonging to the sociology of religion but which says little or nothing about religious culture is regarded as of only secondary interest—studies, for example, of recruitment to religious organizations which say nothing about the cultural orientations of the members of the organizations. More positively, the analysis deals in a persistent fashion with the relationship between religious orientations and other orientations to the problems of meaning and significance in socio-cultural systems, particularly the explicit or implicit philosophic dispositions of the sociologist. This general theme gets an even more crystallized focus in the discussions of modern theology which occur at a number of points—most notably in the penultimate chapter. (It should be stressed that this is not a sociology of theology. Weber warned us long ago (although too dogmatically) about the dangers of taking the statements of religious intellectuals too seriously in analysing the religious phenomenon as a whole. If the analysis does stray rather dangerously into an overconcentration on theology this is because of the almost complete neglect of it by sociologists.[4])

Finally, it will be clear to the initiated sociologist that all that has been said in this introduction implies an essentially macrosociological approach. The primary reference is to the society or to the societal context. In one obvious sense this is also a focus which marks the book's faithfulness to the major concerns of Weber and Durkheim. On the other hand, the interest is in modern ways of posing the classical problems—in, for example, the relationship between the religiosity of individuals in a system and the overall religiosity of the system itself. It needs also to be said that virtually nothing is included by way of discussion of psychological aspects of religiosity. Nor is there very much reference to the 'individualistic' approach to the sociological analysis of religion.[5] We are not concerned with the processes by which individuals *as such* search for, maintain or reject religious interpretations of their own and others' life-situations. This is not to say that such an approach is rejected as wrong or worthless. Indeed the claim would be that this type of approach is largely subsumed under the one which is adopted here.

The second chapter is primarily an overview of the early development of the sociology of religion and the major directions of interest which have been sustained or initiated since that period. The chapter also serves to pinpoint some key interpretive problems, in the context of explicating the more prominent themes in the field. The third chapter takes up most of these problems and proposes some solutions. This is the most abstract and analytical chapter and it concludes with the presentation of a schema which, it is suggested, embraces many of the problems which have plagued the sociology of religion. The remaining chapters rest to a considerable extent on this schema. Chapter four deals with the well-tried theme of the relationship between 'religion and society', including problems having to do with relations between church and state. Chapter five takes as its focal point the social organization of religion. Chapter six is concerned with religious culture. In chapter seven there is an extended discussion of the relationship between religious and sociological conceptions both of social processes generally and the contemporary religious situation. The book concludes with a brief statement on the problem of secularization.

While much effort has gone into *introducing* topics within the sociology of religion, many points are stated which go well beyond the usual introductory themes. A large proportion of these are made in the rather numerous footnotes. This is a very deliberately conceived device. The footnotes in this book serve mainly the function of indicating the directions in which the important themes have been or may be pursued more thoroughly. They fall broadly into two categories: first, those which 'take-off' into sociological issues which lie beyond the sociology of religion as typically envisaged; second, those which 'lead back' precisely to the more typical concerns. Thus the reader is advised to pay special attention to the footnotes in order that he or she may become equipped both to explore more thoroughly much that is of importance in the field, but which is not dealt with comprehensively in the body of the book, *and* to comprehend the wider sociological context of the sociology of religion.

This comment on footnotes in itself indicates the substantive path taken in this book; which travels between the more specific issues in the sub-discipline and those which underpin it. Thus the chapters which follow frequently raise themes deriving from philosophy and theology and invoke points made, for example, by sociologists of complex organizations and political sociologists. Again, this is a consciously chosen tack. As we have already suggested, this choice derives mainly from the author's conviction that sociology cannot be neatly parcelled into sub-disciplines—that the atomization of sociology hinders and stultifies our thinking. Arguments and theses cannot be satisfactorily argued in the sociology of religion or elsewhere without considering their general sociological underpinnings and ramifications.

Notes to Chapter 1

1. Two important books were published as the writer was working on the present essay: Thomas Luckmann, *The Invisible Religion: The Transformation of Symbols in Industrial Society*, New York, 1967; and Peter L. Berger, *The Sacred Canopy: Elements of a Sociological Theory of Religion*, New York, 1967. (Luckmann's book was originally published in Germany in 1963.) Both of these, but Berger's in particular, are major exceptions to the generalizations about philosophical and theoretical neglect. Although there are major points of divergence, some statements indicate an agreement on a number of significant issues as between Berger and myself. Two other books have dealt with important general issues: Charles Y. Glock and Rodney N. Stark, *Religion and Society in Tension*, Chicago, 1965; and N. J. Demerath III, *Social Class in American Protestantism*, Chicago, 1965. (In a rather different respect the work of Talcott Parsons and Robert Bellah has been of great significance.)

2. The term figures prominently in Luckmann's criticisms of recent work in the field: *The Invisible Religion*, op. cit.

3. Ralf Dahrendorf, *Essays in the Theory of Society*, Stanford, London, 1968, p. vi. König's term is cited by Dahrendorf.

4. Peter Berger's work is a very notable exception to this. (His most recent book could not be considered here: *A Rumor of Angels*, New York, 1969.) For Weber's warning, see Max Weber, *The Sociology of Religion* (translated Ephraim Fischoff), New York, 1963, London, 1965, ch. VIII.

5. The phenomenological approaches of Berger and Luckmann come into this category. For a general statement see Peter L. Berger and Thomas Luckmann, *The Social Construction of Reality*, New York, 1966.

2

The Development of the Sociology of Religion

The study of religion is one of the oldest of sociological concerns. Indeed, many if not most of the sociologists of the nineteenth century and early part of the twentieth century made the analysis of religion central to their more general conceptions of social and cultural life. This tendency was particularly prominent in the work of men of the classical period of sociology, extending from the 1890s up to about 1920, the period when Durkheim and Weber compiled their comprehensive sociological studies. Religion loomed large in such works for two closely connected reasons. First, there was a sociological and philosophical tradition of inquiry into religion as a 'mainspring' in the operation of human societies—a tradition which in turn rested on the basic cultural premises of European societies of the time. In the study of religion Weber saw the key to the understanding of the major differences between Oriental and Western societies, whilst in a much less historical vein Durkheim focused on the respects in which religion was a major factor making for social solidarity, cohesion and integration, and at the same time arguing that religion itself was a manifestation of man's dependency on, and subservience to, the collective social life which 'surrounded' him. As we shall see, most of the variations in academic sociological interest in religious phenomena can be located within the terms of reference of either of these two different perspectives. Second, the classical sociologists wrote at a time when religion was still an 'issue' in the societies of which they were members and in the societies in close social and cultural proximity to these. Two major trends in the Western world contributed to the problematic status of religion. On the one hand, industrialization and urbanization had involved the rapid proliferation of numerous spheres of social functioning, such as the economic, political and familial—these had become relatively *differentiated* from each other. The relations between them were unclear and, more relevantly, the relationship of religion to each and all had been called into question. On the other hand, the second half of the nineteenth century witnessed a rapid accumulation in knowledge about the characteristics of non-European and so-called primitive societies, this being reflected notably in the work of early social and cultural anthropologists, to which Durkheim directed much of his attention. (There had also been a late eighteenth-century development in comparative religion, mainly with reference to Islam, Hinduism and Buddhism.) These two trends were of course closely linked, both hinging on economic and political changes internal and external to European societies of the period.

These two trends and the development of a comprehensive academic interest in religion cannot of course be attributed simply and only to the later part of the last century and the early part of the present one. The roots of each extend far back in history; but notably to the eighteenth century at the time of the flowering of rationalist philosophy and the occurrence of the French Revolution and,[1*] even further, to the Protestant Reformation and Catholic Counter-Reformation of the sixteenth century. Throughout the period since the end of the Middle Ages, or thereabouts, most Western societies had undergone marked social differentiation, most notably so-called 'horizontal' differentiation, that is the separating out as relatively separate spheres of social activity of the economic from the political, the political from the religious, the economic from the familial, the educative from the familial and so on. One of the most important of such phases of differentiation which gave special cause for socio-political tension (notably in Britain) during the period of classical sociology was the partial differentiation of the educative from the religious sphere. Another kind of differentiation, 'vertical' differentiation, is closely (and complexly) related to such processes. This concerns the separation out of distinctive classes and statuses and, concomitantly, relations of power, authority and prestige. Such processes of social differentiation continually give rise to new problems of maintaining orderliness in social relations and in integrating the separated activities and social groups. Partly because

* Notes for this chapter begin on page 29.

of the acceleration of such processes and partly because of autonomous developments in the sphere of relatively detached intellectual
inquiry the old, traditional cultural assumptions about the over-
arching and all-embracing significance of religious commitment and
religious sociation came increasingly to be regarded as inadequate.
And yet amongst numerous social elites the belief remained that
what was needed were mere adjustments in religious doctrines and
modifications in religious organizations, rather than any fundamental changes. Thus a commitment to the notion of religiosity
itself remained even amongst many of those far-removed from the
effective operation of religious orientations (a tendency which
persists notably in the United States of today). In fact in nineteenth-
century Britain, in particular, the areligiosity of 'the masses' gave
rise to a substantial and explicit interest in the *instrumental* significance for society of religion—religion being regarded by some
social elites as a *means* by which dispositions in the direction of
political and industrial agitation and various preoccupations considered to be subversive of the social order could be eliminated.[2]
Thus it was at the culmination of a long-drawn-out series of processes which continually 'prised open' the socio-cultural order for
analysis and observation and created needs for fundamental re-
appraisals that men such as Durkheim and Weber wrote. The
general and diffuse social *interest* in religion and religiosity was
strong; and a fairly resilient commitment to its social significance
and benefits remained amongst the members of various social
elites, particularly the educational and political.

There have of course been other recent traditions of a much less
ambitious kind which owe little to the influence of Weber or
Durkheim, but which, nevertheless, stem from contexts in which
religion appeared as socially (as opposed to sociologically) problematic. One of these is a tradition which is really much more
sociographic in nature and owes relatively little in itself to the mode
of disciplined inquiry with its own distinctive perspective, which is
known as sociology. It is only sociological in so far as it deals with
the collection and collation of data from social life. For many years
there has been an interest in France, principally under the influence

of Gabriel Le Bras, in the mapping of religious commitment by geographical region. This tradition has, over the years, become more genuinely sociological by virtue of the utilization of systematic methods of data collection and manipulation and has therefore sought to discover, for example, precise correlations between religiosity and other variables such as urban-rural differences, occupational status and so on; but it has tended to eschew involvement in the larger, more complex questions calling for analytic sophistication and, indeed, explanation. Its close relation to pastoral theology and its essentially 'practical' intention has precluded this.[3]

In a rather similar respect, but more complexly, a tradition of inquiry into the conditions of religious commitment developed in the United States during the 1920s and 1930s; which was, like the French tradition, principally concerned with patterns of religiosity in an increasingly industrialized society—more specifically, the challenge presented to the churches by the exigencies of urban living. The complexity in locating this relatively independent tradition hinges largely on the fact that sociology in the United States emerged from a distinctively Protestant religious matrix. In other words, early twentieth-century sociology in the United States was itself distinctively *social*-problem-oriented, manifesting a concern with problems of social welfare from a Protestant Social Gospel perspective. This characteristic of American sociology was rapidly attenuated during the 1930s and subsequently, under the pressures of increasing professionalization of the discipline and the influx of European émigrés who brought with them an interest in more wide-ranging intellectual problems of interpretation and explanation. But partly because of the nature of the earlier emergence of American sociology and partly because of the socio-cultural characteristics of American society itself, the study of religion has remained, on a somewhat ethnocentric basis, an important if not vital ingredient of the discipline. The most important socio-cultural characteristic of American society in this connection is the admixture of religious orientations and the way in which they have mingled together in a pluralistic pattern. This pattern is held by many American intellectuals not only to be unique but also a central factor in the functioning of American society.[4]

The rapid growth in the study of sociology in the United States and the latter's dominant status in the development of the discipline in the Western world has meant that many of the trends in the sociology of religion have been initiated and sustained by American sociologists. Indeed, one of the more interesting features of the sociology of religion in the last two decades has been the extent to which the 'parish studies' of Catholic sociologists, having much in common with the French tradition mentioned previously, have been penetrated by the general and more self-consciously 'neutral' sociological insights of American sociology.[5] Much of the French sociographic tradition and the analyses of Catholic sociologists in the United States are frequently assigned to a category *religious sociology*, as opposed to sociology of religion—on the grounds that what sociological apparatus is involved in such studies is regarded as a means to a religious end, whereas a sociologist of religion is primarily a *sociologist* whose major professional interest is in the study of religion as a social and cultural phenomenon. In many specific, concrete cases the dividing line, however, becomes blurred; this being particularly true of some recent developments in the study of religion which have involved professional sociologists putting their services at the disposal of religious agencies and religious intellectuals utilizing sociological modes of analysis.[6] In fact, although it is crucial that the basis of interest should always be ascertained by the reader of material on social aspects of religion, the two categories in their generic senses are not very helpful and it is perhaps preferable to use the term religious sociology almost exclusively in reference to the French Catholic setting from which it self-confessedly derives. Thus 'sociologie religieuse' tends to apply best to a study-focus based on the theological assumptions of Catholicism.[7] Catholic sociologists in America have, under the pressures of the extensive professionalization of sociology in the United States, been less restricted in their foci and willing, partly also because of the greater pluralism of American religion, to venture into wider fields of inquiry and to contribute to debates on more general sociological problems. But there are dangers even in this generalization; since to take but two examples, the Holland-based journal *Social Compass* and the France-based *Archives de sociologie des religions* are both forums where primarily religious interests, on the one hand, and primarily sociological interests, on the other, come together in intellectual debate. The last twenty years or so have, then, witnessed a greater openness on all sides to indulge in fairly detached inquiry into the bases of religiosity. Naturally, there remains a series of unresolved problems having to do with the value assumptions of the inquirer into religion in its social aspects, which we shall encounter from time to time in the chapters which follow.

We said earlier that it was possible to regard most contemporary foci in terms of the broad orientations of Durkheim and Weber.[8] It is now necessary to specify the nature of their respective impacts, while at the same time stressing that these two sociologists were each part of vigorous intellectual milieux in their own societies. Each in turn also referred back to previous social-scientific analyses of religion. In the case of Weber one of the most important references was that of Marxist sociology. The Marxist tendency was to regard, indeed to try to explain, specific religious forms, notably doctrinal forms, as manifestations or reflections of the socio-economic infrastructure, particularly relations between classes. In its more extreme form this perspective is much less in evidence in the work of Marx himself that in that of some of his followers, notably Engels and Kautsky.[9] Although taking pains to emphasize that he was trying merely to show that by adopting the opposite perspective interesting and intriguing results could be obtained, Weber's main contribution to the sociology of religion was actually to *demonstrate* the conditions under which religion could be, to use Parsons' phrase, a source of 'creative innovation' in sociocultural systems.[10] Weber's most famous study, but in many respects not his most convincing or well-substantiated, was *The Protestant Ethic and the Spirit of Capitalism*, in which he attempted to show that emergent Protestantism, most notably in its Calvinist predestinarian form, functioning in a conducive commercial and technological setting, sharpened, focused and to a considerable extent promoted that set of values and beliefs which Weber claimed came to characterize nineteenth-century capitalistic orientations—frugality and ascetic devotion to work to the greater glory of God.

Durkheim's 'reference back' in the field of religion was mainly to those social anthropologists and sociologists of the nineteenth century who had adopted evolutionist perspectives and had tried to account for religious phenomena primarily in terms of religious belief as a response to ignorance. Thus a major interest of such social scientists was in arriving at 'theories' of the origin of religion—among the most prominent of which were so-called *animist* and *naturist* theories. Very broadly, animist accounts emphasized the imputation by primitive societies of spirit-like qualities to animals; whilst naturist theories stressed the attribution of spiritual qualities to natural phenomena.[11] The former kinds of theory relied a great deal on the theses advanced by Tylor and Spencer; that originally spirit beliefs emanated from such practices as ancestor worship and from dream experience; i.e. dreaming gave rise to belief in a soul separate from man's everyday being. Naturism, on the other hand, rested on the claim that belief in spiritual phenomena arose out of the feelings of awe aroused by such natural entities as mountains and the sun or such natural occurrences as storms and volcanic eruptions. There were other kinds of theory as to religious origins; but wha was common to most nineteenth-century evolutionists was the conviction that primitive religion (and magic) arose out of ignorance of the 'true' nature of and relationships between social, psychological and natural phenomena. Corollarily, the more 'advanced' a society became the less appropriate were religious beliefs, until eventually religion would disappear from the most advanced societies. What is important in the present context is that Durkheim was concerned particularly to refute the view that religious beliefs were false. Moreover, he was committed to the belief that social phenomena should be explained in social terms and not reduced to individual-psychological factors or natural ones. This twofold commitment led him to argue in connection with his study of indigenous Australian religion that religious beliefs were not false since they were manifestations of social life itself. In a sense, then, religious belief and practice constituted a recognition of man's dependence on society. Social life was inherently religious, maintained Durkheim, and religious ceremonials were celebrations of social life. We should note two vital elements in Durkheim's thesis. First, his definition of religion was a highly inclusive one—that religion had to do with *sacred* things, things set apart from the mundane, or in his word, the *profane* necessities of existence. Second, Durkheim attempted to prove his thesis, interestingly enough, by examining what he took to be the most primitive kind of religion available for study, namely totemic 'religion'.

One important distinction between the sociology of Durkheim and the sociology of Weber is independent of the actual substance of their respective theories. This concerns the characteristics of their *styles* of analysis. Weber has tended to remain particularly influential in this respect through two features of his work. First, his *broad empirical* thesis about the contribution of the great religious traditions to the differential development of the Occidental as opposed to the Oriental 'world'; more specifically, the claim that Islam, Judaism, Catholicism and Protestantism, in increasing order of significance, were more productive of the *rationalization* of social, economic and political activities than were Hinduism, Buddhism and Confucianism. Second, arising mainly from the development of this thesis, Weber made a number of very important *conceptual* contributions to the sociology of religion. Probably the most frequently utilized of these has been his sociological differentiation between churchly forms of religious organization and sectarian forms. Another such conceptual distinction was that between *ethical* prophecy, which Weber characterized as being productive of 'breakthroughs' from traditional social patterns and which was typical of the group of (mainly monotheistic) religions of the Occidental world, and *exemplary* prophecy, which typified the qualities of religious leadership in Oriental religions, and which emphasized the necessity to live up to traditional-mystical social standards of conduct, rather than promulgating new standards. Furthermore, in more general sociological vein, Weber established conceptual distinctions in the spheres of bureaucratic modes of organization and types of leadership which have, with modifications, been used to good effect in subsequent studies of various facets of religion; and his work in the field of social stratification, partly developed in his studies of the major religious traditions, has continued to possess great sociological utility.

Durkheim, on the other hand, contributed relatively little in these two areas, the empirical and the conceptual. Certainly, he presented empirical findings in his major work on religion; but he did not link these with propositions cast in the clear-cut form which would make them susceptible to further investigation in other socio-cultural systems. What was of lasting importance was his discussion of the definition of religion, and the, more complex, attempt to demonstrate that religious belief was a representation of the morphological properties of the society in which it was located and that religious practice was a 'celebration' of the reality of the social sphere, binding the participants together. Thus we can say that the significance of Durkheim's impact has been primarily that of providing explicit *perspectives*, whereas Weber's impact has been on the one hand *conceptual* and on the other hand *empirical-propositional*. It should additionally be pointed out that there *is* a noteworthy perspectival component in Weber's sociology of religion—his emphasis upon religious orientations being responses to a posited universal need for 'salvation', the need for the individual to possess a system of basic beliefs by and through which he can understand and make sense of the social situations in which he typically finds himself.

Thus the influence of Weber has principally been in relatively discrete and concrete spheres of the sociology and history of religion; while Durkheim's influence has been in terms of analytic style and in the provision of general assertions about the social significance of religion. Attempts to rectify the relative neglect of the more general aspects of Weber's sociology of religion have, however, appeared increasingly in very recent years.

The kinds of problem which Durkheim faced and some of the ways in which he dealt with them have been followed up in two main areas of inquiry. First, his most permanent and directly acknowledged influence has been amongst social anthropologists. The attractions of Durkheim's theory of religion have lain in the fact that, as he articulated it in relation to Australian religion, the emphasis was upon the integrative, cohesive consequences of religion for the members of each clan and for the relationships between clans. Anthropologists, particularly during the 1930s and 1940s, but less so in recent years, have tended to lay great stress on primitive societies as functionally integrated wholes; that is societies in which sets of activities, beliefs, values, and so on, complement each other and, in a sense, 'need' each other. In fact they took functional integration as a *premise* of their inquiries and then sought out the precise respects in which such integration was sustained. A theory of religion which laid emphasis above all else on its integrative qualities was obviously well-suited to such endeavours; and, moreover, to regard the system of religious beliefs, values and symbols as representations of structural traits was a very useful heuristic device for uncovering the 'real' social structure. Finally, Durkheim's definition of religion in terms of the sacred and the profane, emphasizing the universality of religion without getting too involved in questions of whether, for example, individuals actually recognized a distinction between the natural and supernatural was well in line with the reluctance of anthropologists to become embroiled in discussions about the rationality or irrationality of religious belief on the model of the nineteenth-century evolutionists. Broadly, the Durkheimian influence has been, then, to stimulate the interest of social anthropologists in how networks of social relationships are sustained, and conceived of, by those implicated in them. Moreover, his emphasis upon religious practice or ritual has been important, since it tended to divert attention away from the purely ethnographic aspects of religion. This was a much needed corrective in anthropological studies in the early period of the century, since there had been a marked tendency to concentrate almost solely on the exposition of the details of 'strange' religious beliefs; in so far as ritual was studied, it was from a purely descriptive, as opposed to an explanatory, standpoint.

But, looked at more closely, the nature of the Durkheimian influence is much more intricate. As we have said, Durkheim explicated his theory of religion in terms of the phenomenon of totemism. Broadly, we may define totemism as the identification of human beings with plants or animals and the designation of kinship groups in such terms.[12] Durkheim claimed that totemism was the most primitive form of religion—that on his definition of religion the *sacralization* of plants and animals relative to specific social groups was the elemental form of the religious phenomenon. This was religion in its 'starkest' and most basic form and other more advanced forms were merely more complex versions of it. It has however become increasingly agreed over the years that totemism *as such* is not a distinctively religious phenomenon. One of the most devastating commentaries not only on Durkheim, but on the whole debate about totemism (which, it is important to emphasize, was an object of controversy before Durkheim's time), is that offered by Lévi-Strauss. At the end of his critique Lévi-Strauss states that 'it is the obsession with religious matters which caused totemism to be placed in religion, though separating it as far as possible—by caricaturing it if need be—from so-called civilized religions, for fear that the latter might crumble at its touch; or else, as in Durkheim's experiment, the combination resulting in a new entity deprived of the initial properties, those of totemism as well as those of religion'.[13]

Our attention is thus directed to a problem which has plagued both the sociology and the social anthropology of religion: How can the analyst of religion determine the boundaries of the phenomenon? Especially in the anthropology of religion a long-lasting temptation has been to operate with very inclusive notions of the sphere of religion; that is, to include a very wide range of social activities, beliefs and values under the heading, 'religion'. The reasons for this are fairly obvious. Primitive societies manifest thought patterns and social activities which to the observer are very remote from those of industrial societies. It is but a short step to the conclusion that these societies are in a sense religious or magico-religious societies and that religious belief tends to constrain all else and penetrates all social activities. Thus ceremonial occasions as such and the naming of clans and marriage classes after animals and plants came under the Durkheimian influence to be regarded as religious phenomena. When Durkheim's importance as a sociologist was rather belatedly impressed upon American sociologists during the 1930s it is not surprising that modern examples of such phenomena should have been regarded as religious phenomena. There has thus been a tendency for Durkheim's impact to be one of searching out and stipulating the religious aspects of activities which involve the affirmation of social solidarity on an intense scale, such as coronations and even American baseball.[14] Moreover, some sociologists have tended to view religious belief and activity as a requisite

C

of all social systems—a dominant force which binds men together and provides the basic cognitive, evaluative and expressive guidelines for the stable operation of the society. The major proponents of this view have been sociologists of a functionalist orientation—men such as Talcott Parsons, Kingsley Davis and Robert Bellah.[15] And where, as in Communist societies, religion in its intuitive sense is disparaged and discouraged, the major belief system and the organizations and activities directly associated with it are either regarded as 'religious' or said to be functional and structural equivalents of religion.[16]

Thus Durkheim's influence on modern sociologists in the field of religion has been a very general one—one of broad interpretations and the drawing of conclusions as to the *functions* of religion—that is, the consequences for a social group or system of religious commitment and religious action. In this broad respect the Durkheimian influence has been extensive, the peak probably having been reached in the 1950s among American sociologists. The utilization of Durkheim's approach in its most general senses by American sociologists was facilitated up to that point in time by two main factors. First, there had been since the early part of the century a tendency to concentrate analytic resources on single societies or on very broad statements about societies in general. Second, many sociologists of religion diagnosed in the American situation a condition of 'denominational pluralism'.[17] This term refers to the coexistence on a relatively tolerant basis of three main religious orientations: Protestantism, Catholicism and Judaism. The coexistence is said to be one predicated on an acknowledgment of the legitimacy of each religious orientation and that the orientations are bound together by a common commitment to the inherent goodness of American society itself. Indeed some have claimed that there is a basic 'religion of Americanism' which underlies the more particularistic orientations of the three major religious tendencies, and which has come about largely through religious affiliation cutting across and supplanting ethnic or national solidarities in the American 'melting-pot'; an affiliation which has been found to be less productive of inter-group tension than ethnic modes of identification.[18] The important point here, however, is that taken together with the non-comparative approach, i.e., the concentration on the analysis of a single society (the United States), this diagnosed characteristic of American religion fits very well with the Durkheimian thesis about religion being a form of society-worship and society itself as being a moral-religious entity. It is thus in such terms that the work of Durkheim has made its impact, although often more implicitly than explicitly.[19]

Another aspect of the Durkheim thesis concerns the attempt to relate the content of religious beliefs to general characteristics of the social structure.[20] One of the foremost anthropologists working within broadly the same tradition, Lévi-Strauss, has found this an inadequate way of posing the problem. He has not focused specifically on a category of thought labelled religion, but has concerned himself much more comprehensively with belief systems in general. This aside, Lévi-Strauss' basic point of disagreement with Durkheim is that the latter concentrated too much on the link between social structure and the beliefs, values and symbols characteristic of the groups constituent of a social structure—so ignoring the relationship between society and *nature*. On the other hand, Lévi-Strauss maintains that a different anthropological tradition, associated with Malinowski, leaned too much in the opposite direction by regarding religion and magic as arising through man's problematic relationship with his natural environment—including man's own biological 'environment'. For Lévi-Strauss, then, man's categories of thought have to do with 'the means (or hope) of transcending the opposition between' nature and culture.[21]

This contrast between the thought of Durkheim and Lévi-Strauss highlights a series of major points of divergence at the most general level amongst sociologists of religion. One of these concerns the difference between the Marxist and the Durkheimian perspectives. Superficially there is a large area of common ground: both schools of thought emphasize the dependency of religious thought on variations in the structure of society. But whereas the Marxist regards the structure of society as only partially autonomous—it is also partially the outcome of man's changing relationship to his natural or, more accurately, material environment—the Durkheimian takes social structure as *given*. Thus a Marxist interpretation of religion does not see the actual structure of religious belief as being a direct reflection of the structured relation between individuals and groups (although there may be elements of this), but as arising from the specific *processes* of interaction. Man's relation to his environment is such that the attempt to master it in the service of his needs creates certain group structures—notably those centred on economic production. It is the nature of the process of production and the relations between the major groups engaged in the production process (socio-economic classes) which create the condition under which religion arises. In a pre-socialist society men stand in an alien relationship both to the means and results of their production, as well as to each other. In such a pervasive condition of *alienation* religious beliefs and practices continue to arise. These are responses to the general sentiment of lack of control over man's destiny; and the persistence of religion is both an indicator of far-reaching alienation and an 'opiate' which perpetuates imbalances and inequalities in the social structure.[22] Thus, to oversimplify somewhat, the Marxist sees religion as a compensatory mechanism in a situation regarded as being devoid of the sociality of which man is theoretically capable; whereas the Durkheimian sees religion precisely as an expression of that sociality, a viewpoint which is well-demonstrated by Durkheim's fear that the decline of traditional Christianity in the West called for a substitute (some kind of liberal nationalism) which would continue the integrative functions previously served by traditional religions. This, incidentally, is not to say that the Marxist denies the integrative functions (i.e. the objective social consequences) of religion. The point is that religion integrates men together in what he considers to be inadequate relationships. Man, it is claimed, is incomplete and human relationships insufficiently social so long as religion is found to be necessary.

What Durkheim and Marx had in common was the contention that in principle the structure of particular religious belief systems as well as the perpetuation of religion could be accounted for in reference to social structure, whether (as in Marx's case) this reference had to be supplemented by further reference to ideas about man's relationship to his environment—or whether (as in Durkheim's case) supplementary reference was made to the emotionalism engendered by social gatherings. Subsequent sociologists have been less willing to claim this much for sociological analysis and indeed there is considerable doubt whether Marxism or Durkheimianism should be taken this far; for there are indications that both schools of thought in effect ascribed to the development of religious belief systems a degree of autonomy inconsistent with the 'ideal' depictions we have just presented. It should be re-emphasized in this connection that Durkheim's thesis was couched in reference to the most primitive religious form he thought was available for analysis; and, as Bellah points out, it is precisely in such a circumstance that one would expect to find a highly intimate relationship between man's group relations (social structure) and his actual beliefs and values.[23] But as a society develops from such a condition there will be an increasing differentiation of these spheres. Beliefs will change or become consolidated by virtue of their having special social groups or organizations 'at their service'. The more that this is the case the more inappropriate it becomes to attempt to relate religious belief and practice directly to the general structural characteristics of a society. Under such conditions religion may either exert a great deal of *control over* social interaction—or, as is the case in the most modern societies, it will become a separated sphere of activity—responsive to changes in the rest of society but not necessarily affected 'across the board' by the general characteristics of the society.[24]

It is around the problems raised here that we can best view the more recent general contributions to the sociology of religion. Talcott Parsons in his *Structure of Social Action* (1937) argued that Durkheim's theory of religion was not tenable; principally on the grounds that it constituted a regression to discredited nineteenth-century views (so-called positivist views) which tried to explain religious beliefs 'as distorted representations of an empirical reality which is capable of correct analysis by an empirical science, this time sociology'.[25] Parsons was willing to accept *in principle* the Durkheimian proposition that God or any other sacred object is a symbolic representation of society. Previous theorists had tried to maintain that the sacredness of natural objects arose out of something intrinsic to such objects, whereas Durkheim maintained that sacredness is 'superposed' upon such properties. The sacred object is a symbol of a specific structural property of society. It is at the point of elaboration that Parsons departs from Durkheim—mainly in a Weberian direction. In brief, the main objection is that religious belief in its symbolic form is on Durkheim's account illusory; it makes something concrete and observable in the real world (group structures) into something else—totemic objects. Parsons' solution to the problem as he saw it was to regard religious symbols as referring not to anything concrete and empirical but to 'aspects of "reality" significant to human life and experience, yet outside the range of scientific observation and analysis'.[26] This 'reality' is a residue left outside the sphere of empirical knowledge. It is part of the social condition that suffering, pain and the meaning of life generally cannot be entirely understood in terms of empirical science. Thus concrete symbols, such as totemic objects, or 'imaginary' symbols, such as gods, are representative of an aspect of the social condition. How satisfactory is this conclusion? For it has been at the foundation of numerous functional approaches to the sociology of religion since the 1930s—a tendency reinforced by the important fact that some 'radical' theologians have adumbrated similar conceptions.[27] In fact Parsons merely pushes the Durkheimian problem one stage further back. Durkheim had argued against those who, like Comte, saw religion as illusory belief, by emphasizing that since it was a manifestation of man's sociality it could not be illusory. Parsons in turn says that there is an element of illusoriness in Durkheim's conception on the grounds that religious belief reflects an empirical property of society. And yet in what accurate sense can fear of death, the meaningfulness of life and so on be regarded as non-empirical? While it is true, for example, that no kind of science can provide a completely satisfactory solution to the problem of meaning, surely various aspects of both natural and social science endeavour impinge increasingly on that area of social problems. Moreover, what is important here is that the spread of 'scientific' values may give rise increasingly to the view that these problems are *capable* of scientific solution even if no such solutions are immediately forthcoming. Parsons' non-empirical residue can and has, in fact, been narrowed by 'science'. But the more serious charge against Parsons is this: Durkheim's position is rejected because it seeks to account for religious conceptions in terms of aspects of social reality open to sociological analysis; but is not a similar charge to be made against Parsons for arguing *in effect* that the sociologist can account for religious phenomena, even though the nature of the factors which give rise to such phenomena are not totally susceptible to sociological analysis as such? That is, the factors giving rise to religion can be specified but not explained. Even this may be misleading; for one interpretation of the Parsonian viewpoint is that religion is accounted for by referring to the fact that social life itself involves problems which from the point of view of the participants are insoluble and that religion is therefore a 'coping mechanism': in one sense it is caused by such problems—in another it is a form of adjustment in the face of or a means of transcending these problems. Thus what begins as an attempt to 'save' religion from reduction to empirical social factors ends up as merely a special version of just such a reduction. On the other hand, Parsons' critique of Durkheim was part of a tendency which became increasingly prominent in the immediate post-war years to ignore self-consciously the problem of the variation in religious belief and practice attendant upon variations in the social structure and to look merely at part of the other side of the coin—the consequences for a social system of religious belief and practice. This is of course only *part* of the other side of the coin, because it focuses on what religion in general does for a social system and not what *variations* in religion do for a social system. This kind of functional analysis of religion-in-general relied primarily on the thesis that religion could be seen only in terms of the 'non-empirical' aspects of social life. But this was an *implicit* rather than an explicit reliance, since the proffering of any theory of how the *content* of religious belief relates to social characteristics was ruled out of order. This preclusion was bound up closely with the concern on the part of sociologists to sustain the value-neutrality of their science. But, more important, it was feared that if particular beliefs could be seen as the result of social characteristics then sociology would be claiming that there was no validity in the beliefs themselves.

Thus there was an extreme reluctance amongst most American sociologists to deal with the question of religious beliefs in any way which ran counter to prevailing social conceptions of religiosity. This did not preclude however the analysis of the more marginal, sectarian forms of religion—in terms of the connections between the beliefs of the adherents and the social characteristics of such adherents. In fact there was an acute dilemma about these matters. The focus on the social functions of religion led to the view that some form of religion was a requisite of all social systems. The sociologist in saying this, however, adopted a standpoint which ran counter to that of the religiously committed. He still tended to account for religion in purely social terms; and to see its consequences as purely social. In saying that the validity of religious beliefs was an irrelevant concern to the sociologist he was in a sense taking up a 'religious' position.[28] It is extremely important, nevertheless, to establish that a large proportion of sociologists of religion are themselves religiously committed in the orthodox sense. What consequences their religious commitments have for their sociological perspectives and interpretations, and vice versa, is an intriguing question.

Sensitivity about impinging upon 'religious territory' has become less marked in recent years. The diagnosis that the general orientation to religious matters of a significant proportion of the American population at large was not all that different from the very views which the sociologists had been propounding (that religion was a social necessity, that it was valued *qua* religion), has, one suspects, been a facilitating factor in this change. Similarly the tendency for some theologians and religious intellectuals to 'sociologize' their religiosity has been partially responsible for the attenuation of the reticence of sociologists with respect to some of the major questions about the significance of religion outside of the sectarian sphere. It is worth noting here that one of the most frequently invoked characterizations of religion amongst American sociologists during the post-war period was in fact originally stated by a Protestant theologian, Paul Tillich—to the effect that God is that which concerns us ultimately. Religion has to do with the problems of 'ultimate concern' which, it is argued, all men as social beings face.[29] This facilitated the feeling that there was in fact no fundamental *sociological* problem in defining religion. The claim here is that sociological and religious interpretations of the world are frequently *competing* interpretations. Both seek in their own terms to probe the basic and 'essential' characteristics of social life. In a very real sense sociology has traditionally sought the *raison d'être* of social life; this being particularly true of the period in the nineteenth century when evolutionary conceptions predominated the field of sociological inquiry. And whilst it has often been stated in reference to physical and natural science that the search for laws and explanations of the phenomena with which those disciplines deal does not necessarily or logically conflict with religious conceptions, it is difficult to argue the same case so convincingly in respect of some of the social sciences, notably sociology, anthropology and psychology—especially when, as we have argued, sociology seeks to comprehend religion itself.[30]

Thus far we have focused on the larger, underlying and fundamental problems of the sociology of religion. That is, we have looked at some of the basic orientations to the phenomenon of religion in general. On the other hand, it was pointed out in discussing the contribution of Weber that there are a number of more narrowly circumscribed aspects of study in the sociology of religion—the analysis of religious movements and organizations, the nature of religious commitment in different social settings and so on.[31] To a considerable extent, these more specific problems have been tackled over the years in *relative* isolation from the kind of fundamental issue indicated in the preceding pages. We have already pointed out that one of the most characteristic of sociological orientations to the study of religion during the 1950s was that of what religion in general 'does' for a social system, with little regard for the social consequences of particular variations in religion or for the kinds of religious conception attendant upon different kinds of social and cultural condition. These problem-areas have certainly not been neglected since Weber's time, but they have relatively rarely been tackled from the cross-cultural standpoint which Weber himself adopted. It will be recalled that Weber was particularly interested in the differences in social, economic and political orientations deriving from the major religious belief systems. The most intensively worked-on theme since Weber's day has, as is well known, been the re-examination of his thesis that Protestantism yields higher

levels of economic motivation than Catholicism.[32] Numerous sociologists and historians have added substantially to our knowledge in
this respect. The major tendency has been to argue that Weber
stated his case much too strongly; notably in under-emphasizing the
extent to which various developments within Catholicism prior to
the Protestant Reformation were productive of innovative economic orientations. Trevor-Roper, among others, has added to this a
very important thesis—that it was not so much that the religion of
Protestants gave rise directly to innovative economic orientations
such as thriftiness, stress on frugality and investment, but rather that
it was the phenomenon of Protestants' *marginal, migrant status* which
led to their being economically innovative.[33] This approach is, in
principle, somewhat similar to parts of Sombart's thesis that it was
not Protestantism but Judaism that 'produced' capitalism; that is, the
marginal, pariah status of Jews created pressures for them to indulge
in relatively free and innovative economic behaviour outside of the
medieval restrictions on such patterns of behaviour.[34]

There have, however, been a large number of sociological analyses
of an even more specific kind—ones which focus on variations in
orientation to economic and political issues as a consequence of
religious commitment within a single society. A great many of these
have, in the Weberian tradition, focused on differences between
Catholic and Protestant and sometimes also Jewish commitments.
One of the most ambitious (and most criticized) of these is Lenski's
The Religious Factor (1961).[35] Many sociologists have found Weber's
position on the Catholic-Protestant distinction to be confirmed—as
did Lenski. The latter discovered that there was a significant differential as between the economic-achievement motivation of Protestants and Catholics. This finding has been the object of criticism,
notably that of Greeley; who has found that there is little or no
difference between Catholics and Protestants in such respects.[36]
Moreover, Greeley's work shows how important it is to locate
religious orientations and attachments within their cultural and
social-structural contexts—ethnic, ecological, stratificatory, and so
on—for the latter may be the really critical variables in accounting
for achievement and other types of motivation. It is not therefore,
on this view, *substantive religious attachment* which counts, so much as

the structural location of the attachment. This is, in general terms, in line with the theses of Trevor-Roper and Sombart indicated above.[37]

Perhaps the main significance of Lenski's work lies in the comprehensiveness of his attempt to systematize and utilize in empirical work a schema of *dimensions* of religiosity. Most, if not all, of previous work had involved using as indicators of religiosity either the expression of religious beliefs of a particular kind (e.g. Protestant) or the practice of religion, notably attendance at a place of worship —or occasionally both. In historical analysis of the kind undertaken under the direct inspiration of Weber such methods were 'excusable' in so far as historical study necessarily requires the analyst to make use of what data are in fact available—the historian or historical sociologist is severely limited in his methodology by being unable to produce genuinely new information. The sociologist of contemporary society on the other hand should not be limited in this way; much inadequate research has been carried out by sociologists into various aspects of the Weber thesis simply through a failure to explore the variety of ways in which religious commitment can be expressed. Hence the significance of Lenski's contribution. Lenski added to religious belief (in his term the *orthodoxy* dimension) and religious attendance (the *associational* dimension) two further dimensions of religiosity: the *devotional*, having to do with such aspects of religiosity as prayer, and the *communal*, that is segregation in terms of religious group.[38]

It is in fact the advent of more rigorous standards of analysis which is a hallmark of contemporary works in the field of the sociology of religion. The present concern with breaking up the unitary concept *religion* into dimension or aspects of religion, which may vary independently of each other, is one of the best examples of this characteristic. Similarly one of the most popular topics of analysis in the field, the study of specific religious organizations or movements, has been penetrated by this self-consciousness as to methodological procedure. Perhaps the only pitfall in this reorientation is that the great empirical knowledge, notably acquaintance with the minutiae of religious doctrine, required for adequate sociological interpretation of religion will be neglected. This, however, is not a necessary corollary of the new-found methodological and theoretical sophistication. Indeed a judicious combination of the empirical-historical and the self-consciously analytic-explanatory approaches may well enable us to tackle anew the large-scale, fundamental problems which were pioneered by Weber and Durkheim. But in order that this programme may be adequately undertaken some very serious problems must be tackled. Among these are the need to establish a viable, 'master conception' of religiosity— one which will at one and the same time transcend the *religious* definitions of particular religious groups and also not be too general as to make redundant such questions as: is society x more religious than society y?

The search for more rigorous analytic procedures has not been the only innovation of recent years. There has been a sharper, more critical reaction to the relative neglect of theoretical issues in the sociology of religion since the time of the classical sociologists. Berger and Luckmann have argued very persuasively that the concentration on institutional forms of religion, that is to say religious phenomena which are bound up closely with visible churches, denominations and sects, has been inhibitive of a genuine sociological theory of religion.[39] Thus they have taken as their points of departure the centrality which Weber and Durkheim accorded to religion in their general conceptions of socio-cultural life. Luckmann has argued that in their works in the sociology of religion both Weber and Durkheim were primarily concerned with the problem of individual existence, with the problem of identity in the socio-cultural order.[40] Thus religious commitment as a means of providing meaning and significance for the individual is the main concern of Luckmann. And both he and Berger have attempted to 'get behind' religion as it manifests itself in institutional forms—to get at the basic 'underlay' of factors which give rise to religiosity. In such an attempt they are returning to the explanatory focus on basic characteristics of religion and religiosity which marked the works of Weber and Durkheim. As we shall see, however, it may be the case that Luckmann's insistence on identifying the problem of the individual's search for and maintenance of an adequate meaning-orientation to his life situation with religion as such is too broad a focus, which, as Berger has indicated, may detract from our understanding of major changes in religiosity[41]—indeed *away from* religiosity—in the modern industrial world. Nevertheless the contributions of both Berger and Luckmann to the resurrection of basic theoretical issues are highly significant.

Notes to Chapter 2

1. With reference to the themes of this book, see especially Carl Becker, *The Heavenly City of the Eighteenth-Century Philosophers*, New Haven, 1932; Peter Gay, *The Enlightenment*, London, 1967.

2. This was a prominent theme amongst political and economic elites in England from the 1820s onwards. Towards the end of the century attention shifted firmly in the direction of mass education as the allegedly necessary preventative. .

3. A fairly recent exposition of some of the major characteristics of French religious sociology is F. Boulard, *An Introduction to Sociology* (translated by M. J. Jackson), London, 1960.

4. There is not a consensus on this, however. For pessimistic interpretations, see Gerhard Lenski, *The Religious Factor*, Garden City, New York, 1963 (revised edition), esp. pp. 362–6; and J. Milton Yinger, 'Pluralism, Religion and Secularism', *Journal for the Scientific Study of Religion*, VI (April, 1967), pp. 17–28. See below, pp. 99–102.

5. See particularly the work of Joseph Fichter: *Dynamics of a City Church*: Southern Parish, Chicago, 1951; *Social Relations in an Urban Parish*, Chicago, 1954; and *Religion as an Occupation*, Notre Dame, Indiana, 1961.

6. See, for example, the number of references to sociological and anthropological insights and findings in Harvey Cox, *The Secular City*, New York, London, 1966 (revised edition). See also Daniel Callahan (ed.), *The Secular City Debate*, New York, 1966. See below, pp. 205–17.

7. See Jackson's introduction to Boulard, op. cit., p. ix.

8. The most important of the works with which we are concerned here are Max Weber, *The Sociology of Religion* (translated by Ephraim Fischoff), Boston, Toronto, 1963; *The Protestant Ethic and the Spirit of Capitalism* (translated by Talcott Parsons), London, 1930; and Emile Durkheim, *The Elementary Forms of the Religious Life* (translated by Joseph W. Swain), London, 1915.

9. See especially Karl Kautsky, *Foundations of Christianity*, New York, 1925.

10. Talcott Parsons, 'Religious Perspectives in College Teaching: Sociology and Social Psychology' in Hoxie N. Fairchild (ed.), *Religious Perspectives in College Teaching*, New York, 1952, pp. 286–337. Weber once referred to his sociology of religion as 'an empirical refutation of historical materialism'. Quoted by Raymond Aron, *Main Currents in Sociological Thought: II Durkheim/Pareto/Weber*, New York, London, 1967, p. 262.

11. For a useful survey of various theories of religion including animistic and naturalistic ones, see E. E. Evans-Pritchard, *Theories of Primitive Religion*, Oxford, New York, 1965. (See also William J. Goode, *Religion Among the Primitives*, Glencoe, Illinois, 1951; and Anthony F. C. Wallace, *Religion: An Anthropological View*, New York, 1966.)

12. Rodney Needham, Introduction to Claude Lévi-Strauss, *Totemism* (translated by Rodney Needham), 1962, pp. 10–11.

13. Ibid., p. 103. For a collection of appraisals of Lévi-Strauss, see Edmund Leach (ed.), *The Structural Study of Myth and Totemism*, London, New York, 1967.

14. For the British Coronation see Edward Shils and Michael Young, 'The Meaning of the Coronation', *Sociological Review*, I–II (1953), pp. 63–81. For American baseball, see Morris B. Cohen, *The Faith of a Liberal*, New York, 1946, pp. 334–6. (For a forceful critique of the former, see Norman Birnbaum, 'Monarchs and Sociologists; A Reply to Professor Shils and Mr Young', *Sociological Review*, III–IV (1955), pp. 5–23.)

15. See Parsons, op. cit. (and footnotes 17 and 25 below); Kingsley Davis, *Human Society*, New York, 1948, ch. 19 (see also Goode, op. cit., pp. 1–55); and Robert N. Bellah (ed.), *Religion and Progress in Modern Asia*, New York, 1965, pp. 168–225.

16. Some sociologists go much further than this and define religion so broadly and inclusively that Communism *is*, from their perspective, clearly a religion; e.g. Yinger, op. cit. For an excellent critique of the functionalist orientation, see Melford E. Spiro's essay in M. Banton (ed), *Anthropological Approaches to the Study of Religion*, London, 1966, pp. 85–126. See also my review of the latter book in *Sociology*, I (January, 1967), pp. 93–5.

17. See Will Herberg, 'Religion in a Secularized Society: Some Aspects of America's Three-Religions Pluralism', *Review of Religious Research*, 4 (Fall, 1962), pp. 33–45. See also Talcott Parsons, *Structure and Process in Modern Societies*, Glencoe, Illinois, 1960, ch. 10. The most famous statement is Will Herberg, *Protestant, Catholic, Jew*, New York, 1955.

18. Cf. Robert N. Bellah, 'Civic Religion', *Daedalus* (Winter, 1967), pp. 1–21.

19. For a comprehensive analysis of American sociology of religion, see

Gerhant Lenski, 'The Sociology of Religion in the United States', *Social Compass*, IX (1962), pp. 307–37.

20. The most clear-cut example of this is Guy E. Swanson, *The Birth of the Gods*, Ann Arbor, 1964. See also Swanson, *Religion and Regime*, Ann Arbor, 1967. Swanson's work is discussed later in this book, pp. 151–154.

21. Claude Lévi-Strauss, *The Savage Mind*, London, Chicago, 1965, p. 91. Cf. Bronislaw Malinowski, *Magic, Science and Religion*, New York, 1948.

22. For Marx's views on religion, see especially 'On the Jewish Question' and 'Contribution to the Critique of Hegel's Philosophy of Right', in T. B. Bottomore (ed.), *Karl Marx: Early Writings*, London, 1963, pp. 1–40 and 43–59. See also K. Marx and F. Engels, *On Religion*, Moscow, 1955.

23. Robert N. Bellah, 'Durkheim and History', *American Sociological Review*, XXIV (August, 1959), pp. 447–61.

24. For some diagnosed similarities between primitive and modern religious systems, see Robert Bellah, 'Religious Evolution', *American Sociological Review*, XXIX (June, 1964), pp. 358–74.

25. Talcott Parsons, *The Structure of Social Action*, Glencoe, Illinois, London, 1949 (second edition), p. 420. For a closely-reasoned subsequent analysis of sociological theories of religion, see Parsons, 'The Theoretical Development of the Sociology of Religion' in *Essays in Sociological Theory*, Glencoe, Illinois, 1954 (revised edition), ch. X.

26. *The Structure of Social Action*, op. cit., p. 421.

27. On the other hand some of these would strongly disagree with the 'gap religion' implications of the Parsonian thesis—at least in a prescriptive sense. See below, pp. 205–17.

28. There have been numerous discussions of the problem. See, *inter alia*, William L. Kolb, 'Values, Positivism and the Functional Theory of Religion: The Growth of a Moral Dilemma', *Social Forces*, 31 (May, 1953), pp. 305–11; and Allan W. Eister, 'Religious Institutions in Complex Societies', *American Sociological Review*, XX (August, 1957), pp. 387–91.

29. For a radical critique of this definition, see Spiro, op. cit.

30. See Charles Y. Glock and Rodney Stark, *Religion and Society in Tension*, op. cit., chs. 14 and 15; and Bryan Wilson, *Religion in Secular Society*, London, 1966, pp. 42 ff. See below, pp. 196 ff.

31. Much of the recent work on religious movements, notably sectarian movements, has been undertaken or initiated by Bryan Wilson. See,

inter alia, Bryan R. Wilson, *Sects and Society*, London, Berkeley, 1961; and Wilson (ed.), *Patterns of Sectarianism*, London, 1967. In the latter I try to apply a number of general sociological insights to a particular religious movement: Roland Robertson, 'The Salvation Army: the Persistence of Sectarianism', ibid., pp. 49–105.

32. For a useful, but by no means comprehensive, survey of the controversy surrounding this thesis, see Robert W. Green (ed.), *Protestantism and Capitalism*, Boston, London, 1959. See also the survey in Kurt Samuelsson, *Religion and Economic Action*, London, 1961, pp. 1–26. For extended discussion, see below, pp. 169–81.

33. Hugh Trevor-Roper, 'Religion, the Reformation and Social Change', *Historical Studies*, 4 (1965), pp. 18–45.

34. Werner Sombart, *The Jews and Modern Capitalism* (translated by M. Epstein), New York, 1962. This may be a rather 'generous' interpretation of Sombart's thesis. But a corrective is needed to the disdain with which the thesis is often viewed. There are other variants of this approach. See below, pp. 174–5.

35. Lenski, *The Religious Factor*, op. cit.

36. Andrew M. Greeley, *Religion and Career*, New York, 1963. See also, *inter alia*, 'Influence of the Religious Factor on Career Plans and Occupational Values of College Graduates', *American Journal of Sociology*, 68 (May, 1963), pp. 658–71.

37. Cf. Swanson, *Religion and Regime*, op. cit., pp. 247–52.

38. Lenski, op. cit. Another much discussed schema of dimensions of religiosity is that proposed by Glock. See Glock and Stark, op. cit.; Charles Y. Glock, 'On the Study of Religious Commitment', *Religious Education*, 42 (1962), Research Supplement, pp. 98–110; Glock, 'Comment on "Pluralism, Religion and Secularism"', *Journal for the Scientific Study of Religion*, VI (Spring, 1967), pp. 28–30. See below for extended discussion, pp. 51–8.

39. Peter L. Berger and Thomas Luckmann, 'Sociology of Religion and Sociology of Knowledge', *Sociology and Social Research*, 47 (1963) Luckmann, 'On Religion in Modern Society', *Journal for the Scientific Study of Religion*, II (April, 1963), pp. 147–62; Luckmann, *The Invisible Religion*, op. cit.; Berger, *The Sacred Canopy*, op. cit. In some senses the work of these men stands in the tradition of *Religionswissenschaft*, the *general* (not simply sociological or historical) study of religion—mainly historical and comparative. This approach was begun in Germany and it was in this intellectual context that Weber crystallized his distinctively *sociological* study of religion. Other important figures included Sombart,

Ernst Troeltsch and Joachim Wach. For some of the major characteristics of *Religionswissenschaft* see Joseph M. Katagawa, 'Life and Thought of Joachim Wach', in Wach, *The Comparative Study of Religions*, New York, 1958, pp. xiii–xlviii.

40. *The Invisible Religion*, op. cit., p. 12 and *passim*.
41. Berger, *The Sacred Canopy*, op. cit., pp. 175–8.

3

Major Issues in the Analysis of Religion

Basic Problems of Definition

It has often been argued that it is fruitless to delve very deeply into problems of definition and conceptualization in the sociology of religion. The authority of Max Weber may be invoked in support of such a contention:

> To define 'religion', to say what it *is*, is not possible at the start of a presentation. . . . Definition can be attempted, if at all, only at the conclusion of the study. The essence of religion is not even our concern, as we make it our task to study the conditions and effects of a particular type of social behavior.
>
> The external courses of religious behavior are so diverse that an understanding of this behavior can only be achieved from the viewpoint of the subjective experiences, ideas, and purposes of the individuals concerned—in short, from the viewpoint of the religious behavior's 'meaning' (*Sinn*).[1]*

Three points should be noted about this passage. First, Weber claims that in so far as definition is possible it can be accomplished only after empirical inquiry and discussion. But, we may ask, inquiry into and discussion about *what*? Second, he speaks of the *essence* of religion. But is this what is required of a definition of religion? Third, Weber refers to religious behaviour. But on what grounds can he logically make such reference since he has declined to define it? Our objections to Weber's position are basically that it is impossible to analyse something without having criteria for the identification of that something; and that it is not the essence of religion which we are after, as if there were something 'out there' to be apprehended as 'religious', but rather a sociological definition which will enable us to analyse in a rigorous and consistent manner.

* Notes for this chapter begin on page 70.

Now it should be emphasized in all fairness to Weber himself that he did quite obviously have criteria as to what constituted the sphere of his inquiry into religion. In his case it was a concern with what Parsons calls 'the grounds of meaning', or the basic perspectives around which a group or society of individuals 'organize' their life —their basic orientations to human and social life, conceptions of time, the meaning of death; in fact the basic cosmological conceptions in relation to human existence. Thus this was Weber's primary point of reference, not 'religion' itself. On the other hand, this point of reference came very close to being what Western scholars usually meant by the term religion—since the grounds of meaning have entailed in practically all, if not entirely all, societies a subscription to beliefs in supernatural entities or forces. More generally these were beliefs which, in Pareto's term, 'surpass experience'.[2] Thus although Weber was reluctant to define religion for sociological purposes he did have a fairly clear-cut conception of the boundaries of the problem-area he was discussing; and these boundaries coincided fairly well with what was widely understood at that time as constituting religion.

Weber did not arrive at a conclusive definition of the religious phenomenon. And yet in his work we can see that it is unlikely that he could really have considered the definitional problem an unimportant one. One major clue to this diagnosis is Weber's frequent emphasis upon rationality as the increasingly dominant mode of cognition and evaluation in early twentieth-century societies. He thought that modern industrial societies were characterized by the tendency for individuals to be guided in their actions by considerations of the most appropriate logical means to specific ends. Moreover the ends themselves were regarded as being of a secular kind— prestige, wealth, particular forms of social organization and so on. The important point to note here is that in spite of tending to equate inquiry into 'the grounds of meaning' with the sociology of religion, Weber did not in the final analysis regard as religious the basic 'ground of meaning' which he considered to be characteristic of modern society. Unlike some later sociologists, Weber did not regard the most general cultural orientations of modern society as being by definition 'religious'.[3]

The value of sociological definitions, classifications and conceptualizations is to be seen in their fruitfulness in theorizing about and explaining social phenomena. There is necessarily an element of arbitrariness in sociological definitions; but we may distinguish basically between types of definition which are in one sense extremely arbitrary, so-called *nominal* definitions, and those which are formulated in reference to empirical phenomena and in the course of an attempt to grapple with the diversity and uniqueness of those phenomena, so-called *real* definitions.[4] Whereas a nominal definition is attractive because it can be fitted into an already adumbrated conceptual scheme, more or less regardless of particular empirical problems; a real definition is used in a very different way—namely, in the statement of a proposition about the empirical world. The proposition tends to be *constrained*, as a matter of degree, by previously explicated conceptual and theoretical schemes.[5] Thus it should be clear that the definitional problem is not a trivially scholastic one. Its solution is indeed closely bound up with the capacity to arrive at satisfactory accounts of religious phenomena. A definition which is very general and 'fuzzy' does not lend itself easily to systematic analysis.

It will probably be illuminating to consider Durkheim's approach to the problem of definition, classification and analytic isolation.[6] In his definition of religion Durkheim immediately faced the problem of the relationship between his own sociological predilections and commonsense, intuitive definitions of religion. One of his foremost concerns was that if he were to adopt a supernaturalistic conception of religion he would thereby rule Buddhism out of analytic court. As Spiro points out, this was an unwarranted worry on Durkheim's part, since Durkheim wrongly assumed that there were no supernatural conceptions in Buddhist religions.[7] (Durkheim's mistake in this respect was the rather common one of focusing upon the philosophical dimension of religious culture and paying insufficient attention to the operative beliefs of 'ordinary' individuals.) Durkheim obviously wanted to incorporate all religions (as intuitively recognized) within his purview, but to avoid the inconsistency manifested in any approach which made beliefs in a god (or gods) a defining characteristic of religion and which, at the same time, called primitive, nontheistic belief systems religious. Hence Durkheim's definition of religion as 'a unified system of beliefs and practices relative to sacred things, that is to say, things set apart and forbidden—beliefs and practices which unite into one single moral community called a Church, all those who adhere to them'.[8] We have already indicated in the first chapter the kind of difficulty to which such a general and vague specification of religion leads. Not only does such a definition 'let in' many phenomena which it is almost impossible to analyse in terms that are applicable to conventionally understood religion; but it is also extremely difficult to handle. The latter deficiency hinges on the point that sacredness is surely a matter of degree. Are we to define as religious all those beliefs and values which are sacredly fundamental to a society—for example, belief in the virtue of worldly success?[9]

Inclusive, broad definitions of religion appear to spring from two sources. First, they have been proposed by those whose conception of a social system emphasizes the need for individuals to be controlled by some overriding loyalty to a central set of beliefs and values. Second, they have been proposed, somewhat negatively, by sociologists who are concerned with more detailed and closely circumscribed problems, such as the study of particular religious organizations. Since basic definitional problems do not impinge directly on their work there is little intellectual incentive to use precise definitions. The pressure to employ more restrictive and exclusive, narrow definitions also arises in connection with particular intellectual stances. First, there are those sociologists who do not see social systems as necessarily held together by homogeneous commitments to a central set of precious values and beliefs. These frequently emphasize the greater importance of power and force. The restrictive or exclusive definition is attractive to some of these because they find that the claim that certain phenomena are religious is a case of special pleading for religiosity, a manifestation of an anxiety about an areligious world. Second, those who wish to assess the extent to which societies operate in terms of religious commitments, or to examine the tensions between religious and non-religious conceptions of the social order, are more likely to prefer exclusive definitions of religion. (As with the two variants of the first category of preferences, these two variants of exclusivism may be held simultaneously by the same sociologist.[10]) These two opposing sets of views and interests confront each other mainly in reference to a number of major changes which have taken place in industrial societies during the twentieth century. In brief the *inclusivist* will see such belief systems as Communism as of the same sociological species as religion, whereas the *exclusivist* will not. The latter will be interested, to continue with the example, in a system which, like Communism, makes an explicit claim to reject all religious commitments as such. The real problem, perhaps, is whether strong commitment to ideals, particularly those which entail an element of sacredness and preciousness and operate as basic premises on which people act or claim to act, should be considered as religious commitments. An associated problem is whether commitment to participation in the affairs of organizations and collectivities that proclaim themselves to be religious should always be regarded as religious commitment. We will deal with each of these problems in turn.

Although Communism is perhaps the most outstanding example, there are a number of 'isms' which the inclusivist tends to regard as religions. Not only political ideologies, such as nationalism and Fascism, but also other belief systems, such as secularism, humanism, psychoanalysis 'as a way of life', and so on, are regarded by the inclusivist as religions—although it is important to note that exceedingly few studies of such phenomena have been undertaken within the framework of the sociology of religion.[11] We are confronted in relation to this problem by a distinction which will recur in this analysis—between, on the one hand, definitions which are *functional*, and, on the other hand, definitions which are *substantive*. This is not the same as the distinction between nominal and real definitions—although there is a close proximity, since functional definitions tend in practice to be nominal definitions and substantive definitions tend to be real definitions. A functional definition is one which uses as the criteria for identifying and classifying a phenomenon the functions which that phenomenon performs: the functions which a system requires are stipulated and then observed social and cultural phenomena are classified and identified on the basis of the functions which they perform.[12] From such a perspective, phenomena such as Communism may become identified as religious in a strong sense—when it is said that Communism *is* a religion, because of the function it fulfils—or in a weak sense—when it is said that Communism is a *functional equivalent* to religion. By this term is meant that Communism performs functions—has social consequences for the system in which it is present—similar to those of conventionally and intuitively understood religion in non-Communist societies. The functional-equivalent thesis is important because it combines an element of substantive definition with the functional definition. That is, Communism is functionally equivalent to religion, *as substantively defined*.

Commitments to, say, humanism or 'psychoanalyticism' pose greater problems than Communism. It is much easier to see features analogous to self-declared, organized religion in Communism than in such orientations and yet some humanist movements have calculatedly espoused a religious style. Many of the recruits to such 'isms' have previously been highly committed to some obviously-religious movement and their new involvement constitutes what we will here call *surrogate religiosity*.[13]

The phenomenon which we have labelled surrogate religiosity bears directly on the present attempt to isolate and define the religious phenomenon. For much of the difficulty in demarcating the boundaries of religion pertains to the kinds of commitment into which people in contemporary industrial societies enter in search of an alternative to a religious adherence which no longer satisfies them. It is basically in the face of this that the present analysis tends strongly towards the exclusivist type of definitional approach. For one of the most interesting and significant characteristics of modern societies would be lost to the sociological perspective if the various 'isms' of which we have spoken were regarded as fundamentally religious for sociological purposes; since their adherents have in many, if not all, cases chosen to renounce contact with the supernatural or spiritual, and the explicit, official values of such groups also obviously deny their reality.[14]

A number of functional definitions are employed within the sociology of religion. First, and least satisfactory, there is that functional approach which defines religion in terms of its concern with 'ultimate problems'—on the assumption that all societies or most individuals in all societies have ultimate problems.[15] In one sense this emphasis may be made into a substantive definition. Yinger has recently suggested that sociologists might attempt to tap the religiosity of individuals by asking them questions about themes sociologically adjudged to be within the domain of 'ultimacy'.[16] In other words, whilst that which sought to solve ultimate problems was regarded as religion—a functional definition of religion—in order to use the concept of ultimacy in empirical inquiry, religion or ultimacy be defined in something approaching substantive terms. The substance of religion therefore consists in beliefs and values relating directly to so-called ultimacy. Aside from the very formidable problem of delineating in a non-arbitrary way what the sociologist is to include and exclude from this domain, one has also to question seriously the sociological validity of research which proceeds by asking people whether they are concerned with ultimate problems, so allowing *respondents* to interpret 'ultimacy'.[17]

Second, another functional approach, most closely linked to the work of Parsons and Bellah, specifies religion as the 'highest' and most general 'level' of culture. In practice, this closely coalesces with the ultimacy approach. But formally the argument is that in any system of human action individuals are 'controlled' by the norms of interaction prescribed by the social system, and that in turn the social system is 'controlled' by the cultural system of beliefs, values and symbols. The cultural system performs the function of providing the general guidelines for human action; at the most general level of the cultural system itself are 'the grounds of meaning' and these are typically identified as the sphere of religious beliefs and values. In this sense, it is said, all societies manifest religious beliefs and values.[18] This is the epitome of the nominal, functional approach to definition. On the other hand it is not an approach which is sustained rigorously by its proponents. They frequently speak in an ambiguous way of the differentiation of the religious sphere from other spheres— suggesting on the one hand that religion in modern societies is still of *fundamental* culture significance, and yet at the same time arguing, in reference to the *empirical* evidence, that religion has become differentiated from other spheres of socio-cultural life in such a way as to make it at best one of a series of interrelated social sectors with no significant degree of autonomy.[19] In effect, these theorists cling to a purely functional and nominal definition when speaking in very abstract terms of systems of action. But, when confronted with concrete cases, they veer, inconsistently, towards a commonsense definition based on conventional, everyday usage. This inconsistency and the intellectual strains arising from it are undoubtedly associated with the acceptability to these theorists of such notions as 'the religion of Americanism', 'secular religion' and 'civic religion'. These notions do *not* conform to the spirit of conventional definitions—which emphasize beliefs about a transcendent or superempirical reality; rather, they overarch and 'contain' religious beliefs and values as normally understood. In this way Parsons and Bellah are able to have the best of both worlds and so maintain some semblance of consistency. A variant of this functional approach, employed most frequently by Parsons, approaches religion in terms of its significance in the social sphere alone. Parsons conceives this sphere in terms of regularized patterns of human interaction—the most salient sociological category being that of values. Committed to the view that in ongoing systems of social interaction values are the dominant factors in guiding and constraining social action, Parsons also sees religion, therefore, in terms of values when he is speaking of the social system. Numerous difficulties arise in this connection—notably the virtual impossibility of deciding whether any particular value, such as democracy or the rule of law, is in any useful sense 'religious'.[20]

Third, there is the functional approach proposed by Luckmann. Luckmann's definition owes nothing specifically to modern trends in functional analysis; but is an extension of Durkheim's approach to the problem. For Luckmann everything human is also religious, religion being the capacity of the human organism to transcend its biological nature through the construction of objective, morally binding and all-embracing universes of meaning.[21] This, although in one sense specific, is also the most inclusive of all functional definitions. And the questions which it raises have mainly to do with the boundaries of the sociology of religion and, indeed, the whole issue of the division of labour within sociology. Basically, Luckmann and Berger (although the latter operates with a much narrower, exclusive definition of religion) see the study of religion as part of the more fundamental enterprise of the sociology of *knowledge*. The pressure towards such an inclusive definition of religion, i.e. that religion is an anthropologically distinctive attribute of the socio-cultural condition, derives from Luckmann's negative estimate of the typical sociologist's focus on institutional religion. He argues against the focus on 'objective' and 'visible' manifestations of religiosity and seeks to rest his own sociology of religion on the 'subjective' and relatively invisible aspects of religiosity.[22] But it does not follow that one has to go as far in the direction of the 'invisible' as Luckmann does in order to bypass the traps and deficiencies of the first approach. The difficulties in Luckmann's stance are highlighted by the distinction he is forced to make between 'the world view' as 'an elementary social form of religion'[23]—a 'nonspecific form'[24]—and 'the configuration of religious representations that form a sacred universe . . . , a *specific historical social form of religion*'.[25] The point of stressing the first seems to be lost once the second is introduced (which it will be noticed must be *substantive*, as opposed to purely functional).

The course suggested in this book is in the direction of a definition which is substantive and real, and also as a corollary it will be exclusive rather than inclusive. One of the most common arguments for this approach is the simple one that it conforms to everyday, intuitive conceptions of religion. But a much more compelling case would rest on other considerations. First, there is the phenomenon which we have already mentioned—that of surrogate religiosity.[26] Second, there is the point that unless we have a fairly tightly circum-scribed conception of the religious phenomenon (or phenomena) we cannot, without extreme difficulty, engage in consistent, systematic analyses and focus on cause and effect relationships; for such exercises necessitate our being able to discriminate between religious variables and non-religious variables. Third, is it not of great sociological significance to inquire into the factors effecting changes in systems of belief and value which are explicitly super-empirical or transcendental in their reference; since nobody could conceivably deny that significant proportions of the individuals in contemporary industrial societies have either given up or come seriously to doubt the validity of such orientations? Implementation of the view propounded by Berger and Luckmann that the study of religious beliefs be located within the wider frame of reference of the sociology of knowledge would indeed enable us to examine shifts from superempirical to empirical referents (and vice versa); but the attractiveness of this approach is considerably mitigated by Luckmann's insistence that we define religion in the very broad terms already indicated.

The category 'religion' is one which has *arisen* in socio-cultural contexts where the Judeo-Christian tradition has predominated. A great analytic difficulty in the sociology of religion is the extent to which our basic conceptual apparatus is derived from the doctrines of Christian religions. The church-sect distinction developed initially in a sociological context by Weber and Troeltsch is the outstanding *specific* example of such a 'Christian' conception.[27] The ideas of religion and religiosity are products of basically Christian thinking because of the tensions expressed in Christian doctrine as between, on the one hand, social and terrestrial reality and, on the other, transcendent spiritual reality; and, more important, the prescription either that the affairs of the former should be brought into line with the latter or that the former constitutes some God-given testing ground, to be lived through, confronted and not eschewed.[28] As Weber put it so often, Christianity is basically an inner-worldly religious orientation. To be religious therefore 'makes sense' in Christianity in a way which is, strictly speaking, alien to other 'religions'—the contrast appearing most sharply as between Christianity on the one hand and Buddhism on the other.[29] The category 'religion' thus arises in a situation in which there is a particular type of ambivalence as to the relationship between this, material world and another 'world'. In different forms the Buddhist orientations and the Hindu orientation are other-worldly, seeking an escape from this world. Christianity, most markedly in its Protestant variations, perpetuates the category 'religion' precisely because it has images of how the world ought to be.

In these terms two basic problems of analysis arise. The first of these relates to Christianity; the second to Eastern religions. Christianity, it may be argued, is in a sense a self-destroying system.[30] Weber's interpretation of the development of Christianity from its earliest to its modern Protestant forms emphasizes the historical trend towards an ever-increasing inner-worldliness. The culmination of this process, as Weber saw it, was the way in which Protestantism promoted economic rationality, a rationality which eventually became autonomous and self-sustaining. Parsons in elaboration and modification of the Weber thesis has tried to demonstrate how, through the successive stages of what are called respectively the 'medieval synthesis', the 'reformation phase' and the 'denominational phase', Christian religious values have become increasingly embedded in the social structure of Western societies (notably, with respect to the modern period, the United States); at the same time religious organizations and religious action become more differentiated from other spheres of social activity.[31] As Parsons develops his thesis the problem is posed very acutely as to what we mean by 'religious' and religiosity. Parsons rightly maintains that it would be wrong to equate religiosity in a simple way with other-worldliness in the Weberian sense. On such an interpretation Protestantism would be the least religious of all religions.[32] How then do we define the sphere of religion in predominantly Christian societies, when the Christian is enjoined to preoccupy himself, and historically has preoccupied himself, with the attempt to Christianize society and in so doing has made religion a differentiated sphere of activity? By Christianization of society Parsons means basically that the social values implicated in Christian culture have become institutionalized in secular society; that is, they have become 'part and parcel' of the everyday operation of social life. Thus we may note an important difference between Parsons and Weber. Whereas Weber appears to say that Protestantism promoted its own eventual destruction by its emphasis on individualism and social involvement,[33] Parsons maintains that such involvement is from the sociologist's standpoint the type-case of the social grounding of religion.[34] Religious values have become more, not less, the keynote of the value systems of modern Western societies. And yet Parsons in the same analysis remains well aware of the kind of problem which has been raised in this chapter:

> Values—i.e., moral orientations towards the problems of life in this world—are never the whole of religion, if indeed its most central aspect. My suggestion is that the principal roots of the present religious concern do not lie in *relative* moral decline or inadequacy (relative, that is, to other periods in our society's history) but rather in problems in the other areas of religion, problems of the bases of faith and the definitions of the ultimate problems of meaning.[35]

In the light of these observations on the relation of the category of religion to Christian doctrine and the history of Christianity, we may crystallize the major problem as having to do with the attempt to delineate sociologically the category of religion *bearing in mind its Christian basis*. In Christian terms, as O'Dea has put it, 'religion both needs most and suffers most from institutionalization'.[36] How can we know when religion has been institutionalized? If we know, can we still say that it is religion?

Although the tension between religious 'purity' and religious 'compromise' is implicit in Christian doctrine in a way which is not true of other religions,[37] it is nevertheless interesting to look at the problem of institutionalization in a very different religious setting. In the post-independence period after 1946, Indian political leaders attempted to establish a secular state, largely along the lines of American society. There was a wish to limit the sphere of operation of religious guidelines; which in turn implies, of course, that Indian society was regarded as 'too religious'. Yet the difficulties in formulating proposals for the establishment of a secular state were considerable. In the main they resulted from the fact that there was no *general*, culturally established distinction between a religious and a secular sphere, or even an acknowledgment that Hinduism was a religion. A distinction between religious and secular was perceived mainly by Western-educated or Western-oriented politicians and intellectuals. Hinduism was to others a way of life, a cultural system. Here then was an attempt to *institutionalize a secular condition* in a situation which culturally made no provision for a distinction between a religious and a non-religious secular sphere. The commitment to the ideal of political secularity necessitated the political elite defining and delineating the sphere of religion and religiosity. This is, of course, not a problem peculiar to the societies of the Indian sub-continent. It is simply that the issue has been a more vexing one in societies such as India and Burma.[38] The source upon which the Indian secular state ideal is drawn, namely the United States of America, has had significant political, legal and constitutional problems in defining the sphere of religion—and this in a society to which the Christian conceptions of religious and secular are in no sense alien.

Primitive societies do not of course face problems of this kind. Both because they are culturally inhibitive of and relatively well insulated from a situational religion/non-religion distinction and because they are almost by definition removed from the political exigencies of having to face the problem, we do not find obvious parallels or analogies to the situation obtaining in the industrialized or industrializing societies of the world. But it is precisely because the distinction arises neither in an intrinsic cultural respect nor in an instrumental political respect that the sociologist is burdened with analytical perplexities. We shall have cause to look at the primitive societal problems at a later stage. Suffice to point out here that indigenous *conceptions* of super-empirical and transcendental realms are often only of minor significance in the thought patterns of primitive societies. And yet of course beliefs in the spiritual and extra- or superhuman qualities of inanimate and non-human animate objects are manifold. In this respect crucial decisions have to be taken about the inclusion or exclusion of the latter from the sphere of religion.[39]

The category 'religion' is historically, then, a societal category. It is only, like many other sociological concepts and categories, by derivation a sociological category or concept.[39a] Bearing this in mind we must ask: What adequate case can be made for extending or violating its usage? To modify it along the lines suggested by some functional sociologists is both to miss the really interesting and demanding *sociological* problems *and at the same time to go beyond the role of the sociologist into the role of the theologian or religious intellectual.* In the final chapter it will be argued that given the present state of theology

—particularly so-called radical theology—some degree of confusion of this kind is inevitable. Theologians and their audiences are resting some of their arguments on quasi-sociological insights and an implicit debate has in this sense been proceeding for some years. The objections to most of the functional definitions hinge, more precisely, on three points. First, if sociologists are going to state the ultimate essence of religion or what it ought to be then the least they should do is to make explicit the *theological* issues and problems. They should not utilize a prescriptive definition of religion like Tillich's as an analytically-neutral definitional statement. Second, they should be aware that any definition which they may propose will inevitably be, at least indirectly, challenged by theologians. This, too, points to the necessity for sociologists to familiarize themselves with the work of theologians, philosophers of religion and religious intellectuals. Third, it must be emphasized that it is functional approaches which get into 'theological difficulties' most easily—since to talk in functional terms is to make far-reaching statements about the overall significance of religion in a society or in societies in general.[40]

That we have argued here for a conformity to the ordinary cultural connotations of 'religion' does *not* mean that we can be content with using the term loosely as in everyday discourse. There has to be some degree of 'tightening' and analytic shaping. The definitions proposed here rest upon the substantive, cultural content of religious phenomena. In these terms we define, first, *religious culture. Religious culture is that set of beliefs and symbols (and values deriving directly therefrom) pertaining to a distinction between an empirical and a super-empirical, transcendent reality; the affairs of the empirical being subordinated in significance to the non-empirical.* Second, we define *religious action* simply as: *action shaped by an acknowledgment of the empirical/super-empirical distinction.* These definitions constitute merely an analytic base-line. The remainder of this chapter introduces more complex problems of definitional and methodological elaboration.

It is common for sociologists to draw a definite line between magic and religion.[41] This is usually done by saying that whereas religion involves submissiveness to the super-empirical and concern with the intrinsic attributes of gods, spirits and so on, magic obtains when the individual subordinates the super-empirical or super-natural to the empirical: he is concerned with the instrumental significance of supernature in pursuit of some extrinsic goal. On the other hand, many anthropologists no longer hold to this over-facile distinction or variants of it. Durkheim found a distinction necessary on the grounds of the individualness of magical action and the collective nature of religious action. Tylor, in a well-known distinction, emphasized the 'personalized' nature of the gods, ghosts and spirits in religious belief and practice, in contrast to the impersonal, unindividualized powers characteristic of magical belief and practice.[42] Although such variations noted by Durkheim and Tylor (and many other anthropologists) are of great significance, it is not clear that to make them into two separate systems of thought is particularly useful. Lévi-Strauss argues that although it can

> be said that religion consists in a *humanization of natural laws* and magic in a *naturalization of human actions* . . . , the anthropomorphism of nature (of which religion consists) and the physio-morphism of man (. . . magic) constitute two components which are always given, and vary only in proportion. . . . Each implies the other. The notion of a supernature exists only for a humanity which attributes supernatural powers to itself and in return ascribes the powers of its super-humanity to nature.[43]

Worsley, in trying to dispel the tendency for social scientists to concentrate too much on the broad cosmologies and theologies of primitive societies instead of what Leach calls 'practical religion', argues that the traditional distinctions between magic and religion 'can easily be dismissed: magical actions necessarily imply some theory of the gods, spirits, "life-force", etc.; and religion is not just abstract theology; it is something acted out, i.e., it is usually most manifest as "magic"!'[44]

Thus what is frequently called magic is assimilated to our simple definitions of religious culture and religious action—and this includes witchcraft, sorcery and the like.[45] We do, however, acknowledge that post-primitive societies manifest a greater emphasis upon moral issues in their religious belief systems. It is perhaps this which is the more important point which emerges from the old debates about religion versus magic. In some primitive societies questions of morality are handled separately from religious issues. It is such phenomena which we will have in mind when we speak subsequently of magico-religious cultures.

Two particular problems arise from these definitions. First, there is the problem of religion in primitive societies, which we have already indicated. This issues from the apparent absence of an *internal distinction* between the supernatural and the natural or the empirical and the super-empirical. There has been some controversy on this point, but it seems clear now that members of many primitive societies do not make such a distinction or separation—at least in terms which are directly translatable into those of the so-called world religions. Drawing on the work of Nadel (in his study of Nupe religion) and Evans-Pritchard (in his work on the Azande and the Nuer), Goody has convincingly concluded that the criteria for 'the isolation of sacred or ritual or magico-religious phenomena are derived not from the actor's but from the observer's assessment of what is intrinsic . . .'[46] (In stating this conclusion Goody also makes the important point that the sacred/non-sacred distinction is not intrinsic or internal.) One of the implications of Goody's statement, as he himself sees it, is to open the way for a partial rehabilitation of the usages of the nineteenth-century anthropologists.[47] This is, of course, well in line with the trend of the present argument—in that the need for criteria of religion and non-religion is clearly stressed and, therefore, the question of the factors promoting religious decline becomes an explicit part of our analytic focus. In what manner, however, are we to conclude that many beliefs and actions in primitive societies are religious? Or, more strictly, *how* do we discriminate between that which is religious and that which is non-religious in such settings?

The discovery of the idea of *mana* in Melanesia at the end of the nineteenth century was an important step in the direction of clarifying the definitional problem. Basically an object which is attributed with *mana* is 'charged' with spiritual power. As Berger notes, the discovery of this phenomenon 'suggested that there might be

E

something like a fundamental religious category of cross-cultural scope'; since similar ideas have appeared in all acknowledged religious forms, even though in, for example, Christianity they have not been central.[48] What is important in the present context is that whereas the notion of *mana* does not readily conform to Christian-based conceptions of transcendence, the attribution of spiritual properties to particular objects does imply that there is a reality which is in some sense *beyond* that of immediate everyday experiential reality. Collectively the members of the society in question have a perception of an 'other'. On such terms we can readily accept Lienhardt's point which he makes in his excellent analysis of the Dinka: That to use the distinction between natural and supernatural beings or events 'implies a conception of the course of laws of nature quite foreign to Dinka thought'.[49] In a sense the Dinka accept what appears to us as supernatural as natural. In acknowledging this observation it should be stressed with respect to the definitions stipulated above that the terms empirical and super-empirical must not be taken to mean factual and fictional, real and unreal or some other proximate dichotomy. Rather, the distinction is almost the same as in the strict scientific sense. Empirical means that which is readily observable and accessible, super-empirical (or in the scientific case non-empirical or theoretical) means accounts or conceptions which are brought to bear on and relate to the empirical. The crucial feature which in this sense marks off religion (and magic, superstition, astrology, etc.) from science is the attribution of 'otherness' to the non-empirical. It is this very attribution which makes the non-empirical best rendered as *super-empirical*.

Another closely related problem is raised by pantheistic beliefs as these have been prominent amongst elite groups in India, Japan and China for many centuries. In the present context we must call this *religious pantheism*, to distinguish it from non-religious forms of pantheism.[50] Swanson succinctly describes the most extreme form of religious pantheism, what he calls universal pantheism, as 'the doctrine that there is no distinction between the life of the infinite godhead and the history of the universe itself; all things being but aspects or activities of the one god, their distinctive attributes or powers only special purposes of his, their careers determined by

their services to his immutable nature'.[51] The ramifications of this
phenomenon in terms of our definition are related to the primitive
societal case in that there is a strong *immanentist* element in each;
immanentist beliefs being those which stress the presence and operation of spiritual forces. In primitive societies immanence is prominent
in the sense that it is believed that spiritual qualities can be *transferred*
from an object or person to another object or person. (The same idea
is of course inherent in many sacramental practices—notably those
of Roman Catholicism.) In pantheism immanence is much more
thoroughgoing—since life itself is the continual operation of 'the
spirit'. But although superficially problematic in relation to our
definition, religious pantheism can be accommodated within it in
either of two ways. First, it may be said that pantheism denies the
empirical altogether—believing in complete 'otherness' to the point
that 'thisness' is dissolved. Second, and perhaps preferably, pantheism
may be said to postulate levels of spiritual reality—'the world' is an
emanation from a higher-order being, agency or realm. (Pantheism
contrasts most strongly with those religious belief systems which
have postulated a radical *dualism*. Zoroastrianism, and subsequently
what has been described as 'that bastard offshoot of Zoroastrianism
and Christianity',[52] Manicheanism, involved commitment to views
that this world was inherently evil and that God had not created the
Devil and sinfulness.)

Dimensions of Religiosity

In the first chapter it was indicated that in recent years sociologists of
religion had become increasingly dissatisfied with the *unitary* conceptions or definitions of religion which had prevailed up to the late
1950s. Thus Lenski and others, notably Glock, began to outline and
subsequently utilize in empirical research schemata of dimensions
of religiosity; that is, of analysis which explicitly proposed
that there are separate aspects of a person's religiosity. These dimensions of religiosity may vary independently of each other—an
individual may be high on one dimension but not on another.
While facilitating more precise and methodologically sophisticated
research, the attempt to utilize dimensions of religiosity has not been

altogether satisfactory. In the attempt to move away from unitary, and therefore usually unwieldy, definitions of religion, Lenski and Glock have probably gone too far in the opposite direction. The criticisms which may be made against them fall into two main categories. First, there is the problem of the meaningfulness of the dimensions as dimensions *of religiosity*. Second, there is the thorny problem of the relationship between measures of the religiosity of *individuals* and the religiosity of the system as a whole; recent research has concentrated almost entirely on defining the religiosity of the individual.

Those who have used dimensional schemata have tended not to see the need for an underlying or master-conception of religiosity. Rather, the dimensions have been established on a fairly *ad hoc*, intuitive basis. The line of reasoning appears to be of the following kind: In empirical work in the sociology of religion, analysts have used the most obvious estimates of so-called religiosity, such as attendance at church services or membership of religious organizations. These are unsatisfactory, in that they fail to distinguish between orientation to the religious organization and orientation to the belief system of the organization, among other important considerations. Most obviously, such indicators as membership and attendance do not have any clear relationship to the definitions of religion, be they functional or substantive, which lie behind such practices, such as the ultimate concern of the belief-in-supernatural- entities definitions.

So far, so good. But the next step—of actually establishing the dimensions—appears to involve little more than listing those features of religious identification or commitment which have cropped up in literature in the sociology of religion. In other words, recent attempts to establish dimensions of religiosity flow not so much from a desire to break down analytically a clearly established or proposed concept of religiosity; but rather to 'add together' available and promising indicators, so arriving *atomistically* at a total, aggregated conception of religiosity. In Lenski's work, the broader definitional problem itself is eschewed as being of relatively little consequence and the definition he actually states is, in his own words, one which makes 'every normal adult member of any human society religious'.[53] In contrast, Lenski's own schema of dimensions of religiosity, consisting in the four aspects of associationism, communalism, orthodoxy and devotionalism, adds up to a much more *specific* conception of religion. *Logically, an individual who is zero-ranking on all of these is irreligious or areligious*; which is, of course, completely incongruent with the remark of Lenski's which we have quoted.

Glock's five postulated dimensions of religiosity are less open to criticism, in so far as they are at least located in a defined category of religious values or perspectives, which stand in substantive contrast to a category of non-religious or secular world-views.[54] The dimensions are: the *experiential* (subjective religious experience or emotion); the *ritualistic* (specific practices expected of religious adherents); the *ideological* (the actual beliefs held by adherents); the *intellectual* (knowledge of basic tenets of faith); the *consequential* (the secular effects of religious belief, practice and experience).[55] The most immediately striking problems here have to do with the separability of the dimensions, most notably the ideological from the intellectual. The experiential would appear very difficult to handle satisfactorily in the survey context, in so far as the sociologist is seeking to tap the depth and scope of the individual's religious emotionalism.[56] It is also difficult to see in what way degrees of overall religiosity could be ascertained—not only for the obvious reason that religious expectations vary considerably from religion to religion—but also because at least one of the dimensions, the ideological, has only to do with sociological *description*: Concrete beliefs in the Glockian sense are not a matter of degree. Indeed, perhaps the real significance of the work of Glock and Stark in this field lies in its usefulness for adequate sociological description of the religiosity of individuals. In any case the effectiveness of this schema is severely reduced by the inclusion of a *consequential* dimension. This dimension of religiosity refers to the extent to which religious commitment has consequences in social, economic, political and other spheres. Important as this theme is, it is difficult to see how in any logical sense one may be permitted to include within a schema of dimensions of religiosity a dimension which is a consequence of religiosity. Something cannot be both an aspect of x and at the same time be a consequence of x.[57]

Such criticisms are by no means intended to denigrate the attempt to dimensionalize religion, or religiosity. The problem is of the greatest importance and adequate research cannot proceed without some resolution of it—save in the sense that such sophisticated procedures cannot be employed in historical work, as was argued in the first chapter. But it is important that there should be consistency between general or master conceptions of religiosity and the dimensions of religiosity. And it is in terms of this proposal that we turn now to a brief discussion of further difficulties in Lenski's approach.[58]

As we shall see more fully at a later point in the present chapter, attempts like those of Lenski to isolate dimensions of religiosity have meaning only in reference to societies where religion is, in the terms of Glock and Stark, both differentiated and organized—that is where, on the one hand, religious belief and activity are distinguished from intrinsically non-religious activities (although these may be infused with religious significance) and, on the other hand, religious orientations are based in bounded, organized collectivities of an ostensibly religious nature.[59] This kind of situation is sometimes called one of *institutional* religion, in contrast to the *diffuse* religious situation of, for example, classical China, and indeed also of all primitive societies.[60] Bearing this in mind we can see that two of Lenski's dimensions refer to *social* aspects of so-called religiosity, whilst the orthodoxy and devotional dimensions have reference to *cultural* aspects. The first two, the associational and the communal, relate therefore to the social context or means of gaining, preserving and promoting commitment to doctrinal tenets and devotional practices. As Lenski himself puts it, the communal and the associational aspects concern commitment of the individual to a 'socio-religious group'; orthodoxy and the devotionalism concern commitment to a type of 'religious orientation'.[61] Now it is no mere semantic quibble to ask whether it is helpful to refer to the former category in a straightforward sense as a dimension of religiosity or religious commitment. Following our previously outlined adherence to substantive, cultural definitions of religion, it may be argued that the communal and associational dimensions are at best only indirect measures of religiosity. On the other hand, Lenski's schema throws

up the possibility of knitting together the social and cultural aspects
of religious activities along rather different lines.

Emphasizing again that we are speaking of religion in societies
where religious activities are both differentiated from other kinds of
activity and also relatively organized, we may establish a typology of
orientations to religious activity—that is, activity defined by the leaders
of the organization or movement in question as having to do with
the themes embraced by our previous definition of religious culture.
This typology is established, first, by drawing a distinction between
social and *cultural* aspects of religious activity and, second, by
distinguishing between *consummatory* and *instrumental* attitudes
towards the affairs of the movement or organization.[62] By cross-
tabulating these distinctions we arrive at the following:

ORIENTATIONS TO RELIGIOUS ACTIVITY

	Cultural	Social
Consummatory	1	3
Instrumental	2	4

First, we have the cultural-consummatory type of participation,
which is close to what many would regard as the 'most genuine'
type of religious participation. In this case religious ideals are held
to be valuable in and of themselves and these ideals are the primary
point of reference for participation in the relevant activities. Second,
we have the cultural-instrumental type of participation. Here
religious ideals are used in a manipulatory respect. Religious symbols
are utilized by one group or one individual in order to persuade
others to a certain course of action. Third, we have the social-
consummatory type of participation in which intrinsic satisfaction is
gained from involvement in a community or association of like-
minded people without direct reference to what it is that the people
concerned actually do 'like'. Finally, we have the social-instrumental
participation. Here involvement in the affairs of the group or

organization is regarded in some way as benefiting the individual with respect to a goal or state of affairs which lies beyond that group or organization. That is, the satisfactions gained from involvement are essentially extrinsic to such involvement.[63]

We come now to the problem of the relationship between the religiosity of the individual and the religiosity of the system of which the individual is a member. Glock has argued that the 'religiousness of a society is subject to measurement through aggregating indicators of the religiosity of its constituent members'.[64] It is on the other hand widely recognized in the social sciences that this kind of reasoning commits what is often called the *individualist fallacy*.[65] It is fallacious because one is viewing the system as no more than the sum or aggregation of the properties of the units within it. What one would wish to say about the degree of political democracy, religiosity or whatever of a *system* cannot be couched in the same terms as statements about whether individuals are democratic, religious or whatever. To take a concrete example from the religious sphere, nobody would surely wish to argue that the Soviet Union is more or less the same with respect to the general religiosity of the society as Britain; and yet the evidence that we have suggests a broadly similar pattern of commitment at the level of the individual. It may well be that an argument against this example would be posed in terms of the inadequacy of the information about individual religious commitment—that the evidence of which we are speaking refers in the main to rates of participation in formally defined religious activities, and does not refer to the critical dimensions of commitment to religious beliefs and values. However, the main point to be made against the aggregation argument is this: the fact that a larger proportion of individuals in society *A* are religious when compared to society *B* does not necessarily mean that society *A* is a more religious society than society *B*. In substantiating this statement one can invoke only a small number of points, amongst many possible ones. First, it may be that in society *A* the larger number of religiously committed is to be accounted for in terms of the anti-religiosity of a dominant minority. The fact that the minority is *dominant* means, of course, that the society does not operate on religious principles. Second, it may be the case that in society A there are a number of different religious traditions, which have had to come to terms with each other in such a way as to preclude the 'religious factor' from public affairs. Third, it may be the situation in society A that its relatively high aggregated degree of religiosity is a response to the secularization of major sectors of its social life. And so on. When it is argued that the religiosity of individuals may be aggregated in order to arrive at the religiosity of the society, is it intended that the 'overall' religiosity of each individual be added up so as to make statements of the kind: society A has 66 per cent believers, whereas society B only has 23 per cent believers? Or is it intended that the *intensity* of religiosity should be the focal issue, in which case a relatively small number of intensely religious individuals could make the system very religious—that is, if one adhered to the aggregation position.

Thus the conclusion must be that in so far as the problem of the relative religiosity of societies is a soluble one, we must pay attention to structural and general characteristics of the system as a whole— the degree of differentiation and autonomy of religious sectors in relation to other social sectors, the strategic location or otherwise of religious leaders, the relationships between religious groups and so on. Those factors which we have mentioned here are social-structural ones—factors having to do with the location of, and relations between, groups. But by religiousness of the overall system Glock may be referring to culture—on the assumption that the religious culture of a society consists in a summation of individual religiosities. But even if we confine our attention to culture, the objection must be made that in estimating the degree of religiosity of a particular culture there is much more to consider than aggregate individual attributes; there is, for example, the religious content in art forms or in language, not to speak of distinctively non-religious culture, such as modern science. Social-structural and cultural aspects of religiosity are notoriously difficult to isolate and assess. But there is no denying their great independent significance.[66] It is indeed quite clear that, contrary to Glock's claim, the religiosity of a society cannot be represented simply as the summation of the religiosity of individuals.[67] On the other hand this refutation should not be interpreted as a denial of the worthwhileness of comparing societies in terms of *religiosity at the level of the individual.*

The Problem of Explanation

In the first chapter we touched upon some of the ways in which the classical sociologists of religion approached the problem of explaining religious phenomena. In the present chapter we have so far talked mainly about the terms in which it is sociologically most fruitful to approach the analysis of religious phenomena. We have thus been concerned primarily with the problem of interpretation, as opposed to explanation. In many ways the line between interpretation and explanation is blurred. By interpretation we mean the analytical context of sociological discussion, the mode of *explication*; whereas by *explanation* we mean the attempt to account for various religious phenomena—the stipulation of the conditions under which the problematic phenomenon occurs and the invocation of some general, plausible statement which links these conditions with the phenomenon itself.

In the matter of explanation, sociologists of religion have paid more attention by far to the explanation of religious beliefs, generally —by ascertaining the conditions under which they arise and persist, and by seeking constant factors among these conditions. Most of the explanations of religion-in-general can be characterized as stating (in many diverse forms) that religious beliefs are found where human beings feel unable to control their own destinies. As we have noted, the quest for an explanation of religious phenomena in these general terms has fallen out of fashion and many sociologists have tended to switch their attention to making propositions about the functions which religious beliefs and values perform for the social system in which they appear.[68]

Philosophers have argued that statements of a functional kind can be transformed into statements of a causal-explanatory kind. Thus if one proposes that one of the major functions of religion is to reduce anxiety, the argument goes that anxiety causes religion. Unless specific conditions are introduced into such a statement, then it would appear that the sociologist is claiming that anxiety always gives rise to religious commitment of some kind. This is, of course, an extremely implausible hypothesis and it is, indeed, illustrative of the confusion and vagueness which reign in sociology of religion in matters of explanation. One of the great difficulties in this area is precisely what one means by explanation. Some have claimed that if one can produce systematic and consistent statements and findings about the kind of personality system which is most productive of religious commitment, then one has, in fact, accounted for the phenomenon of individual religiosity.[69] There can, it is argued, be no other explanation for the persistence of religious belief than a specific type of human personality. From a sociological point of view, such arguments are extremely unsatisfactory, since psychological explanations of this kind do not in any way account for the *nature* of the religious commitment. They say nothing about the type of religious belief or value which is held by the individual concerned. What is ideally needed, therefore, in sociological terms is an account of the conditions under which religious beliefs and values are sustained by groups of individuals, and the ways in which they are transmitted and modified. Some anthropologists and sociologists have tried to retain a focus upon personality variables by regarding the personality system as a variable which intervenes between one sociological variable and another. In this case, the personality system is seen as transmitting the effects of a social-group characteristic into a religious-cultural characteristic. Spiro, for example, maintains that the crucial social-group variable is family structure; and that by an examination of family structures in different kinds of societies we will be able to see what kinds of personality are produced by a system of social relations in the family, and to see how the personality type in turn produces a specific variant of religious belief and value.[70] A difficulty about this argument is that it seems unsatisfactory to begin at the point of family structure; since family structure itself is constrained by other more general characteristics of the society in question. In any case, it is only by examining the *context* in which the individual personality operates that we can get at the important sociological questions having to do with variations in religious belief and commitment.

The only way out of such dilemmas appears to be that sociologists should regard as open the question of causal priorities in each specific case which they examine, rather than attempt to discover an ubiquitous and universal set of social processes which are productive of religious phenomena. This means that we should realize that in some social systems religion is a relatively independent variable and that in other social systems it is a relatively dependent variable. Thus religion at some time and in some place may be relatively autonomous and determinate with respect to other processes and structures within a social system and at other times and places it may be 'at the mercy' of political, economic and other social factors. In arguing for such an approach, it should be emphasized that we must always stipulate what aspect of religion we are talking about—the major distinction which is always necessary being that between cultural and social aspects of religion. Religious functionaries may be extremely influential in a particular society (as political individuals, for example) without their influence involving the shaping of religious beliefs and values other than, perhaps, a subservience to the idea of religion itself. In such a case, it is clearly a social aspect of religion which is being assigned some kind of causal priority. On the other hand, in cases where political decisions, for example, are taken with respect to religious beliefs or values, then equally clearly it is a cultural aspect of religion which enjoys autonomy. The most complete case of religious autonomy in these terms would, of course, be that in which both cultural and social aspects of religion were synchronized and equally influential.[71]

It is important to note that many so-called explanations of religion proposed by functional theorists are couched in terms of properties of individuals rather than properties of social groups or systems. To speak in terms of anxiety and uncertainty is to argue usually at the level of the individual. Such arguments, as we have noted, do not say anything about the relationship between religious factors and other inter-individual, social factors. The major exception to this tendency amongst functional theorists is to be found when emphasis is laid upon religion as the most fundamental aspect of culture—religious beliefs and values provide a kind of pattern or template in terms of which individuals interact and organize their life, both as individuals and in terms of their group interaction.[72]

One of the few comprehensive attempts to state specifically the social conditions under which patterns of religious belief emerge is that of Swanson in his book *The Birth of the Gods*.[73] Swanson's basic proposition is essentially a Durkheimian one: that the group structure of a social system significantly affects the character, and more particularly the form, of the religious belief system. More specifically, Swanson proposes that it is the number and nature of what he calls the sovereign groups in a society which determine the structure and form of the religious belief system. In these terms, he produces on the basis of an analysis of a large number of primitive and pre-industrial societies a set of findings about the relationship between sovereign group structure and religious beliefs in spiritual entities which symbolize experiences that men have with the activities and purposes of independent and organized groups. Regardless of its exact content (which we look at in chapter six) Swanson's approach is important because it does come close to the appropriate explanatory principles. Swanson produces a general proposition which can be applied to all cases where religion is found, that is to say, the relationship between group-structural experience and religious belief; and then proceeds to account for all specific cases in terms of this general proposition. One difficulty, however, in interpreting Swanson's findings is the problem of the degree to which religious beliefs become autonomous and therefore themselves are determinate with respect to the structure of social systems. However, this point notwithstanding, Swanson provides valuable insights into the correlations between religious beliefs and the structure of human societies, and although the problem of substantive explanation and the assigning of causal priorities may still be problematic, it is only in this way that some of the larger questions in the sphere of religious behaviour can be approached.

There are a number of similar problems in the sociology of religion which can be, perhaps more fruitfully, attacked in explanatory terms. As we shall see, one of the more promising areas of inquiry in the field is that of the conditions under which religious organizations change over time. Much is now known about the conditions under which religious sects either retain their sectarian characteristics or become modified and move into a more mainstream position in the socio-cultural system. Explanation in this sphere involves the specification of the initial characteristics of the religious movement, the social and cultural conditions which it encounters, and the statement of generalizations about the characteristics and conditions which lead (as a matter of degree) to continued insulation from the wider society or absorption into it.[74]

In order to highlight the complexities involved in coping in explanatory terms with religious phenomena we will here focus on a concrete example which has given rise to recent controversy. In general terms this example has to do with the famous thesis advanced by Weber that Protestantism (particularly in its Calvinistic version) was a major determinant in the development of a specific ethos or 'spirit' of capitalistic economic orientations; the latter being characterized by frugality, a disposition to defer immediate gains for long-term benefits—in broad terms, economic rationality.[75] More specifically, we are concerned with a recent controversy in the United States about the differential dispositions on the part of Catholics and Protestants in the direction of economic, scientific and intellectual achievement. The controversy was stimulated by Lenski's *The Religious Factor*. Lenski had tried to ascertain whether religious commitment was playing, and would be likely in the future to play, a crucial constraining and directing role in the main spheres of American life. Taking four categories, White Protestant, Negro Protestant, Catholic and Jew, Lenski geared his inquiry to an examination of the linkage between religious commitment and 'non-religious' commitment, in terms of the four dimensions of religious commitment we have already adumbrated.[76] Lenski's most relevant findings were marked and significant differences between Catholicism and White Protestantism—Catholics being less highly motivated economically, educatively and scientifically than Protestants and more likely to vote Democrat and favour state intervention than Protestants. Partly by extrapolation and partly through the invocation of further sociological considerations, Lenski came to the conclusion that American society was being increasingly *compartmentalized* along socio-religious grounds—that whereas previously ethnic attachment had been a major basis of solidary grouping this was being steadily supplanted by attachment to subcommunities consisting in individuals of similar religious commitment, as indicated, for example, by the tendency for Americans to marry across ethnic boundaries but less frequently across religious boundaries.

Lenski's findings, interpretations and predictions have been subjected to considerable criticism by Greeley, notably in his book, *Religion and Career* (1963).[77] Greeley presents findings arising from a national survey of the aims, ambitions and dispositions of members of graduating classes in American universities and colleges, which to all intents and purposes show little significant differences between Catholics and Protestants—for it is around the Protestant/Catholic issue that the controversy revolves. In interpreting his results, Greeley makes a number of objections to Lenski's approach. The principal of these is that Lenski did not allow for ethnic variation within the Catholic category and that in any case the Detroit sample was, relative to national proportions, overweighted within the Catholic category in favour of Catholics who had recently immigrated. (Note that Lenski did make an ethnic distinction within the Protestant category from the outset.)

The major point of interest which this debate raises in the context of a consideration of explanatory problems is this. Greeley acknowledges that Lenski's book demonstrates 'that religious variation cannot be dismissed merely as the result of the operation of current economic and social forces . . .'[78] The question remains, nevertheless, says Greeley: 'to what extent are the formal creed, code, and cult of a given religion responsible for the variations observed among members of the different groups? Are religious differences the result of the theology and the morality of a religion or are they the result of the social experiences of the group which are, in turn, the result of historical "accidents"?'[79] As Greeley further points out, in some respects the answer is obvious. Catholic beliefs and values with respect to family morality obviously relate *directly* to Catholic dispositions in respect of birth control and sexual behaviour. But in many other instances the connections are far from clear.

What needs to be taken carefully into account in dealing with this kind of problem is the actual socio-historical experiences of the religious group under consideration, as Greeley notes. We have already seen that the thesis proposed by Sombart, for example, as to the significance of the Jews in the development of modern capitalism can be interpreted (perhaps rather 'generously') as resting on such an emphasis—that is, to regard the historical experiences and, more particularly, the structural *location* of the Jewish people as a major factor.[80] We can therefore propose that any particular religious orientation as expressed by its adherents should be viewed in terms of the specific historical and contemporary socio-cultural circumstances in which it has survived and maintained itself. Historically, any religious orientation will have undergone particular changes which are contingent, at least to a substantial degree, on the original and subsequently changing nature of the settings in which it obtains. Thus at any given point in time the social dispositions and behaviour of the self-defined adherents to a religious tradition are a consequence of (a) the original beliefs and values of the tradition, (b) the socio-historical experiences of the tradition attendant upon the beliefs and values in the tradition (both of these factors continually interacting with each other) and (c) the 'present' socio-cultural circumstances of the self-defined adherents in relation to their 'presently' espoused religious beliefs and values. In these terms it becomes much less easy to talk of the autonomy of the religious factor—because what is included in the alleged consequences of the religious factor may be due not to anything unique to adherence (be it associational, communal, devotional or orthodox-cognitive) to the religious position in question; but rather to historical, social and cultural factors. Or, as Greeley has pointed out, the structural location of a particular self-defined religious group may overcome or compensate for secular disadvantages attendant upon the orthodox doctrine in question. The fact that Catholics are relatively overdistributed in centres of urban industrialism in the United States may account for the fact that on Greeley's evidence they do not have lower rates of secular achievement-orientation as compared to Protestants. It should be noted that this interpretation is not the same as saying that if we control, in a statistical sense, for such factors as urban/rural distribution the Protestant/Catholic differential would be restored. What the interpretation states is that there are significant differences among self-defined Catholics as to secular orientations. These secular orientations are not the direct consequence of religious factors; but have primarily to do with the social and cultural contingencies of the location of self-defined Catholics.

We have been utilizing the term 'self-defined' quite frequently and it is in this connection that a further problem presents itself. Most inquiries into religiosity and religious commitment have worked in terms of the individual's adherence (or non-adherence) to a substantive, empirical religious body or tradition. The difficulty with such a procedure is that it automatically biases the investigation towards particular religious orientations in the 'real world'. Thus religiosity becomes defined in terms of particular, existential conceptions of such.[81] As Yinger has pointed out, this means that 'religious liberals' (those deviant with respect to particular established orientations, but nevertheless highly committed to unorthodox religious stances) get classified as relatively non-religious.[82] Furthermore, such conceptions of religiosity allow for little cross-societal comparison—except across societies broadly similar with respect to religious tradition. On the other hand, the solution proposed by Yinger and others is not much more attractive than the kind of procedure under criticism. Yinger himself has proposed that the 'ultimate concern' definition be utilized to facilitate 'across-the-board' analyses of, say, the United States. But as we have already noted, this kind of approach involves a prescriptive line of argument —that problems of ultimate concern is what religion is 'really about'. Here we are proposing the adoption of an approach midway between that of Yinger and those operating on the principle of self-definition—an approach based on our previously delineated definitions of religious phenomena, making a distinction between religiosity in the cultural sense and participation in religious activities in the social sense.

A General Analytic Framework

The previous sections of this chapter have committed us to the following modes of inquiry. First, that we should utilize an exclusive, substantive definition, focusing on concrete beliefs. Second, that we should bear clearly in mind the distinction between social and cultural aspects of religious activities—the former referring to beliefs

F

and values espoused, the latter to the social means by and through which these beliefs and values are held and 'carried'.[83]

These emphases now facilitate the explication of an analytic schema which will be utilized, if somewhat loosely, in the remainder of this book:

	Religion	Non-religion
Culture	1. Religious culture	3. Secular culture
Social structure	2. Social aspects of religion	4. General social structure

The four sub-spaces of this diagram are the major categories of analysis which we will use in the more substantive chapters which follow. Much of what has been emphasized so far concerns the relative absence in the sociology of religion of clear-cut indications of *variables*. These four categories of analysis may in fact be regarded as variables. Theoretically we are therefore mainly interested in the ways in which a variation in one, two or three of these categories effects variation in the fourth category; or how variations within two effect the other two; and so on. Since we are concerned with religion as such we are obviously not concerned here directly with relationships between categories 3 and 4. More schematically the major, direct relationships between the categories may be indicated as in the diagram on page 67.

Line *a* refers to the relationship within the religious sphere; line *b* to the relationship between religious and secular culture; line *c* to the relationship between religious culture and general social structure of the wider society; line *d* to the relationship between the social structure of religion and secular culture; line *e* to the relationship between social structure within the religious sphere and social structure generally. The dotted line *f* has to do with matters outside of the religious sphere. It seems analytically convenient to take these relationships in clusters. Thus we can take *a* as an interesting problem in its own right; then we shall take *b* and *c* together—focusing, therefore, on religious culture; finally we shall deal with *d* and *e*—concentrating on the social structure and organization of religious practices and beliefs in relation both to secular culture and the wider social structure. It should be remembered that in real life the effects of changes in one of the four variables will be, at least partially, mediated to its 'final source' through a third (intervening) variable. But we shall not complicate matters unnecessarily and will be content to deal in this book only with the relationships as explicated in the diagram.

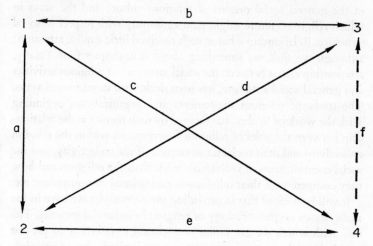

Thus we have three clusters of major problems. It may be helpful at this stage to indicate how our schema relates to work done within the sociology of religion to date and briefly point up the range of themes facilitated by the schema. Relationship *a* has been typically focused on by those sociologists dealing with the internal dynamics of religious movement and organizations; whilst social anthropologists have analysed in these terms when trying to see the relationships between the various aspects of religion in primitive societies—religious beliefs in relation to the roles of religious functionaries for example. Relationship *b* was a major concern of early sociologists such as Comte, who was very interested in the ways in which a religious orientation to the world was being supplanted by a scientific orientation. In more recent times this relationship has been a major focus of those talking in terms of the process of secularization. But probably the most famous work on this problem is that of Weber— concerned as he was with the ways in which general cultural characteristics of modern societies were historical outcomes of a specific religious heritage. Relationship *c* is also, of course, an area in which Weber worked extensively. Indeed this was the main sustained focus of sociologists during the classical period of the sociology of religion. As we have seen, both Marx and Durkheim were vitally interested in the general social origins of religious culture and the ways in which religious culture might gain autonomy with respect to social structure. Relationship *d* has as such received little *explicit* attention; although we shall say something about it in chapter four. Finally, relationship *e*, that between the social structure of religious activities and general social structure, has been dealt with in numerous ways. The study of religious movements and organizations, beginning with the work of Weber, has focused on such themes as the relationship between the roles of religious functionaries within the religion collectivity and their social status outside of the collectivity, and the social commitments of individuals other than the religious and how they compete with their religious-organizational commitments; etc.

It will be noticed that in providing these examples we have in the main drawn on the sociology of religion in industrial societies. The ease with which we can utilize our schema in reference to pre- or non-industrial societies is somewhat more limited—but in principle it is a viable procedure. It may help at this stage to pinpoint the problem of the terms of employment of our schema by explicating the previously mentioned point about the *institutional* characteristics of religion in industrial societies as contrasted to the *diffuse* characteristics of religion in other societies. Here we invoke a set of distinctions suggested by Glock and Stark (see page 69).[84]

Type 1 is obviously that relationship between religion and the wider society which is most pervasive in the industrialized part of the world. Religion is contained within fairly clear-cut organizational boundaries and is regarded as a sphere of activity separate from, for example, the economic, political and educative spheres. Type 2 is historically to be found most frequently in centralized, bureaucratic empires, such as the Egyptian—in which there were strong theocratic tendencies.[85] That is, religion was organized at the

TYPES OF RELATIONSHIP BETWEEN RELIGION AND THE WIDER SOCIETY

	Relatively organized religion	Relatively non-organized religion
Relatively differentiated religion	1	3
Relatively undifferentiated religion	2	4

state level and religion was fused with political, economic, educative and other activities. In the modern period some Roman Catholic societies such as Portugal and Spain are the nearest such examples, with some Islamic societies also approaching this type. Islamic societies generally have tended to manifest organized and yet relatively undifferentiated religious forms. Type 3 is, empirically, as Glock and Stark point out, relatively unusual; the best example they give being cultic religions in the United States of America which are separated from other spheres of activity and yet only very loosely organized through the distribution of religious literature and, in some cases, occasional gatherings.[86] Finally, type 4 is that which obtains in primitive societies, where religion *is* organized to the extent that there are closely stipulated procedures for participation in religious activities, but the activities do not occur in, nor are they regulated, by specialized religious collectivities. Moreover, religion is not a separate sphere of activity, but is often all-embracing and certainly always bound up with activities which in industrial societies and so-called transitional societies are regarded as relatively independent spheres of activity.

Notes to Chapter 3

1. Weber, *The Sociology of Religion*, op. cit., p. 1.

2. See the discussions of Pareto in Parsons, *The Structure of Social Action*, op. cit., chs. V–VII; and 'The Theoretical Development of the Sociology of Religion', op. cit.

3. See particularly Max Weber, *General Economic History* (translated by Frank H. Knight), New York, 1961, p. 270.

4. See the important discussion of definitional issues in the sociology and anthropology of religion by Spiro, op. cit. See also the very recent statement of Berger which makes similar points to those promulgated in this chapter: Berger, *The Sacred Canopy*, op. cit., pp. 175–8. Slightly older, but still important discussions include: Jack Goody, 'Religion and Ritual: The Definitional Problem', *British Journal of Sociology*, 12 (1961), pp. 142–64; and R. Horton, 'A Definition of Religion and its Uses', *Journal of the Royal Anthropological Institute*, 90 (1960), pp. 201–26.

5. Thus the use of the term 'real' has here *nothing* to do with 'essence'—as it has in the work of some philosophers.

6. As in *The Elementary Forms of the Religious Life*, op. cit.

7. Spiro, op. cit., pp. 88 ff. Spiro's argument points up the dangers of the sociologist relying too heavily on the most visible doctrinal expressions of major religious traditions and thereby ignoring the 'popular' manifestations of such traditions. See also E. R. Leach (ed.), *Dialectic in Practical Religion*, Cambridge, 1968.

8. *The Elementary Forms of the Religious Life*, op. cit., p. 62. Durkheim's influence in the matter of definition has been considerable. There is, however, a rather different tradition which has emphasized the property of sacredness. This stems from Rudolph Otto's *The Idea of the Holy*, London, 1929 (first published in Germany in 1917). Peter Berger thus proposes as a viable definition: 'religion is the human attitude toward a sacred order that includes within it all being—human or otherwise. In other words, religion is the belief in a cosmos, the meaning of which both transcends and includes man.' (Berger, 'Religious Institutions', in Neil J. Smelser (ed.), *Sociology: An Introduction*, New York, London, Sydney, 1967, p. 338.) The accusation that sacredness is a matter of degree does not apply so easily to Berger's definition. The worry is that, at least as he states if informally, it lacks specificity.

9. In effect this *is* what is done in Thomas Luckmann and Peter Berger, 'Social Mobility and Personal Identity', in *European Journal of Sociology*, 5 (1964), pp. 331–44.

10. Furthermore, extra- or pre-sociological commitments and preferences are at work on both sides of 'the fence'. This point crops up again at various points in the book. One of the most important of these is that in some intellectual circles 'religion' tends to be used *pejoratively*.

11. But see Luckmann, *The Invisible Religion*, op. cit., chs. VI and VII and the references cited in those chapters. A number of people have pointed up the allegedly religious character of communism. See, for example, Donald G. MacRae, 'The Bolshevik Ideology', *The Cambridge Journal*, 3 (December, 1954), pp. 164–77.

12. For a recent statement of the basic issues see W. Goldschmidt, *Comparative Functionalism*, Cambridge, 1966.

13. On lower-class ideological surrogates, see Weber, op. cit., ch. VII.

14. Self-conscious surrogate religiosity is particularly manifest in some of the humanist societies which have developed in Britain during the past one hundred years. The National Secular Society, for example, exhibits a functional kind of 'religious' opposition to religion. For a survey, see Susan Budd, 'The Humanist Societies: The Consequences of a Diffuse Belief System', in B. R. Wilson (ed.), *Patterns of Sectarianism*, op. cit., pp. 377–405.

15. This concern with 'ultimacy' is so widespread in the orthodox literature that any single citation or series of citation of its usage would be very misleading—so common has been its invocation. The really important point to note is that it derives from the work of a theologian, Paul Tillich. The attractiveness of such a definitional approach inheres in its generality and, one suspects, the fact that it has been religiously legitimated. One should note, with emphasis, that whereas sociologists seek to use the 'ultimacy' definition in a neutral, analytic sense, Tillich's formulation is *religiously prescriptive*. In any case sociologists utilizing Tillich's approach have yet to come to terms with his conception of God or such statements as: there is 'no place *beside* the divine . . . no possible atheism . . . no wall between the religious and the non-religious. . . . The holy embraces both itself and the secular.' Paul Tillich, *The Protestant Era*, Chicago, 1957, p. xi. Cf. the statement on Tillich by Robert Bellah in 'Words for Paul Tillich', *Harvard Divinity Bulletin*, 30(January, 1966), pp. 15–16.

16. J. Milton Yinger, 'Pluralism, Religion, and Secularism', *Journal for the Scientific Study of Religion*, VI (Spring, 1967), pp. 17–28, esp. pp. 22–4.

17. Yinger actually proposes this: ibid., p. 23.

18. See, *inter alia*, Bellah, *Religion and Progress in Modern Asia*, loc. cit., and Parsons, 'Introduction' (to 'Culture and the Social System'), in Talcott

Parsons *et al.* (eds.), *Theories of Society*, Glencoe (Illinois), 1965 (one-volume edition), pp. 963–93. See also Clifford Geertz, 'Religion as a Cultural System', in Banton (ed.), op. cit., pp. 1–46; and J. P. Nettl and Roland Robertson, *International Systems and the Modernization of Societies*, London, New York, 1968, pp. 152–6.

19. In addition to many previously cited references to Parsons' work, see Talcott Parsons, 'Religion in a Modern Pluralistic Society', *Review of Religious Research*, 7 (Spring, 1966), pp. 125–46. See also Talcott Parsons, *The Social System*, London, 1951, ch. VIII.

20. Cf. Talcott Parsons, 'Christianity and Modern Industrial Society', in Edward A. Tiryakian (ed.), *Sociological Theory, Values and Sociocultural Change*, Glencoe (Illinois), 1963, pp. 33–70.

21. Luckmann, *The Invisible Religion*, op. cit., esp. ch. 3.

22. Ibid., p. 25.

23. Ibid., p. 53.

24. Ibid., p. 78.

25. Ibid., p. 61.

26. See above, p. 39.

27. See above, p. 14; Ernst Troeltsch, *The Social Teaching of the Christian Churches* (translated by Olive Wyon), 2 volumes, New York, 1931.

28. This statement is only intended as a brief indication of the major socio-cultural characteristics of Christianity. The theme is returned to at greater length in the next chapter.

29. Difficulties in the uses of the terms 'other-worldly' and 'inner-worldly' are treated in the next chapter, pp. 89–95. Here it suffices to utilize Weber's term without reservation.

30. Independently, Berger has said that 'historically speaking, Christianity has been its own gravedigger'. Berger, *The Sacred Canopy*, op. cit., p. 127. Cf. Ernst Troeltsch, *Protestantism and Progress*, Boston, 1958. See below, pp. 169–81.

31. Parsons, 'Christianity and Modern Industrial Society', op. cit.

32. But see below, pp. 89–95.

33. For detailed discussion, see below, pp. 169–81.

34. Parsons' view might be best expressed by the aesthetically unattractive neologism, *social religionization*. Cf. Bellah, 'Religious Evolution', op. cit.

35. Parsons, 'Christianity and Modern Industrial Society', op. cit., pp. 68–9. Parsons' emphasis here upon morals and the normative signifi-cance of religion, whilst conforming to many interpretations of what 'religion ought to do', runs against the grain of analyses which have

stressed its 'meaning' or *cognitive* significance. For an earlier, more systematic and satisfactory attempt to delineate religious beliefs analytically, see Parsons, *The Social System*, loc. cit.

36. Thomas F. O'Dea, 'Sociological Dilemmas: Five Paradoxes of Institutionalization', in Tiryakian (ed.), op. cit., p. 74.

37. This tension is extensively analysed in J. Milton Yinger, *Religion in the Struggle for Power*, Durham (N. Carolina), 1946. For the Buddhist sphere, see the excellent essays in Leach (ed.), *Dialectic in Practical Religion*, op. cit.

38. The Indian case is particularly well analysed in Donald Eugene Smith, *India as a Secular State*, Princeton, Oxford, 1963. See also *idem, Religion and Politics in Burma*, Princeton, Oxford, 1967. See the review article on *India as a Secular State* by Marc Galanter, 'Secularism, East and West', *Comparative Studies in Society and History*, VII (January, 1965), pp. 133–59.

39. The attention of the uninitiated reader should be drawn to the fact that the discussion is proceeding at two levels: not only at the sociological interpretation of religion, but also at the way in which sociologists have interpreted it. In spite of much recent philosophical debate of these problems sociologists and anthropologists have paid far too little attention to them.

39a. This is in line with Schutz's distinction between first-order, commonsense concepts and second-order, scientific concepts. Alfred Schutz, 'Concept and Theory Formation in the Social Sciences'. *Journal of Philosophy*, 51 (1954), pp. 272–3.

40. The type of theological writing with which we are concerned here has to do particularly with the so-called radical theologians of the 1960s. See, *inter alia*, Thomas J. J. Altizer and William Hamilton, *Radical Theology and the Death of God*, New York, 1966; and C. W. Christian and Glenn R. Wittig (eds.), *Radical Theology: Phase Two*, Philadelphia, New York, 1967. For relatively rare examples of a sociologist involving himself in theological issues, see Peter Berger, *The Sacred Canopy*, op. cit., pp. 179–88; and Harold Fallding, 'Secularization and the Sacred and Profane', *Sociological Quarterly*, 8 (Summer, 1967), pp. 349–64. Also relevant here is the work of the philosopher of religion, Mircea Eliade. See, *inter alia, Patterns in Comparative Religion*, New York, 1958; and Eliade, *Cosmos and History*, New York, 1959. For other relevant contributions see Chapter 7 below. Compare the present concern with religious intellectuals' analyses and the position of those who argue for closer attention to invisible, practical or popular religion. The present

writer is sympathetic to this position; but believes the more general issues must also be tackled.

41. Goode depicts religion and magic as being empirically interpenetrative in a variety of respects. That is, a particular action will be more religious and less magical than another kind of action. William Goode, *Religion Among the Primitives*, op. cit.

42. E. B. Tylor, *Primitive Culture*, London, 1871. See also Malinowski, op. cit.

43. Lévi-Strauss, *The Savage Mind*, op. cit., p. 221.

44. Peter Worsley, *The Trumpet Shall Sound*, London, New York, 1968 (revised edition), p. xxviii.

45. For a brief summary statement on these phenomena, see John Beattie, *Other Cultures*, New York, London, 1965, ch. 11.

46. Jack Goody, 'Religion and Ritual: The Definitional Problem', op. cit., p. 157 and *passim*. S. F. Nadel, *Nupe Religion*, London, 1954; E. E. Evans-Pritchard, *Witchcraft, Oracles and Magic Among the Azande*, Oxford, 1937; *idem*, *Nuer Religion*, Oxford, 1956.

47. Goody, op. cit.

48. Berger, 'Religious Institutions', op. cit., p. 336. See also Swanson, *The Birth of the Gods*, op. cit. The nearest equivalent in Christianity is belief in the *immanent* presence of the Holy Spirit. What we have been discussing here raises difficult philosophical problems. See below, p. 224, n. 2. See the rich argument in Steven Lukes, 'Some Problems about Rationality', *European Journal of Sociology*, VIII (1967), pp. 247–64.

49. Godfrey Lienhardt, *Divinity and Experience: The Religion of the Dinka*, Oxford, 1961, p. 28. See also the valuable evidence in Nadel, *Nupe Religion*, op. cit.

50. One has in mind here that kind of naturalistic pantheism manifested in the work of the Romantic poets of the late eighteenth century and early nineteenth century. (One might observe here the links between German romanticism and the immanentist notion of the dialectic so central to Marxist thought.)

51. Swanson, *Religion and Regime*, op. cit., pp. 5–6.

52. Norbert Wiener, *God and Golem, Inc.*, Cambridge (Mass.), London, 1966, p. 16. For a good analysis of Zoroastrianism, see R. G. Zaehner, *The Dawn and Twilight of Zoroastrianism*, New York, 1961.

53. Lenski, *The Religious Factor*, op. cit., p. 331. See above, p. 38, for elaboration.

54. Glock and Stark, *Religion and Society in Tension*, op. cit., ch. 1.

55. Ibid., ch. 2. (These have been fruitfully renamed and elaborated since

the present book was completed in Rodney Stark and Charles Y. Glock, *American Piety: The Nature of Religious Commitment*, Berkeley, 1968.) For other older, dimensional schemata, see the discussions in ibid. See also Demerath, *Social Class in American Protestantism*, op. cit., and below, p. 55. It is important to point out that much of the interest in dimensions of religiosity grew out of the controversy about the so-called religious revival in America in the 1950s.

56. This is very much a psychological problem which, strictly speaking, lies outside of the sphere of interest (and competence) of the present discussion. The classic in the field remains William James, *The Varieties of Religious Experience*, New York, 1899. See also Gordon Allport, *Religion in the Developing Personality*, New York, 1960. (See also below, n. 63.)

57. In *American Piety . . .*, op. cit. (p. 16), Stark and Glock show considerable uneasiness about the consequential dimension. Bryan Wilson has suggested to me that this dimension might be reformulated as a *moral* dimension. For findings which *do* suggest independence of the remaining dimensions, see Stark and Glock, ch. 9.

58. Lenski's work has already been the object of much criticism. Here our picking on his *The Religious Factor* should be regarded both as a tribute to the importance of Lenski's contribution and a means of introducing or elaborating on vital analytic themes. Note particularly Gibson Winter, 'Methodological Reflections on "The Religious Factor"', *Journal for the Scientific Study of Religion*, 2 (Fall, 1962), pp. 53–63.

59. Glock and Stark, op. cit., pp. 12–17. See below, p. 69.

60. Cf. the utilization of this unidimensional distinction in C. K. Yang, *Religion in Chinese Society*, Berkeley, 1961. (Yang derives this from the work of Joachim Wach.)

61. *The Religious Factor*, op. cit., p. 18.

62. This second distinction derives mainly from the work of Talcott Parsons. See also David Apter, *The Politics of Modernization*, Chicago, 1965.

63. Here we are thinking of the situation in which there is a prevailing sentiment that people ought to belong to some religious group—as in the U.S.A.—and individuals then attend church in order not to receive social disapproval or, more positively, to enhance their prestige. My attention has been drawn to the importance of Allport's work in reference to the instrumental/consummatory distinction. He distinguishes between 'extrinsic' and 'intrinsic' religiousness. Gordon Allport, 'Religion and Prejudice', *Crane Review*, II (1959), pp. 1–10; 'The

Religious Context of Prejudice', *Journal for the Scientific Study of Religion*, V (Fall, 1966), pp. 447–57.

64. Charles Y. Glock, 'Comment on "Pluralism, Religion, and Secularism" ', *Journal for the Scientific Study of Religion*, op. cit., p. 29.

65. See the excellent discussion in E. K. Scheuch, 'Cross-National Comparisons Using Aggregate Data: Some Substantive and Methodological Problems', in Richard L. Merritt and Stein Rokkan (eds.), *Comparing Nations*, New Haven, London, 1966, pp. 131–67. See also Peter M. Blau, 'Structural Effects', *American Sociological Review*, XXV (April, 1960), pp. 178–93.

66. The distinction in this book follows, broadly speaking, A. L. Kroeber and Talcott Parsons, 'The Concepts of Culture and of Social System', *American Sociological Review*, XXIII (October, 1958), pp. 582–3.

67. It may be that the inclusion of a *consequential* dimension of religiosity in Glock's schema is an attempt to come to terms with some of the problems raised here. Even so he is still talking about *individual* consequences of religiosity. For other comments on the social structure/culture distinction, see Berger, *The Sacred Canopy*, op. cit., p. 107.

68. The work of Berger and Luckmann goes, of course, against this latter trend—as does that of Swanson.

69. See discussion in Michael Argyle, *Religious Behaviour*, London, 1958, esp. ch. 12.

70. Spiro, op. cit. Spiro finds much of use in Freud's theory of religion. (See discussion in Philip Rieff, *Freud: the Mind of the Moralist*, London, 1959, New York, 1961, ch. VIII.)

71. Cf. Luckmann's statements on the synchronization or non-synchronization of 'official' religious culture and individual, subjective religious dispositions: *The Invisible Religion*, op. cit., pp. 74 ff.

72. See particularly Geertz, op. cit., and Bellah, *Religion and Progress in Modern Asia*, loc. cit.

73. Op. cit., see also Swanson, *Religion and Regime*, op. cit. See below, pp. 151–54.

74. In my analyses of the Salvation Army I have tried to conform to such explanatory procedures. See Robertson, 'The Salvation Army . . .', op. cit.

75. Weber, *The Protestant Ethic and the Spirit of Capitalism*, op. cit.

76. Above, pp. 52 ff.

77. Greeley, op. cit.

78. Ibid., p. 125.

79. Ibid.

80. See further discussion below, pp. 174–75.

81. This would, taken to its extremes, conform to the sociologically unfollowable advice of Peter Winch, *The Idea of a Social Science*, London, New York, 1958, p. 87: What is religious can only be decided in terms of criteria drawn 'from religion itself', says Winch.

82. Yinger, 'Pluralism, Religion, and Secularism', op. cit.

83. I have briefly introduced and utilized this schema in a previous publication: Roland Robertson, 'Factors Conditioning Religious Belief', *Cambridge Opinion*, 49 (1967), pp. 13–15.

84. Glock and Stark, op. cit., pp. 12–17. See also Luckmann, op. cit., pp. 66–7.

85. See S. N. Eisenstadt, 'Religious Organizations and Political Process in Centralized Empires', *Journal of Asian Studies*, 21 (May, 1962), pp. 271–294.

86. Note that this example does not relate to a *societal* pattern, like the other three. Bryan Wilson has indicated that the candombles of Brazil provide an example of type 3. These are loose client-practitioner systems with very little organization beyond the practitioner's establishment and virtually no organizational constraints on clients: the occasions are not haphazard, but the attendance of any one client must be. They have virtually the character of performances for those who turn up.

4

Religious Systems: Cultural and Social Aspects

We have shown that the category 'religion' derives from an essentially Christian matrix. The same applies to the frequently utilized distinction between church and sect. In theological terms, churchly religious forms constitute the mainstream of religious history, the orthodox path of Christian development; whereas sectarianism is a form of religious deviance. Sectarianism is a relative matter. What from the standpoint of, say, the Anglican Church in the seventeenth century constituted sectarianism was from the point of view of the newly emerging religious movements of Congregationalism or Baptism the correct and the true Christian perspective. Similarly from the standpoint of twentieth-century Congregationalism or Presbyterianism, fundamentalist holiness movements are sectarian. In a somewhat different respect it is often observed that the church/sect distinction within Christianity has to do with the degree to which the religiously committed should be involved in 'the world' and the extent to which doctrinal prescriptions should be interpreted literally and kept 'pure'.[1]* It is clear that in these terms the polarity, church versus sect, is closely related to the notion of being religious —what religious commitment 'really is'. In order to understand the distinction between church and sect and to understand the category 'religion' we have to comprehend the distinctiveness of Christianity as a general conception of the world.

For many centuries the Catholic Church was very successful in maintaining the tension and ambivalence concerning degree of religiosity and secular involvement within its own boundaries. Two institutional characteristics were of major importance in this success. First, the institution of *monasticism* made provision for those who were especially religious—for the 'full-time' religious virtuosi.[2] Thus many Catholics were able to sustain a deep, ongoing religious

* Notes for this chapter begin on page 106.

commitment relatively untrammelled by the exigencies of political and economic considerations. Second, the institution of *sainthood* enabled Church leaders to recognize and applaud certain types of religious deviance by legitimating it in a circumscribed manner. The saint and his followers were either contemporaneously or post-humously accorded special recognition. Their religious deviance was institutionalized generally without challenge to the mainstream religious tradition.[3] This is not to say that there were no secessionist forms of sectarianism in the medieval Church.[4] But the real beginnings of sectarianism *in the sense of separate movements* came into full prominence with the Protestant Reformation. Then the territorially demarcated boundaries of religious allegiance and the fairly clear-cut accommodation between Church and State in Europe were broken up and the problem of the relationship between 'religion and society' began to emerge as something more than an implicitly recognized tension inherent in Christian doctrine. It is the emergence of the state which is crucial in this connection. Feudal emperors had required religious legitimation; nation states needed stable, but subservient, religious institutions. In the centuries which followed the Protestant Reformation the 'influence-versus-purity' or 'involvement-versus-withdrawal' problem gave rise to a multiplicity of religious movements; this process being accelerated during the period of Civil War in England in the middle of the seventeenth century. On the other hand, some of the movements which grew out of the latter period, such as Congregationalism, Presbyterianism and Baptism, subsequently became the bearers of a new solution to the sect-church dilemma—the solution of denominationalism. The denominational solution was one midway between the polarity of sect versus church—involving an 'accepting' of the wider society but not seeking to dominate it or change it in any fundamental way. (This position became most viable in America—in the absence of an established church.)

The Christian orientation to the world is one which has historically stressed a tension between 'the world' and 'the religious sphere'. It has sought, in its mainstream tendencies, to 'push' the latter into the former. At the theological level there have, of course, been many different emphases over the centuries. The *relatively* high degree of success of classical Catholicism in maintaining religious hegemony, that is in maintaining a high degree of social power and control over the shaping of societal values, was finally broken by the Protestant Reformation—and the Catholic Counter Reformation did little to restore the former state of affairs. Thus since the sixteenth century various theological positions have been elaborated, notably within mainstream Protestantism, many of which have focused precisely on the issue of the relationship between religion and 'the world'.

The church-sect distinction is a useful point of entry to the general discussion of relationships between religion and society because sociologists have been sensitized to a tension between religion and society through the initial Christian-cultural grounding of sociology and, more particularly, the penetration of the sociology of religion by Christian insights and perspectives. This is not to say, however, that the distinction cannot be generalized sociologically in such a way as to be useful in the analysis of *other*, non-Christian religious traditions. There are major difficulties in utilizing the church/sect distinction outside of the Christian complex, but the more generic problem of the relationship between 'religion and society' appears in a number of other religious situations. The point we are therefore seeking to emphasize is that the Christian, and subsequently the Western sociological, perception of the relationship is one which facilitates a particularly comprehensive view of the relationship—at least in the great religious traditions. This is precisely because the Christian perspective is the one which posits the most severe tensions between religion and the wider society—the one which of all major religious orientations involves inherent strains and ambiguities. It is vitally important, however, to establish that in speaking of 'religion and society' we are not taking these terms to imply literally that there is, on the one hand, religion and, on the other hand, society—in the sense of there being two separate spheres from the detached, objective standpoint of the sociologist. Rather we utilize the distinction as it derives from the logic of the beliefs and values of religious adherents themselves. Religion is just as much social and cultural as is society from the sociological standpoint. But in religious terms adherents to particular traditions have specific conceptions, *as a matter of degree*, of what is taken to be genuinely spiritual and/or what constitutes the realm of godliness.[5]

There are a number of ways in which the major religious orientations of the world may be delineated. If we were to confine ourselves purely to the mid-twentieth-century situation we could perhaps state merely that the global religious situation consists in Christianity, Judaism, Islam, Hinduism, Buddhism, possibly Shintoism, and what in effect would be a residual category of primitive religion. In fact this is a fairly typical procedure amongst analysts of religion. This method is one characterized by its *ad hoc* and intuitive nature. Another alternative is to include within one's range of focus religious orientations which have in some sense been significant over a wide area and for a long historical period, no matter whether the orientation in question has survived on a major scale into the modern historical period. This procedure would automatically lead to the inclusion of Confucianism—although some have expressed reservations as to whether Confucianism qualifies as a genuinely religious orientation, in so far as its supernatural referents were not very clearly articulated. (In its literal origins Confucianism contained no supernatural referents.) Finally, a truly adequate typology of religious orientations on a world-historical scale would make provision for a delineation or series of delineations within the primitive category. Wallace suggests that there are or have been four major types of religious culture: (1) *Shamanic*; (2) *Communal*; (3) *Olympian*; and (4) *Monotheistic*.[6]

1. *Shamanic religious culture* covers those religious forms which involve the performance of rituals by non-specialists and part-time specialists. Shamanic religion of the pristine Siberian variety involves a part-time practitioner 'endowed by birth, training, or inspirational experience with a special power' and who 'intervenes for a fee with supernatural beings or forces on behalf of human clients'.[7] But more generally we may include within the shamanic category not only magico-religions involving diviners, medicine men, mediums, spiritualists and the like, but also individualistic cults such as mortuary rituals and magic and taboo customs. In these latter each individual is a specialist for the magico-religious occasion. One finds such

G

phenomena amongst the Iroquois (dream cult) and the Trobrianders (sailing magic).[8] What characterizes this category of religion (or rather magico-religion) is a very simple 'theology', ranging from the relatively well-articulated mythological symbolism of the Eskimos to the much more elemental mythology of the Andaman Islanders. There are rarely major deities of particular, ongoing and everyday significance; and ritual is not tied to seasonal occurrences.[9]

2. *Communal religious culture* also manifests individualistic and shamanic magico-religious orientations. But in addition it involves pantheons of deities, which are related in a categorical manner to aspects of nature, to seasonal occurrences and to events in the individual's life-cycle, such as puberty, marriage, illness, old age and so on. Whilst such deities assume much greater significance in everyday life than in the shamanic case, the 'intervention capacity' of such deities and spirits is relatively low. Thus gods and spirits are more autonomous in the negative sense that they have 'elusive' locations; they are accessible only through the performance of specific rituals.[10] And although there is wide participation in such rituals there is a much greater degree of specialization in the communal as compared to the shamanic type. It should indeed be stressed that scope of group-communal participation in religious activities goes hand-in-hand with degree of role specification, and specialization in the performance of religious activities. Some of the major examples of communal religion are to be found historically in many Melanesian cults, in Polynesia and in African societies of the non-kingdom type.

3. *Olympian religious culture* is distinguished by the centrality of orientation to a pantheon of several high gods. These gods are conceived as being active in human life. Being significant in the operation of the society they are worshipped and propitiated in permanent temples through the mediation of a full-time priest-hood.[11] Historically, the major examples of this type of religious culture are the religions of the Inca and the Aztecs and that of the African Negro kingdoms, such as Ashanti and Dahomey.[12]

4. *Monotheistic religious culture*, in terms of Wallace's classification, includes all the so-called 'world religions', Hinduism and Buddhism, Judaism and Christianity, Islam and, finally, Chinese religion

(a syncretic mixture of Confucianism, Buddhism, Taoism and to some extent Islam).[13] In monotheism the 'pluralism' of olympian religions is transcended by belief in a single supreme entity or being; who either controls other supernatural beings or expresses himself in terms of them. Wallace's compelling argument for including Chinese religion in the monotheistic category rests on the unifying function of Confucianism, in relation to the multiplicity of faiths in ancient and classical China, including not only other monotheistic faiths, but also communal and olympian cults. Confucius functioned as 'a kind of humane focus of divine wisdom . . . sanctioning . . . all cults and . . . the state . . .'[14]

In terms of our present focus on relationships between religion and society we may now observe that types one to four constitute a kind of scale; such that type 2 (communal) implies the presence of some degree of shamanism, type 3 implies some communal and shamanic features, and type 4 (monotheistic) implies some shamanic, communal and olympian features.[15] But, more relevantly, we can discover important differences in types of relationship between religious beliefs and symbols and the socio-cultural context in which they occur. The first, shamanic, type primarily relates the individual and the small group to nature. Social structure and social life-cycle experience is relatively undifferentiated and in this sense there is an implicit, unselfconscious fusion of the religious and the social experience. In the second type, the communal, the defining characteristic is that a more elaborate structure of society and of the individual life-cycle is explicitly related to spirits and deities; and these deities are also linked to 'departments of nature'. This type of society is the one in which there is the clearest elaboration of norms pertaining to the location of individuals within the overall system—in terms of kinship rules, rites of passage, initiation rites, age-sets and so on. Anthropologists have differed as to whether it is more appropriate to regard features of the social structure as yielding the attributes in the religious sphere or whether, on the other hand, structural arrangements are contingent on religious beliefs. Questions of this sort are, as we shall see in the fifth chapter, not fully answerable. But in this type of system 'religion and society' are meshed together in such a way as to raise no situational problem about competing domains of attention and focus. Religious symbols are embedded in the social structure.[16] In the absence of literacy, culture is closely tied to social circumstance (literacy being a prerequisite for the autonomy of culture, in the sense that beliefs and values can be recorded and stored separately from social circumstance).[17] Ritual practices appropriate to specific social-structural contexts facilitate this systematic articulation of religion and social circumstance—and of human life and nature.

When we move to the olympian type, the systematic cohesion within the sphere of religious beliefs and symbols disappears and the pluralism or polytheism of such religious forms does not facilitate a close articulation between social structure and social circumstance, on the one hand, and religious referents on the other. Lack of correspondence and articulation as between overall social structure and religious pantheon is a major characteristic of such systems; this being particularly the case with the religion of ancient Greece. In the absence of a clearly articulated theology to systematize the belief in gods, religion consisted primarily in the discrete contact with gods according to specific social circumstance. That is, both the religious spheres and the social spheres were relatively uncoordinated internally. In such a situation we find neither the close association of religious ideas and social reality, as in communal systems, nor the systematized separation of these spheres as it appears in the monotheistic type.

It is, then, only in the monotheistic type that the relations between a social and a religious sphere are manifested in an enduringly problematic fashion. This situational difficulty is absent in the shamanic type because of the subordination of religion and magic to particular circumstances of social need. It is absent in the communal type because of the (in ideal-typical terms) synchronization of religious beliefs and societal characteristics—they are interdependently meshed together. Finally, this tension is absent in the olympian type, or at least it appears only discretely, because the religious realm tends to lack consistency and coherence.[18]

The present mode of exposition at one and the same time avoids overweighting the significance of the major religions of fairly recent origin and also highlights what is distinctive about these religious forms. Within the monotheistic category we need to pay particular attention to Confucianism, Buddhism, Judaism, Islam and Christianity. Hinduism we omit here as a special consideration, in spite of its general historic significance and the fact that it was the matrix from which sprang Buddhism, because of its highly syncretic nature. Hinduism is a compound of a wide variety of cults and doctrines with a special emphasis upon ritual. Ritualistic conformity is the prescriptive norm of Hinduism; and, as we have already noted, Hinduism is in this sense a culture, a way of life—in which it is possible to be an atheist and yet a respected Hindu. (In this respect many sociologists have tended to assume, following the work of Weber, that Hinduism is, in and of itself, an other-worldly religion. While such a characterization was extremely useful for Weber's analysis of those cultural forms which were conducive or unconducive to the development of entrepreneurial capitalism, it is somewhat misleading—in that it overstresses the significance of the problem of the relationship between religion and society in Indian religion.[19])

The Major Religious Traditions

In proceeding to a brief depiction of relations between religion and 'the world' in the major religious traditions we need to stress again that in the monotheistic category the degree of monotheism varies considerably from the marginal Confucian case to the clear-cut monotheism of Judaism.[20] Buddhism lies much closer to the Confucian end of the continuum as far as degree of monotheism is concerned, while Christianity and Islam approach the Judaistic end. Confucianism is, of course, difficult to handle in the monotheistic category—but relative to our other types of religion this is where, by virtue of its unifying principle, it must stand.[21] The basic principle of Confucianism as far as the religion-versus-society problem is concerned is that religious beliefs are essentially subordinated to the discerned facts of social structure. The world itself was regarded as an immanent sacred harmony. This harmony was maintained by the so-called Mandate of Heaven. Thus, while there is a clear acknowledgment of a transcendent realm, that 'realm' actually sustains social life. The Emperor was, at least officially, believed to be higher in the hierarchy embracing both heaven and earth than some of the lower spiritual beings in the heavenly sphere.[22] Thus although there was emphatically a world beyond this phenomenal world the two were regarded as interpenetrative and to this extent there was no fundamental tension between commitment to the two spheres. The religious and the social ethic were roughly coincidental.[23] Another way of putting this characteristic of Confucianism is to say that in the latter there is nothing within the logic of Confucianism which points to the option of withdrawal from the present state of affairs.

In Buddhism the situation is very different. Here 'the world' is regarded doctrinally as being illusory, *a psychological condition* from which the Buddhist should seek to escape. This is but one way of stating that the notion of withdrawal from the world is central to Buddhism—withdrawal being accomplished by self-imposed religious discipline. There is then a transcendent realm, the real realm of Nirvana which is more or less unambiguously acknowledged in 'pure' Buddhist form as the state of affairs to which the Buddhist should aspire. The interpenetration of each realm is regarded as being slight. Yet we must bear very much in mind that the layman, as opposed to the Buddhist monk, cannot, because of his secular preoccupations, attain Nirvana. The 'lowest' form of religious activity involves the seeking of prosperous rebirth through meritorious support of monks and temples.[24]

Islam is like Confucianism in so far (but only in so far) as there is a rough coincidence of the social and the religious ethic. But in the Islamic case the worldly sphere is, so to speak, enclosed within the religious sphere. *Within* the boundaries of Islam the affairs of mankind are contained within the spiritual commitment—the idea being crystallized in the Islamic messianic ideal which historically has involved the 'onward sweep' of Moslems through individual processes of *submission* rather than conversion. Thus subscription to the religious point of reference, Allah, in and of itself, is assumed to entail involvement in a religiously bounded social sphere. This emphasis upon the simple act of submission says a lot about the unique features of Islam. In contrast to Confucianism and Judaism, Islam has definitely been a religion of evangelization—that is, it has sought to widen its social and cultural scope and bring large numbers of individuals within its boundaries. Judaism, and also of course Christianity, has manifested a sense of historical mission. But the self-conceived historic mission and destiny of Jews has been almost entirely *ascriptive*. That is to say that Jews are Jews largely by virtue of being born so.[25] And it is Judaism in this ascriptive sense that has a historic mission. Conversion to Judaism is of course possible—in Roman times it was relatively easy—but is not often actively encouraged.

Confucianism was not a missionary or an evangelical religion for two closely related reasons. First, classical China—indeed China right up until relatively modern times—was regarded as the centre and core of the world by high-ranking Chinese and because of this the rest of the world was regarded as inferior, distant and basically not worthy of being embraced culturally by China. Second, the function of Confucianism and the religious orientations it subsumed was to sanction the existing harmony of the social order. Since the only social order which mattered in this respect was Chinese-Confucian society the question of conversion outside the boundaries of Chinese society did not arise. Although, of course, Buddhism, taking a hold in China between the first and third centuries A.D., did operate in a sense as a conversion religion. It did so not through any inherent advocacy of conversion as such—this would have been incongruent with a religious orientation which negated the significance of any given state of worldly affairs—but rather through the adaptability of Buddhism to various kinds of socio-cultural contexts. This compatibility derived mainly from its emphases upon *individual* salvation without any particular judgment of the context in which such salvation occurred, and upon release from sin, suffering and 'ephemeralness'. As Weber put it, in 'authentic ancient Buddhism there is no predestination, but neither is there any divine grace, any prayer, or any religious service. Rewards and punishments for every good and every evil deed are automatically established by the *karma* causality of the cosmic mechanism of compensation.'[26]

Finally, in contrast to Christianity, Islam through its emphasis on submission, rather than on conversion and induction, reveals again its unique form of dynamism—embracing the social world and sustaining it through the religious impulse. This is of course a statement of historical tendency. The entrance of predominantly Islamic societies into the global international system, and their subjection to the exigencies of industrialization and modernization, have severely mitigated missionary zeal. Perhaps, in this sense, Islam in the societies of the Middle East comes closer to the sanctioning, legitimating function of religion as exemplified by Confucianism—although there is one crucial difference, in that Islam does not in the mid-twentieth-century situation sanctify a static socio-cultural situation, except in the sheikdoms of the southern Middle East.[27] Economic and political considerations have primacy within a loosely conceived Islamic framework in such societies as Egypt and Syria—with vigorously invoked religious principles coming to the fore mainly through the special contingency of the Arab-Israeli conflict (but also involving suppression of the more intense religious manifestations, such as the Muslim Brotherhood). This modern characteristic of Islam should, on the other hand, be compared to the maintenance of a more demanding religious conservatism in the case of Burmese Buddhism—Burma, unlike the more advanced Middle Eastern societies, being relatively speaking an isolate within the modern system of societies.[28] Christianity's distinctiveness is that the sphere of religion and the sphere of society are in a *positively* tense relationship—as compared to the negatively tense relationship inherent in Buddhism.[29] This means that whereas the ideal-typical Christian regards both the world and the problematic relationship between the world and the spiritual realm as a 'testing ground'—the terms under which he can and has to be religious—the Buddhist regards the world as something to escape from, even if the lay Buddhist cannot realistically anticipate the ideal of Nirvana. Within Christianity there are of course sectarianism and monasticism. But neither of these is an 'escape mechanism' in the sense of world-negating Buddhism. Sectarianism within Christianity has been typically directed at a diagnosed failure of existing religions within the immediate societal context. Occidental monasticism is an institutionalized religious specialism within the context of a church (whether it be Roman, Anglican or whatever)—the legitimacy of involvement in the wider society on the part of the church being fully acknowledged by the monastic individual.[30] In contrast monasticism has been an essential, central part of the Buddhist tradition; it was not a lay religion in origin.

It must be pointed out that under certain exigencies of contemporary political situations Buddhism becomes transformed to the point where Buddhists do in fact become generally involved in a more positive fashion in the practical affairs of the 'political world'. Notwithstanding the traditionalistic, withdrawal tendencies of Burma relative to the structure of the contemporary international system, Burmese Buddhists do obviously have to be less world-rejective than their ancient forebears—simply in order that Burma may function as a political state. In a rather different fashion Buddhists in South Vietnam have engaged positively in political secular affairs with a well-known degree of militancy. On the other hand, the distinctiveness of Buddhism as a religious orientation is well exampled by their capacity to use suicide and self-destruction as a political weapon, a frequent occurrence under the Catholic regime of Diem.

Weber's thinking on the socio-cultural characteristics of the major religious belief systems has dominated sociological analysis for many decades. His characterizations and analytic dissections were presented in terms of, and have persuasively persisted with reference to, one basic problem—that of the historic divergence and differential rate of development of Occidental and Oriental 'civilizations'. Nearly all of what Weber said about Christianity, Hinduism, Buddhism, Chinese religion, Islam and Judaism, was shaped by this interest. Judaism, Christianity and Islam were regarded as belonging to one category of basically inner-worldly religions, Hinduism and Buddhism being other-worldly religions.

Underlying the distinction between other- and inner-worldliness was Weber's concern with the *need for salvation*.[31] Parsons, in his extremely helpful interpretation of Weber's sociology of religion, describes this as 'the need for a basis of personal legitimation which is in accord with ... ultimate standards, themselves conceived as standing in essential conflict with those of *any* institutionalized order'.[32] The problem of salvation has a specific and emphatic reference to 'the world'. The distinction between other- and inner-types of worldliness thus arises as the two basic *directions* in which salvation may be sought. Since Weber was above all interested in the religious bases of socio-cultural change it may be seen that this dichotomy held special attractions. Change of 'the world' could, it seemed, only be stimulated religiously by an orientation to the world. But there is a major problem here: there is a difference between a changeful orientation to the world and a 'mere' orientation to the world as such. We will argue that full acknowledgment of this and related distinctions necessitates modifications of Weber's characterization of the major belief systems.[33]

The general tendency of such modifications is highlighted initially by indicating Weber's interpretation of Confucianism. In contrasting Puritanism (the most thoroughly inner-worldly, activist religious orientation) and Confucianism, Weber stressed the *acceptance* of the world in Confucianism, and the Puritan tendency to regard the world as inherently evil. Thus although not actually describing the Confucian orientation as other-worldly (which it would be totally impossible to do), Weber did, nevertheless, regard it in a negative sense as of the same overall significance as Buddhism and Hinduism. The main point here is that Confucianism was in a major sense inner-worldly. But since Weber appeared to regard Confucianism as *fundamentally* inimical to a doctrine of radical salvation, we may consider also the relationship between Islam and Christianity in terms of the distinction between other-worldliness and inner-worldliness. For Weber, Islam was less inner-worldly than Christianity. Yet the argument, advanced by Hodgson, that relative to Christianity Islam has been more this-worldly is a persuasive one.[34] Hodgson maintains that Islam, Judaism and Zoroastrianism are distinctively more this-worldly than Christianity and Manicheanism. Christians have traditionally conceived of their religion as consisting in a sacramental church with 'a sacred dogma *acting upon* a profane world', whereas Muslims have regarded theirs as 'a body of universal law and a community which is bound thereto and which *is* the world at its best'.[35]

Hodgson's distinction is a radical one. The critical point here is that concerning the idea of *acting upon* the world. What we know of classical and medieval Christianity in Europe strongly backs up

Hodgson's thesis. The problem is further illuminated in Weber's observations on American Protestantism.[36] It has been remarked by many analysts that American Christianity is very different from the European Christianity which is historically most familiar to us.[37] In structural terms the absence of a church establishment is the most prominent feature of American Christianity. More important, American Protestantism, which has set the tone of American religion generally, is notable for its 'primitivism'—religious orientation developing in terms of specific social contexts and exigencies with an emphasis upon the uses of religion. It is therefore very 'worldly'. But the 'worldliness' of American Christianity is in large part explicable in terms of factors having to do with the nature of the founding and development of American society. It is not permissible to see American Christianity as a kind of final unfolding of inherent characteristics of the Christian tradition.[38]

Such criticisms of the Weberian approach bring us very close to an appraisal of his thesis about the link between Protestantism and the capitalistic ethos. But this is dealt with in some detail in the fifth chapter. What needs to be stressed here is that in spite of Weber's many analyses of the social-structural aspects of religion— the affinity between specific status groups and certain types of religious belief, the attributes of religious leadership and so on—his characterization of the major motifs of Christianity in relation to other major religious belief systems was considerably biased by his interpretation of modern Christianity, and his failure to pinpoint the full range of socio-historical circumstances which give rise to the various strands of modern Christianity.

For a particular religious belief system to have played a large part in changing 'the world' does not require that it should have been inner-worldly. It is the Christian emphasis upon such themes as suffering, death, evil, consolation and redemption which marks off Christianity from Islam. Emphasis also upon mystery and paradox in historic Christianity have contributed particularly to other-worldliness as compared to the inner-worldliness (in the sense of *embracement*) of Islam, at least in the main Sunnite tradition. Whereas Islam traditionally has involved the prescription that one submits to God and then joins in the general diffusion of Godly-enjoined principles, Christianity in its emphasis upon paradox and mystery makes the relationship to God a basically problematic one—hence the significance of conversion in Christianity. In this sense we may see that Islam differs from Judaism in its stress on the prescription that there is an element of *achievement* involved in the process of becoming religious, whereas historically the Judaistic conception has been an ascriptive one.[39] The emphasis upon demonstrable and wide-ranging religious achievement is, then, perhaps that character-istic which marks off Occidental from Oriental religious forms, crystallized in the Christian emphasis on conversion.[40] Achieve-ment orientation in respect of religiosity is likely to have (often unintended) socio-cultural consequences beyond the religiously conceived act.

Thus we may remain faithful to many of the conclusions advanced by Weber, but without utilizing his misleading emphasis upon this-worldliness. Other-worldliness is a defining attribute of religious culture and commitment and it may be argued that the more directly there is 'otherness' the more will be the emphasis upon achievement within the religious domain. Thus the relatively unspecific nature of 'otherness' in Buddhism tends to minimize the range of 'religious effort'. Moreover what are usually called magical elements in a religious belief system reduce the degree of achieve-ment motivation—in the sense that magic is a kind of 'short cut'. The actor 'leans on' nature in order to achieve his goals or adapt to their unattainability and does not value contact with 'the other' so intrinsically as in the religious case. All of this is of course in line with Weber's stress on the importance of the elimination of magic in the Christian tradition, culminating in Protestantism.

It is the basically incompatible and incongruent demands of Christianity which account for both its capacity for exerting a leverage on socio-cultural change and for its basic instability. (Instability, not of course in an organizational, but in a doctrinal sense.) Indeed these two factors, change-inducing and instability, tend to reinforce each other. Further, it is then not so much the inherent 'rationality' of Christianity, but its lack of closure, its indeterminacy and openness, plus, of course, the particular social circumstances its adherents have encountered which relate to its changefulness and significance in major socio-cultural changes. We repeat that none of this actually, in and of itself, directly denies the viability and validity of Weber's main points. What we have sought to do is to offset some misleading emphases in his work, particularly those which veer in the direction of positing a kind of dichotomy between 'religion' and 'society'—a presentation which is probably much less due to Weber himself than the sociologists who have interpreted and relied on his work.

Historically, then, Christianity has manifested a high degree of so-called other-worldliness. Lovejoy notes that Western religion as a whole has from the time of Plato possessed 'two Gods'—which were in principle 'two antithetic kinds of being'. On the one hand there was 'the Absolute . . . [who was] self-sufficient . . . needing no world of lesser beings to supplement or enhance his own eternal self-contained perfection'. The other conception was of a definitely non-self-sufficient God—'one whose essential nature required the existence of other beings, and not of one kind of these only, but of all kinds which could find a place in the descending scale of the possibilities of reality . . .'[41] Thus historic Christianity manifested a theological dualism, involving, respectively, transcendental and immanentist tendencies. Lovejoy characterizes the first conception as other-worldly and the second as inner-worldly, in the light of the fact that the first, the transcendent tendency, is more akin to the Puritanist view, whilst the second, the immanentist, is much closer to the Catholic stance rejected by Puritanism, especially Calvinistic Puritanism. Thus what emerges is that transcendent 'other-worldliness' much better connotes Occidental religious traditions *relative to* Oriental ones, which tend to be more immanentist and 'innerworldly'.

Swanson illustrates some combinations of immanentism and transcendentalism in the following fashion:[42]

Immanent?	Transcendent?	Illustrations
Yes	Yes	Catholicism
Yes	No	{ Buddhism Hinduism
No	Yes	Protestantism

Swanson picks out for special attention Parsons' interpretation of Weber's *Sociology of Religion* as being of outstanding significance in our understanding of the relations between *society* and *culture*.[43] The twist which Swanson gives to this observation is pertinent to the present discussion. Transcendence represents the differentiation of culture from the social structure which it guides and from which it grew. In these terms we may conclude that what is frequently spoken of as the 'religion/society' problem is really better appreciated as the culture/social structure problem. Broadly when we speak of the differentiation of culture from social structure we are referring, on the one hand, to a condition in which there is both a self-awareness of, and an objective demonstration of, a distinction between what is held to be desirable and generally believed about a society (culture) and, on the other hand, what actual patterns of social relationship and social experience obtain in the given society (social structure). Weber's characterization of Christianity as being basically and inherently inner-worldly relative to Buddhism and Hinduism can be re-expressed along these lines. What Weber called inner-worldliness is in effect a condition in which the members of a society have at their disposal the capacity for reflection upon that society and therefore the potential to understand and comprehend it. The tension between how things are and how they could be or ought to be[44] was basically the religious problem *par excellence* as it emerged in the Judaistic and Christian traditions—and to some extent in the Islamic. The legalism of Judaism and Islam constituted a stable bridge between 'cultural otherness' and social reality which in different ways 'softened' the full societal impact of a thoroughgoing transcendentalism. Christianity, historically much less monotheistically transcendental than either of these, gave rise acutely to the problem of religiosity and was more fragile with respect to holding the cultural and social-structural domains in stable alignment. In clear contrast the syncretism of Hinduism, and particularly its emphasis upon ritual and *relative* lack of firm scriptural referents, involved little situational distinction between a social-structural and a cultural domain. In large part the same is true of Buddhism, notwithstanding important differences in the respective belief systems. Buddhism in its classic form takes the existing social and material circumstances as the only point of reference. It is in this sense that it is, in purely Weberian terms, more this-worldly. It accepts 'this world' as all that is possible socially. The fact that Buddhism negates any existing social condition makes no difference to this contention about its *initial point of reference*.[45]

Church-State Relations

In the Christian tradition the problem of the right relationship between church and state has been a persistent one. In a major respect the problem is a corollary of the more general issue of 'religion and society'. As we shall see the actual phrase, church-state relations, is somewhat misleading in the present sociological context. The word 'church' is too limiting for most purposes, whilst to focus only upon relations between religious collectivities and 'the state' suggests a legalistic or constitutionalist approach.[46]

We may proceed to an analysis of some of the more detailed aspects of church-state relations by making an initial distinction, following Stroup, between religions of a people; religions closely supportive of a people; religions of withdrawal; and religions of universal scope.[47] *Religions of a people* include Judaism, Sikhism and Shintoism. Such religions have generally not claimed universal application and have been relatively bound to specific political territories. As Stroup points out they have, to a large degree, been identified with the social and cultural boundaries of the population within the relevant territory. 'They may support the distinction between the social institutions of religion and the state, but they perceive them to be completely harmonious because the goals are almost completely identical.'[48] Of the specific examples mentioned here only Judaism and Sikhism (initially a syncretic mixture of Islam and Hinduism) have been closely bound up with the formation of nations as such, Judaism with the state of Israel and Sikhism with the separate state of the Punjab (1966).

Religions closely supportive of a people shade into those which have been directly supportive of a people. Perhaps the best examples are Confucianism and Hinduism, in so far as we may call them genuine religions. Historically Hinduism was very closely related to the general qualities of the Indian socio-political system. The closest intimacy in this respect has been the relationship between Hindu religious beliefs and the caste structure of Indian society. As we have noted, India is now officially a secular state—following the implementation of the 1948 Constitution.

Religions of withdrawal include Jainism, Taoism, Zoroastrianism and variants of Buddhism. These manifest withdrawal tendencies in so far as they reject the surrounding culture and political structure. In the case of Buddhism this has historically been much truer of Hinayana Buddhism than the Mahayanan version which spread in Japan and China. Mahayana Buddhism has been much less isolationist than has Hinayana. Religions of withdrawal usually sustain values and norms which are held to be superior to those which obtain in the wider society—and there is a tendency for withdrawal religions to maintain separateness in monastic orders and engage in ascetic practices. (However, in Ceylon and Siam Hinayana Buddhism came to be very closely associated with the state.) As Stroup notes these may not be in conflict with the state—as is shown by the fact that Asoka was the Buddhist ruler of India, while Ardeshir I, a Zoroastrian, led the establishment of Persia's independence in the third century B.C.[49]

Religions of universal scope are exampled best by Christianity and Islam. In one important sense Buddhism should be included here, since it stresses principles of universal application. But the eschatologies of Islam and Christianity, as we have noted, have historically constrained adherents to involve themselves very actively in the global spreading of their religious beliefs.

This brief survey reveals the inherently problematic nature of church-state relations in the case of religions of universal scope. In exploring the latter, with special attention to the Christian case, we should note that there is a difference between speaking of the philosophy of church-state relations adumbrated by a particular school of thought and the actual, objective relationship holding between 'church' and state at any given time. Moreover, the situation is complicated further by the existence in some societies of a plurality of competing religious collectivities or traditions, none of which in any formal sense is predominant. The problem then becomes one of analysing the relationship between religious collectivities or simply 'religion' and the state. In the modern world something approximating to this situation is to be found in many societies.

In looking primarily at the objective patterns of relationship in this sphere, we may generalize that prior to the development in the modern period of societies manifesting a plurality of religions or 'confessions', the commonest situation was that in which religion was 'neither state-controlled nor yet a state in itself', one in which the religion 'harmonizes with its society without being entirely dominated by it . . .'[50] In such a circumstance the religion functions as 'a moral force, an influence on public opinion, but which becomes a political force only in exceptional circumstances'.[51] In fact it is the Islamic state-religion relationship which historically most nearly approximates to this pattern, notwithstanding the common tendency to attribute a definite theocratic tendency to Islam.[52] Even in 'pure' form the Islamic state has been more strictly a *divine nomocracy*. According to Quincy Wright a nomocracy exists if 'a supreme law regarded as of divine or natural origin is the source of governing authority'.[53] Clearly on this definition Christianity has also constituted the basis upon which divine nomocracies have been erected. The doctrine of the divine right of kings relates closely the nomocratic ideal.[54] But Christianity tended, in its classical and medieval phases, to produce conflicts with respect to the implementation of the nomocratic ideal. While on the other hand the firm and definite *legalistic* core of Islamic religious beliefs and values was productive of a more harmonious relationship between religion and the state— one in which the caliph was 'the head of both the church and the state, as one institution, monopolizing, at the same time, all the powers of Caesar'.[55] It should be emphasized strongly that the description of harmony applies to the relationships between religion and politics *per se*. It follows from there being a relatively undifferentiated relationship between religion and politics that conflict will take on a politico-religious form. As Strayer notes, it was very difficult to have conflict between political institutions and religious institutions simply because Islam has as such manifested very little

H

institutional apparatus—no church or separate organizations devoted to the preservation of faith.[56] Preachers, teachers and theologians had influence and authority, but no institutionalized loci of power and, therefore, no sanctions at their disposal.[57]

Such characteristics of Islam made the divine nomocracy much more of an objective reality than was the case with Christianity. Whatever the ideals of Christianity, its heavy emphasis upon its institutional structure, developed *partly* in response to its initial minority, persecuted status within the Roman Empire, led to frequent conflicts with political authority and power.[58] The most crucial phase in the development of such conflict was in the immediate period following the fall of the Western portion of the Empire at the end of the fifth century A.D. By that time the Christian Church had developed an elaborate institutional structure extending far beyond the Mediterranean area. The uniqueness of this period lies in the fact that at the fall of the Empire the Church took over much of the latter's political machinery and law. The further development of institutional Christianity led to its becoming in the medieval period much 'more of a state than most of its secular rivals'.[59] The church had a centralized government, and even, at times, an army, in a period when political authority was relatively decentralized and indeterminate. When real states began to develop again in Europe (which was in part made possible by the very fact that the church had not become totally secularized in political terms), conflicts between religious leaders and collectivities, on the one hand, and political leaders and collectivities, on the other, were inevitable. But we must realize that these conflicts were frequently not between church and state but, as Strayer puts it, 'purely political conflicts between two states, an old clerical state and a new secular state'.[60]

This historical background aids considerably in the comprehension of the church-state problem as it appeared so frequently in the period leading up to the Protestant Reformation. The Reformation had itself of course a significant political component—in the sense of a struggle for national political independence from Roman Catholic hegemony. The major difficulty in establishing an adequate and analytically consistent pattern of church-state relations for the period since the Reformation lies in the fact that societies have varied considerably since that time in the degree to which they have had a variety of religious belief systems represented within their boundaries. It is not easy to compare a society which is overwhelmingly Catholic with one which has large numbers of Catholics and Jews and a large variety of Protestant denominations. The difficulties are highlighted by invoking the distinctions which Stokes makes with respect to church-state relations.[61] He distinguishes: (1) the Erastian pattern, where the state dominates the church; (2) the state-church pattern, where the official church is only loosely 'established', with other religious collectivities allowed freedom; (3) the jurisdictional pattern, in which there is equal status for several confessions; and (4) the separation pattern, which involves state and religion being kept separate. In this 'typology' Stokes concentrates almost entirely upon legal aspects of the problem. Yinger notes that the relationships between religion and politics (that is to say formal, governmental politics) 'are embedded in a whole social structure and will vary with variations in that structure'.[62] It is clear that an adequate sociological depiction of the problem has to include, as a critical variable, a reference to the nature of the relationships between religious groups within the society, independently of a variable pertaining to the relationship between central government and 'religion'.

Patterns of Religious Commitment at the Societal Level

It may thus in fact be an unnecessary task for the sociologist to focus specifically on church-state or state-religion relations as such. In the modern period the question does not assume the social and political importance that it used to do, notwithstanding periodic strains with respect to state support for 'sectarian' schools in the U.S.A., conflicts between religious groups and Communist governments, and so on. In any case these problems themselves can only be understood through analyses of the structure of the relationships between religious collectivities and cultural tendencies at the societal level. Indeed we may propose that state-church relationships in the modern period are primarily dependent on variations within this domain. In order to get at such variation an initial distinction has to be made between pluralistic and monistic societal systems of religion. In a primitive sense this simply discriminates between those societies characterized by a plurality of religious 'clusters' and those manifesting a single religious tendency. Along such lines we would contrast the situation in the U.S.A. (pluralistic) with that of Spain (monistic). But what of a seemingly pluralistic situation such as that obtaining in the Netherlands, where there are religious *columns*—where mutually exclusive and antagonistic religious commitments exist?[63] In Britain there is a plurality of religious collectivities, but these are not culturally welded together in the positive way that many commentators have claimed to be the case with religious collectivities in the U.S.A.[64] Even more problematically there is the situation obtaining in Java: a coexistence of three major religious forms which correspond quite clearly to structural divisions within Javanese society.[65]

It is apparent that the simple term 'religious pluralism' is not a sufficiently precise one. The most basic problem has to do with the range and relative distributions of religious positions manifested in a particular society. In these terms, the situation in the United States is very different from that obtaining in Britain. In Britain the proportion of Catholics and Jews is relatively low, while most of the Protestant collectivities are fairly close to each other in terms of espoused doctrine. In the United States on the other hand there are many Catholics.[66] Moreover religious commitment has been a major mode of self-location and identification in American society. Thus in speaking of religious pluralism we need always to pay attention to two variables: the range of religious positions manifested in the society—in terms of the 'doctrinal distance' between religious tendencies—and the extensiveness and the intensiveness of the respective positions. But even after such variables have been taken into account there is further need to consider what, so to speak, is 'made' of the situation of religious pluralism. There is an important difference between depicting the distribution of religious commitments and the 'distance' between them, and discovering how these relate to each other in terms of modes of orientation between them. Of the societies so far mentioned, it is only American society which displays anything like a genuine religious pluralism in the sense that the virtues of pluralism are explicitly proclaimed by Americans. (This is currently mitigated by racial conflict.)

Thus in trying to grasp the essential characteristics of the general structure of the religious situation on a cross-societal basis the most relevant variables would appear to be: firstly, the extent to which the situation is rigid and solidified; and, secondly, the range of religious positions in the society. The second of these is much easier to identify than the first. Although it is certainly not unproblematic: we need not only to grasp the range of positions in numerical terms, we need also to take into account whether one (or more) religious cluster(s) predominates over the rest. We might therefore describe this variable, concerning range of religious positions, in terms of a *monopolistic* versus a *competitive* tendency. The first variable, the degree of *rigidity* (or, conversely, *flexibility*) in the religious situation, has to do with the strength of commitment in terms of religious particularism. One useful indicator of this variable would be the salience of political voting in terms of religious commitment. For example, voting along lines of religious cleavage in Great Britain is low in comparison to Canada, Australia and the U.S.A.[67] In the Netherlands it is very high. An indicator of very high rigidity would be where the political system operated in an institutionalized manner according to religious cleavage, as it does in the Lebanon. (Although the fact that such cleavage *is* highly institutionalized will make for a relatively stable situation.)

An example of a *monopolistic, flexible* religious situation at the societal level would be that of France, where Roman Catholicism predominates, and where there is a tradition of taking positions on a pro- or anti-clerical basis, but where there is no legal or general harassment of minority religious groups. An example of a situation approximating to the *competitive, flexible* type is the U.S.A., with three prominently represented major orientations, Protestant, Catholic and Jew, with numerous explicit variations within the Protestant category, some in the Jewish and a few (albeit minor) in the Catholic. The American situation also manifests various bridging mechanisms—organizational ventures which cut across the major religious divisions or have arisen in response to the felt need to adapt to American society. The *competitive, rigid* situation is best exampled by societies like the Netherlands and the Lebanon, which are columnized or compartmentalized on a religious basis, such that not only does religious or anti-religious commitment tend to determine a variety of other types of commitment at the individual level (as it does in the U.S.A.) but where religious collectivities as such operate extensively on a political basis—with political parties and trade unions being organized in ostensibly religious terms. Finally, a *monopolistic, rigid* situation is well illustrated by the cases of Spain and, much less significantly, Portugal, where the Roman Catholic church operates as a dominating force in most spheres of social activity and where non-Catholics are placed in positions of definite disadvantage. The same applies to a number of Latin American societies. (Italy is an intriguing case, in so far as it has a Catholic *religious* monopoly, but this is competitive with respect to the Communist Party.)

State-governmental policies as such tend to cluster around the following: maintaining, neutral or constraining. The latter is most applicable to the Communist society, where religious commitment is controlled through limitations upon the activities of religious collectivities. Constraint involves a purposeful attempt to circumscribe the significance of religiosity as such. Some societies, such as Japan and India, stand midway between the constraining policy exhibited in Communist societies and the maintaining policy to be found in the U.S.A. In Japan religious collectivities are supervised by governmental agencies, as they are in Communist societies; but the supervision does not amount to harassment. In the monopolistic, rigid situations we have indicated, in particular Spain, we also have a midway position between constraining and maintaining. Some societies such as Britain fall midway between maintaining and neutral policies. In respect of the formal links between the state and the Church of England there is maintenance; but in so far as there is no positive encouragement to maintain a pattern of relationships between religious collectivities the British situation is one of state neutrality.[68] On the basis of what we have said already about Islam we may describe Middle Eastern societies as principally manifesting policies of maintenance (Turkey being an interesting exception in its neutrality).

A Note on Syncretism

An added complication arises in connection with the phenomenon of syncretism. Religious cultures are syncretic to the extent that they involve a fusion and combination of elements from two or more religious traditions. In the present context syncretism is relevant mainly because of the possibility that separate groups, classes or strata may be the bearers of distinctive cultural elements. Thus the problem is posed of *distinguishing between syncretism and pluralism*.

In the strictest terms all religious doctrines are syncretic. For example Christianity was historically composed of elements from Eastern and Near Eastern religions (e.g., virgin birth, baptism, burial services), from Greek religions (asceticism, cosmology, eschatology), from Judaism (monotheism) and from gnostic religious doctrines.[69] But in so far as all these and many other elements became crystallized into a relatively coherent doctrine, there seems little point in speaking of Christianity as a syncretic religion, except in respect of the historical periods when the elements were actually being assembled and incorporated. Hinduism is, as we have noted, much more clearly syncretic in the sense that it lacks systematization into a coherent doctrine. The process of syncretization, like that of Christianity, is of very long standing—much longer than that of Christianity.

The real sociological interest in the phenomenon of syncretism arises when we can examine precisely the *processes* of syncretization and when the relationships between the component aspects of the overall syncretic products are problematic for the individuals and groups within the society in question. One of the best studied of such cases is that of Javanese religion. In his analysis of the religion of Java, Geertz notes that there are three principal elements in the Javanese syncretism. First there is *abangan*, which stresses animism and broadly relates to the peasantry. Second, there is *santri*, which involves an emphasis on Islamic beliefs and most directly relates to traders, but also to 'certain elements in the peasantry'. Thirdly, there is *prijaji*, which is mainly Hinduistic and is related to the bureaucratic stratum.[70] In such a situation of religious cleavage along vertical lines it may be wondered in what sense the situation may be said to be syncretic at all. One does not describe the situation in Northern Ireland as syncretic. There the society is *polarized* in terms of a Protestant, privileged stratum and a Catholic, underprivileged stratum. Nor does one describe the situation in the Netherlands as syncretic, where the divisions are primarily horizontal, cutting across class and strata divisions in the form of *zuilen* (columns). (A particularly intriguing problem is posed by the association between caste divisions and Hindu culture. The castes as such do not contribute separate elements to Hinduism. The latter is syncretic independently of the caste structure; the culture prescribes and sustains these structural divisions.)

It may be that Geertz exaggerates the extent to which there is genuine syncretism in Java. But the important point is that there are various beliefs and commitments which cut across the religious divisions. For example the Hinduistic mystical beliefs—*prijaji* mysticism—involve a high degree of tolerance of, and respect for, a variety of religious forms. At the time of his study Geertz noted two main integrative elements in Javanese society, both of which contributed to a sense of common culture: first, a tendency to denigrate the present in terms of the past, and, second, the growing strength of nationalism. Additionally, a great deal of *santri* (Islamic) ideology is stated in generally Javanese terms, whilst certain rituals, notably that of the *slamatan* communal feast, are more or less commonly practised. 'All Javanese—santri, prijaji, and abangan—hold certain truths to be self-evident, just as behind the division into Catholic, Protestant, and Jew, Americans cling to certain over-arching values which in many ways make, for example, an American Catholic more similar in his world-view to an American Protestant than, say, to a Spanish Catholic.'[71] Thus it is not easy to speak of *a* religious syncretism in Java. There is at least as of now no final product of the syncretic tendencies. What obtains in Java is a series of interpenetrations of major religious belief systems plus some overarching, common cultural themes. A more general and thoroughgoing syncretism is to be found in those contexts where there is selective borrowing from two or more distinctive religious traditions. One finds this in society such as Guatemala where there is a selective knitting together of indigenous, primitive religious beliefs and Catholic beliefs on the part of native members of the society; one finds it in Brazil and Chile where there is a knitting together of Catholic, Protestant and indigenous primitive religious beliefs.[72] This applies mainly to lower strata. Belief in spirit possession and the therapeutic assistance of spirits are prominent themes. (Pentecostalism is the main Protestant contribution to these.)

In this chapter we have dealt firstly with the main types of religious culture and the ways in which they relate to social structure and, secondly, with the problem of the relationship between religion and the society as a bounded collectivity. These two themes together comprise the more general theme of systems of religion. Of the four types of religious culture which we delineated, the shamanic, the communal, the olympian and the monotheistic, it is only in the latter two that there is in fact a problem of the relationship between religion and the wider society *qua* society. The olympian and the monotheistic progressively mark the development of a competitive relationship between religious commitment and societal commitment. In terms of the typology of relations between religion and society at the social level which we stipulated in chapter two olympian and monotheistic cultures tend to connect respectively (but only very loosely) to the organized, undifferentiated and the organized, differentiated kinds of situation. This circumstance of religious organization, however tentative and embryonic, operates in conjunction with the differentiation of religious culture to produce strains in the relationship between religious and other types of commitment. The strains are obviously most manifest where there is a full conjunction of religious-cultural monotheism and social differentiation of organized religious commitment.

Notes to Chapter 4

1. See Yinger, *Religion in the Struggle for Power*, op. cit.
2. For a discussion of the distinction between the community of religiosi and the religious order, see E. K. Francis, 'Toward a Typology of Religious Orders', *American Journal of Sociology*, 55 (March, 1950), pp. 437–49.
3. See particularly John M. Mecklin, *The Passing of the Saint*, Chicago, 1941. See also K. and C. H. George, 'Roman Catholic Sainthood and Social Status', *Journal of Religion*, 35 (April, 1955), pp. 85–98.
4. See, *inter alia*, Troeltsch, *The Social Teaching of the Christian Churches*, op. cit., Vol. I; R. A. Knox, *Enthusiasm*, Oxford, 1950.
5. These points are taken up in detail below, pp. 85–95.
6. Anthony F. C. Wallace, *Religion: An Anthropological View*, New York, 1966, p. 88. In the next few pages we rely considerably upon Wallace's discussion. It should be noted that the first two types involve a considerable intermingling of phenomena frequently labelled as 'magic' and religion. In primitive-societal belief systems there is a particularly close relation between magico-religion and *survival* problems. This contrasts with the greater emphasis upon religion in relation to *moral* problems in non-primitive contexts. See above, pp. 48–9. (Lévi-Strauss distinguishes between 'cool' societies in which the culture/nature relationship is relatively direct and unmediated and 'hot' societies where the relationship is indirect and complex. *The Savage Mind*, op. cit.)
7. Wallace, *op. cit.*, p. 86.
8. Wallace notes that we find this kind of phenomenon in industrial societies. But in industrial societies the individualistic cult orientation— where the individual enters into a relationship with spiritual power for purposes of need—frequently obtains within a contextual culture of monotheistic religion, thus constituting a kind of magico-religious substratum. We have in mind the use of lucky charms and patron-saint protectors. See also below, pp. 237–38.
9. On the functions of creator spirits and gods in primitive societies, see Swanson, *The Birth of the Gods*, op. cit.
10. This function of ritual is to bridge the 'gap' between magico-religious culture (which is more autonomous than in the shamanic case) and the actual circumstances of the social structure. On the evolutionary significance of this, see Wallace, op. cit.; Talcott Parsons, *Societies; Evolutionary and Comparative Perspectives*, Englewood Cliffs (New Jer-

sey), 1966; and Robert N. Bellah, 'Religious Evolution', op. cit. More generally, see Bellah, 'Durkheim and History', op. cit. For the significance of ritual in Hinduism, see below, p. 85. It will be noted that in these characterizations of religious cultures we speak in the shamanic and communal cases not only of beliefs, symbols and values, but also of practices and institutional structures. The fact that we include reference to the latter is indicative precisely of the relative lack of differentiation of culture from social-structural circumstance in such societies.

11. For the development of the role of the priest see E. O. James, *The Nature and Function of Priesthood*, New York, 1961.

12. Ancient Greek religion is important in this connection. We do not mention it specifically within the olympian category because in many respects it bridges the olympian and monotheistic categories. For in spite of its polytheism Greece also produced, notably in the work of Plato, a theme which has lasted in some form or other to the present day—namely the conception of an ineffable realm beyond the mundane world of everyday affairs. Such notions as 'the completely other', 'the One', 'the Absolute' and 'the Good' relate closely to this. Lovejoy attributes to Plato the philosophic genesis of the idea of 'The Great Chain of Being', a persistent theme in the history of Christian thought. See Arthur O. Lovejoy, *The Great Chain of Being*, New York, 1960 (first published in 1936), especially pp. 45 ff. Religious ideas of cosmic continuity and gradation are of course very much more widespread than the Christian sphere. For example, see Yang, op. cit., for classical Chinese conceptions; and E. E. Evans-Pritchard, *The Nuer*, op. cit. (For Greek religion specifically see Frank Russell Earp, *The Way of the Greeks*, London, 1929, especially pp. 67 ff.; Gilbert Murray, *Five Stages of Greek Religion*, New York, 1955; Jane E. Harrison, *Prolegomena to the Study of Greek Religion*, New York, 1955. More generally see Alvin W. Gouldner, *Enter Plato: Classical Greece and the Origins of Social Theory*, London, 1967.)

13. Syncretism as a special topic is discussed below, pp. 103–5.

14. Wallace, op. cit., p. 101.

15. In fact Wallace explicitly utilizes his schema in an evolutionary sense. For his specific evolutionary arguments, see ibid., pp. 255–70. Cf. Bellah, 'Religious Evolution', op. cit.

16. For this see Bellah in ibid.

17. See Jack Goody and Ian Watt, 'The Consequences of Literacy', *Comparative Studies in Society and History*, V (April, 1963), pp. 93–114.

18. These statements relate to a number of critical themes which have been

objects of considerable controversy, especially in recent years in reference to the work of Lévi-Strauss. We are unable to explore these in any comprehensive way in the present context. See, *inter alia*, Claude Lévi-Strauss, 'The Structural Study of Myth', *Journal of American Folklore*, 68 (1955), pp. 428–44; Edmund R. Leach, 'Lévi-Strauss in the Garden of Eden: An Examination of Some Recent Developments in the Analysis of Myth', *Transactions of the New York Academy of Sciences*, Series 2, 23 (1961), pp. 386–96; Leach (ed.), *The Structural Study of Myth and Totemism*, op. cit. For Wallace's critical comments in terms of Lévi-Strauss' neglect of ritual, see *Religion: An Anthropological View*, op. cit., pp. 243 ff.

19. See Max Weber, *The Religion of India: The Sociology of Hinduism and Buddhism*, Glencoe (Illinois), 1958.

20. This part of the analysis rests a great deal on the insights of Weber—as have nearly all sociological discussions of the past thirty years or so. (In addition to previous citations, see H. H. Gerth and C. Wight Mills (eds.), *From Max Weber*, London, New York, 1948, Pt. III; Max Weber, *The Religion of China: Confucianism and Taoism*, Glencoe (Illinois), 1951; *Ancient Judaism*, Glencoe (Illinois), 1952.) See also Reinhard Bendix, *Max Weber: An Intellectual Portrait*, London, New York, 1960. On the other hand, there is one major point of disagreement with Weber's conceptions. See below, pp. 89–94.

21. It is, we repeat, the unifying principle of Confucianism, transcending in classical China many other more 'spiritual' ancestral cults, as well as, at various times and places, Taoism and Buddhism, on which we are focusing.

22. This is emphasized in Yang, op. cit.

23. David A. Martin, *Pacifism: An Historical and Sociological Study*, London, New York, 1965, p. 20.

24. S. J. Tambiah, 'The Ideology of Merit and the Social Correlates of Buddhism in a Thai Village', in Leach (ed.), *Dialectic in Practical Religion*, op. cit., pp. 41 ff. More generally see Melford E. Spiro's valuable *Burmese Supernaturalism*, Englewood Cliffs, 1967.

25. The basis for this lies of course in the central idea of the Jewish covenant with God—analysed so brilliantly by Weber, *Ancient Judaism*, op. cit.

26. Weber, *The Sociology of Religion*, op. cit., p. 266. For an excellent critique of Weber's conceptions of salvation and theodicy, see Gananath Obeyesekere, 'Theodicy, Sin and Salvation in a Sociology of Buddhism', in Leach (ed.), *Dialectic in Practical Religion*, op. cit.

27. For some good essays on the Middle Eastern situation see Leonard Binder, *The Ideological Revolution in the Middle East*, New York, 1964.

28. Nettl and Robertson, *International Systems and the Modernization of Societies*, op. cit., pp. 160 and 175. For modern Burmese Buddhism in relation to the Burmese state, see Smith, *Religion and Politics in Burma*, op. cit.

29. This and related points are stated succinctly in Martin, op. cit.

30. One must also note the historic importance of (basically individualistic) mysticism in Christianity. See below, p. 243, n. 14.

31. Weber, *The Sociology of Religion*, op. cit., especially chs. XI–XII.

32. Talcott Parsons, 'Introduction' to ibid., p. xlix. Cf. Obeyesekere, loc. cit.

33. The doubts which are expressed here about Weber's inner- versus other-worldly distinction are by no means new. Others have entered reservations, including: Bellah, 'Religious Evolutions', op. cit.; (by implication) Lovejoy, op. cit.; Bryan Wilson, 'Millennialism in Comparative Perspective', *Comparative Studies in Society and History*, 6 (October, 1963), pp. 93–113; Marshall G. S. Hodgson, 'A Comparison of Islam and Christianity as Framework for Religious Life', *Diogenes* (Winter, 1960), pp. 49–74. Cf. Parsons, 'Christianity in Modern Industrial Society', op. cit.

34. Hodgson, op. cit.

35. Ibid., p. 68.

36. See Gerth and Mills (eds.), *From Max Weber*, op. cit., pp. 302–22; and Weber, *The Protestant Ethic and the Spirit of Capitalism*, op. cit.

37. For example, Kenneth Scott Latourette, *A History of the Expansion of Christianity*, New York, 1962, Vol. IV, p. 424.

38. This misleading conception is very strongly present in Parsons' various essays on American religion and in Bellah, 'Religious Evolution', op. cit. For the charge that Weber overemphasized the 'Protestant' tendencies within ancient Judaism, see Peter L. Berger, 'Charisma and Religious Innovation: The Social Location of Israelite Prophecy', *American Sociological Review*, 28 (December, 1963), pp. 940–50.

39. In a different and very important sense Jewry is highly achievement-oriented. That is, by virtue of being ascribed Jewish status the Jew is then enjoined to achieve particular 'worldly' goals.

40. To be sure, there is an important stress on achievement in Buddhism, both monastic and lay; but this is fairly narrowly circumscribed to a specific range of actions. Christian achievement is more 'open-ended'.

41. Lovejoy, op. cit., p. 314.

42. Swanson, *Religion and Regime*, op. cit., p. 257. (The diagram is an adaptation of Swanson's presentation.) The full implications of this

approach in relation to Weber's discussions of types of radical salvation cannot be explored here. Cf. Parsons' dissection of Weber's position in 'Introduction', op. cit., pp. xlix ff. Cf. Obeyesekere, op. cit.

43. Swanson, *Religion and Regime*, op. cit., pp. 258–60. The meaning we attribute to Swanson's point is an *extension* of his position.

44. Cf. the distinction between ideal and actual structures—used extensively in Marion J. Levy, Jr., *Modernization and the Structure of Societies* (two volumes), Princeton, 1966. Cf. John Dewey, 'Union of the Ideal and the Actual', in J. Milton Yinger, *Religion, Society and the Individual*, New York, 1957, pp. 609–11. For a discussion of the widespread use of such distinctions in American sociology, see Roland Robertson and Andrew Tudor, *The Sociology of Talcott Parsons* (forthcoming), ch. 6.

45. Much of the above discussion raises an even more profound problem. This concerns the extent to which religious belief systems have been governed and constrained by societal cultural patterns which are much more basic than religious beliefs as such. Lovejoy's emphasis upon the importance of certain Platonic notions points to the significance of this suggestion. Serious entertainment of the idea that religious belief systems are subject to 'cultural control' would involve a radical recasting of orthodox thinking. Eister has argued that both religion and sociology are governed and controlled by the 'orientational institutions' of societies. Allan W. Eister, 'Addendum' to 'Ideological and Organizational Characteristics of New Religious Movements in Secular Societies', 1967 (mimeo).

46. For a general discussion of related problems, see Joachim Wach, *The Sociology of Religion*, Chicago, 1944, Pt. II.

47. Herbert Stroup, *Church and State in Confrontation*, New York, 1967, pp. 136–52.

48. Ibid., p. 138.

49. Ibid., p. 147.

50. Joseph R. Strayer, 'The State and Religion: Greece and Rome, the West, Islam', *Comparative Studies in Society and History*, I (1958), p. 43.

51. Ibid.

52. See the analyses of classical Islamic societies in Karl A. Wittfogel, *Oriental Despotism*, New Haven, 1957.

53. Quincy Wright, *A Study of War*, Chicago, 1942, Vol. II, p. 942. Quoted in Majid Khadduri, 'Nature of the Islamic State' in S. N. Eisenstadt (ed.), *The Decline of Empires*, Englewood Cliffs (New Jersey), 1967, p. 33.

54. Quite clearly a distinction must be made between a nomocracy and a theocracy, in which political and religious are fused and co-terminous.

The god-king situation is obviously theocratic. See the discussion of ancient Egypt in Parsons, *Societies: Evolutionary and Comparative Perspectives*, op. cit., pp. 53–62. Perhaps the only genuine theocracy of modern times was that of Llamaist Tibet.

55. Khadduri, op. cit., p. 35.

56. Strayer, op. cit.

57. Cf. Eisenstadt, 'Religious Organizations . . . ', op. cit.

58. On the early development of the Christian church see T. G. Jalland, *Origin and Evolution of the Christian Church*, London, 1950; and Karl Kautsky, *The Foundations of Christianity*, op. cit., pp. 350–96.

59. Strayer, op. cit., p. 126.

60. Ibid. Cf. Vatro Murvar, 'Max Weber's Concept of Hierocracy', *Sociological Analysis*, 28 (Summer, 1967), pp. 69–84.

61. Anson P. Stokes, *Church and State in the United States* (3 vols), New York, 1950. Cited in Yinger, *Religion, Society and the Individual*, pp. 242–3.

62. Ibid., p. 242.

63. See David O. Moberg, 'Social Differentiation in the Netherlands' *Social Forces*, 39 (May, 1961), pp. 333–7. Lenski predicts a rather similar situation in the U.S.A. See *The Religious Factor*, op. cit. (See the articles on pluralism in *International Yearbook for the Sociology of Religion*, 1965.)

64. See particularly Will Herberg, *Protestant, Catholic, Jew*, op. cit.; Herberg. 'Religion in a Secularized Society: Some Aspects of America's Three-Religion Pluralism', op. cit.

65. See Clifford Geertz, *The Religion of Java*, New York, 1960.

66. Jews comprise only about 3 per cent of the U.S. population; but their 'presence' is much more clear-cut than in Britain, where accommodation to long-established British traditions has been very marked.

67. Robert Alford, *Party and Society*, Chicago, 1964.

68. There are still constitutional restrictions on the religious commitment of monarchs and certain governmental officers (e.g. the Lord Chancellor).

69. Thomas F. Hoult, *The Sociology of Religion*, New York, 1958, p. 59. See the warning about perceiving too much unity and coherence in religious belief systems in Worsley, *The Trumpet Shall Sound*, op. cit.

70. Geertz, op. cit., pp. 6–7 and *passim*.

71. Ibid., p. 366.

72. See Emilio Willems, 'Religioser Pluralismus und Klassenstruktur in Brasilun und Chile', *International Yearbook for the Sociology of Religion*, 1965, pp. 189–211. In more cataclysmic form, millennial movements typically involve the fusion of Christian emphases upon eschatological hope and indigenous magico-religious ritual. Syncretic combination of

Christian and primitive beliefs also occurs in many non-millennial religious movements in Africa, Asia and Oceana. For a useful discussion of types of African religious movements with specific reference to their location in the wider cultural and social context, see James W. Fernandez, 'African Religious Movements—Types and Dynamics', *Journal of African Studies*, 2 (1964), pp. 531-47. See also Roger Bastide, *Les Religions Africaines au Brésil*, Paris, 1960; Maria Isaura de Queiroz, 'Classifications des messianismes brésiliens', *Archives de Sociologie des Religions*(January-June, 1958), pp. 111-20. See also below, pp. 163-7.

5

Religious Collectivities

In this chapter we develop as a theme in its own right the characteristics of the social 'vehicles' through which religious doctrines are
expressed. As we noted in the second chapter, by no means all
religious beliefs, values and symbols are actually sustained on an
organizational basis.[1]* There it was stated that there are two
principal types of non-organized religious systems. The first of these
—where religion is not differentiated from other socio-cultural
spheres—has historically been the most prominent. It is, as we have
noted, a major characteristic of primitive societies that religious
activities are not readily distinguished from other activities. Thus,
in such cases, it is possible to analyse the social-structural characteristics which impinge most directly on the performance of religious
activities. The concern there is with roles and positions in the social
structure which have to do with the performance of rites of passage,
the giving of sacrifices and so on. Necessarily exercising some degree
of selectivity, we only attend fleetingly and intermittently to primitive societies in the present chapter.

In the typology presented in the second chapter, two types of
organized religious systems were adumbrated: the differentiated
type and the undifferentiated type.[2] The differentiated type of
religious system is found where religious activities are both relatively
highly organized in terms of some procedural rationale, and where
the organizations are in the main *independently* oriented towards the
implementation of a set of religious ideals. With respect to the
second type there are societies in which religious activities, although
also relatively highly organized in terms of procedural rationale, are
not independently oriented towards the implementation of religious
ideals. In this second type the organizational vehicle is closely linked

* Notes for this chapter begin on page 142.

I

with, or actually implicated, in *a set* of organizational preoccupations. These types of religious system are by no means 'pure'; i.e., they shade into one another in the real world. Empirically, the relationship is most clearly seen in the variations of church-and-state. The most highly and genuinely differentiated type of religious system is that in which religious organizations are completely separated from the central political agency. The least differentiated type is that of the theocratic society—where the political apparatus is heavily infused with a religious significance, indeed is based upon religious principles.

A deliberate if flexible distinction is made here between movements and 'mere' organizations; although the terms are by no means mutually exclusive. A religious movement is of course organized—although not so explicitly and formally in many cases—as a religious organization. The major difference between the two is that a movement is geared to effecting a specific series of alterations in the condition of the wider society or at least in the environment of the collectivity, while a religious organization exists to serve the needs and desires of members and clients. A movement is a dynamic collectivity, concerned with the mobilization of individuals and groups in the pursuit of, or the defence of, specific objectives; whereas an organization is a collectivity concerned primarily with ensuring that certain values and beliefs are upheld in a given society or set of societies. Some such distinction is indispensable; for it is only in these terms that we can adequately indicate the full range of religious collectivities and groups. This is an important consideration, even though this chapter is primarily about religious collectivities in highly differentiated societies.

It is clear that, in terms of this loose distinction between organizations and movements, a collectivity may at a given point in time be an organized movement. Many sects in industrial societies began their 'lives' as collectivities explicitly geared, in dynamic fashion, to rapid mobilization of adherents in pursuit of radically conceived values and goals. Smelser has depicted all collectivities manifesting commitment to a generalized belief system as passing through a phase of *mobilization*.[3] This phase is one in which there is a preoccupation with the articulation of beliefs, values and goals and rapid recruitment of members. The modern, industrial-societal context, then, requires the collectivity typically to move into a phase of *organizational consolidation*. In contrast, the nature of pre-industrial societies was and is such as to be relatively unconducive to such a shift. More typically, we find that the collectivity either accomplishes its objectives or simply dissolves. The cultures of most pre-industrial (or perhaps more crucially, pre-*literate*[4]) societies were and still are unconducive to organizational consolidation for many reasons; one of the key factors being the 'extensive incapacity to trust strangers'.[5] Modern organizations require impersonality and routinized procedures which are alien to the ascriptive, kin-based solidarities of pre-literate societies. Stinchcombe notes that in such contexts organizational structure is limited to 'that which can be built out of combinations of kinship loyalty and force'.[6] To this we should add that religious movements in societies of this kind, and indeed in many so-called transitional societies, have very often been charismatic —resting on an almost familial allegiance to a leader or group of leaders.

The attempt to establish an adequate analytic depiction of the main tendencies in the sphere of religious collectivities has been made most frequently in reference to American society. Troeltsch's initial typology was, strictly speaking, not a typology at all, but rather a dichotomous classification of religious collectivities in terms of their empirical characteristics. In the European society of the sixteenth century to which he primarily directed his attentions, Troeltsch noted that religious collectivities were either supportive or rejective of the existing socio-cultural order.[7] In the Reformation period, religious collectivities could be accurately described as churchly or sectarian; that is, with or against the established order, be it Anglican, Lutheran or Roman Catholic.[8] Established churches tended on the whole to be the focus of loyalty on the part of members of the upper class in any particular society, while religious sects tended to be the focus of loyalty of underprivileged, displaced or new social strata. American sociologists, historians of religion and theologians became increasingly conscious during the 1930s and 1940s that such a characterization did not conform in any meaningful way to the religious situation in the U.S.A. Since the American

Revolution of 1776 there had never been any societally established church, while the last state-established church had disappeared in Massachusetts in 1833, with the breaking of Congregational hegemony.[9] Thus the extended discussion of denominationalism by Niebuhr in the late 1920s heralded a series of attempts to expand and modify Troeltsch's original formulation.[10]

The Church-Sect Approach to the Analysis of Religious Organizations[11]

Troeltsch characterized the church as an institution endowed with grace and salvation, able to receive the masses and adjust itself to the world 'because, to a certain extent, it can afford to ignore the need for subjective holiness for the sake of objective treasures of grace and redemption'.[12] Troeltsch also noted that the church manifested such important attributes as the tendency to utilize the state and the ruling classes in attempting to stabilize and determine the social order; and that individuals are born into the church. In contrast, the sect is a voluntary community, whose members join of their own free will: 'The very life of the sect . . . depends on actual personal service and co-operation; as an independent member each individual has his part within the fellowship; the bond of union has not been indirectly imparted through the common possession of Divine Grace, but it is directly realized in the personal relationships of life. An individual is not born into a sect; he enters into it on the basis of conscious conversion. . . .'[13] Troeltsch emphasized the repudiation of the compromises made by the church—the failure of the church to yield emotional satisfaction, and its support of allegedly unjust features of the society. Sects thus tend to be connected with the lower classes or at least with those groups in a society which are opposed to the state: they 'work upwards from below, and not downwards from above'.[14] Finally, Troeltsch contrasted the asceticism of the church with that of the sect. Churchly asceticism 'is a method of acquiring virtue'; sectarian asceticism consists in a 'simple principle of detachment from the world'.[15]

Criticisms of Troeltsch have been numerous. There is in his schema a lack of analytic clarity and parsimony, and little indication of the ways in which the attributes are related. On the other hand, it is also now recognized that, in the main, these characteristics stem from the particular societies and historical period about which Troeltsch was writing. The fact that his depiction was a dichotomous one is thus merely an analytic manifestation of the fact that the societies about which he was writing were, *relative to* the modern condition of those same societies and to modern American society, *polarized* and *undifferentiated*.[16] They were relatively polarized in terms of class structure and relatively undifferentiated in respect of the relations between political, economic and religious spheres of belief and action. Thus protest against injustice or exploitation was simultaneously political, economic and religious, as was the attempt to perpetuate inequality and privileged status. It is important to note that while discussion of Troeltsch's contribution to the analysis of religious collectivities has revolved around his distinction between church and sect in reference to the Reformation period in its broadest sense, his own discussion of religion in the modern historical period did suggest the need for an extension and elaboration of his original distinction. By the late nineteenth century societies which were not predominantly Catholic had become much more structurally differentiated and integrated. Thus Troeltsch spoke of the modern period as one in which there was a greater consciousness of membership in a wider societal community. Many sects were both less persecuted and, reciprocally, less alienated from the wider society.[17]

The next major contribution to the analysis of the relations between religious collectivities and the wider society was that of Niebuhr, whose principal contributions were to provide stable referents for the denomination as a type of religious organization and to stress the importance of adopting a dynamic perspective in this problem area. In this latter respect Niebuhr was primarily interested in the processes of change in the relationship between religious organizations and the society in which they were located. More specifically, he was concerned to explain how theological ideas are mediated by the character of the social structure to influence the course of religious organization. (In the context of the emphasis in the present book on the relationship between sociology and theology this aspect of Niebuhr's contribution cannot be underscored too heavily.) Denominationalism for Niebuhr is 'a compromise between Christianity and the world'. It is the 'accommodation of Christianity to the caste-system' [*sic*] of human society, along the lines of ethnic and economic divisions in the social structure.[18] Thus Niebuhr diagnosed in the American situation that the transcendentality and inclusiveness of churchly forms of collectivity had increasingly given way to collectivities specifically adapted to social-structurally generated needs. Theology and the relationship of the collectivity to the wider society were thereby modified.

Niebuhr also maintained that religious sects had either to effect a reconciliation with the wider society or suffer dissolution. By its nature sectarianism, with its emphasis upon the pristine effervescence of 'the message', was valid for one generation only. 'The children born to the voluntary members of the first generation begin to make the sect a church long before they have arrived at the years of discretion.'[19] The socialization of children into the sectarian pattern induces a preoccupation with the means of education and control to the detriment of sustaining the distinctiveness of the doctrinal stance. Niebuhr backed this thesis with the argument that the asceticism and self-denial of the sect automatically increases wealth, which in turn brings greater involvement in 'the world'. (This generalization is often labelled 'Wesley's Law', following an observation of John Wesley as to the effects of the Methodist emphasis upon the performance of economic duty in a spirit of devotion and thriftiness.[20]) The weaknesses of Niebuhr's analysis derive mainly from his paying relatively little attention to the *internal* dynamics of religious collectivities, notwithstanding his point about the accommodative consequences of the development of educational agencies within religious sects. As we shall see, one of the key themes of relevance in the analysis of religious sects (indeed of all kinds of collective deviance from a mainline societal culture) is the range of organizational provisions which have been erected in order to maintain distinctive and unique religious belief systems. The very notion of being separate implies in and of itself a high degree of *discipline*. Thus commitment to discipline is a *given* feature of religious sects; and it is not therefore the development from 'scratch' of disciplining procedures which is the crucial variable affecting degree of accommodation to the world, as Niebuhr implies in his emphasis upon educative imperatives, but rather the *effectiveness* of the disciplinary procedures. In Niebuhr's terms, Jehovah's Witnesses and Seventh Day Adventists would have to be typified as denominations or churches, on the grounds that they both have exceeded the first generation of membership and both have developed educational agencies; whereas they have in fact been very successful in sustaining world-views which diverge radically from those of both the prevailing societal culture, and the most highly legitimized religious organizations in all the societies in which they operate.[21]

The first self-conscious attempt to establish a *typology* of religious collectivities after Troeltsch was that of Von Wiese, on the basis of whose work Becker formulated a typology consisting in the *ecclesia* (typified by its compulsory character); the *sect* (typified by its elective principle); the *denomination* (regarded as an advanced state of the sect with the original fervour disappearing); and the *cult* (characterized as a private, personal form of religion of the mystic type).[22] Becker agrees with Niebuhr that the sect is valid for one generation only.

In two separate contributions to the typological problem Yinger considerably clarified sociological thinking about the relations between religious collectivities and the wider society, and relations amongst religious collectivities themselves.[23] It had been by no means fully explicit just what criteria were being utilized in the delineation of the typology before Yinger's contributions. Thus Yinger argued that the task of a typology was both to encompass the relevant range of empirical data and at the same time oversimplify that data by disregarding minor differences and emphasizing major similarities. He utilized two criteria in his delineation of a sixfold typology: first, the degree of inclusiveness/exclusiveness of the organization; second, the degree of attention to the function of social integration (as contrasted with the function of personal need).

The six types which Yinger derives are as follows: The *Universal Church* (one which transcends national-societal boundaries) combines sectarian and churchly tendencies, in that it is relatively successful in both supporting the integration of society and satisfying individual needs. The best example of 'success' in this respect is the Catholic church of the thirteenth century.[24] The *Ecclesia*, which is characteristically an established national church such as the Church of England, is less successful than the universal church in respect of both integrating the society and satisfying a variety of individual needs. It is also less inclusive than the universal church. The *Denomination* is still less successful in achieving universality, since it explicitly caters to particular groups within the population. The *Established Sect* is primarily an outgrowth of the sect and is Yinger's most important contribution to the general theme of religious organizations. The *Sect* is characterized in broadly the same terms as those employed by Troeltsch. It is particularly unsuccessful in contributing to the integration of society, while it *is* very successful in catering to individual needs. Finally, the *Cult* is concerned almost wholly with individual needs and desires, with little or no specific orientation to the social order. It is typically lacking in organizational structure and is grouped around a charismatic leader, with a strong tendency to disintegration.

A Typological Reformulation

Over the years sociologists of religion have dipped into what has been written in the Troeltschian tradition of research and analysis for a variety of different purposes, whilst the church-sect perspective has persisted to the point that the contributors to a recent symposium largely decided that the only thing left to say on the subject was that it was time to call a halt.[25] (The one exception to this trend argued for a return to the original Troeltsch position—although on a more rigorous analytic basis than that espoused by Troeltsch himself.[26])

One of the main points of discussion and controversy has been the utilizability of the church-sect typology, in whatever form, outside of the Christian sphere.[27] There has been a majority view that the typology is inapplicable to societies which are primarily non-Christian; whilst some have sought to establish that it is inappropriate even to use it on societies which are primarily Roman Catholic. When sociologists have sought to restrict the application of the typology to Christian societal spheres they appear to have rested their case on the fact that the church-sect distinction, and also such concepts as 'denomination', derive from a Christian theological and doctrinal perspective and therefore make 'no sense' outside of Christianity. Some also appear to think that some of the more detailed typologies are inapplicable on the grounds that non-Christian societies are insufficiently complex to 'take them'. This latter argument is inadequate. The purposes underlying the explication of typologies in sociology frequently include their capacity to facilitate comparative analysis. If a typology is *in principle* applicable to a given range of reality then it is in itself illuminating to discover that particular types specified in the typology are not found in certain contexts. But the problem of the European-Christian origin of the church-sect distinction is a much more serious one. Objections can and have been made against the use of this distinction in reference to the American situation; since the European church arrangement never took hold in the U.S.A. and was foreign to American culture. (In contrast the notion of the sect 'has long applied to groups in Hinduism, Buddhism, Judaism and Islam in ways which make it at best difficult, at worst presumptuous, to try to preempt it for special use in Western Christendom in contradistinction with *church*'.[28]) Thus the very extensive usage of the church concept in reference to American society is in itself a 'violation' of its native-cultural origins —although it should readily be conceded that the great stress on the concept of the denomination amongst American *sociologists* derives precisely from unease about talking in terms of American churches or churchliness.[29]

The really crucial point about the applicability or otherwise of the church-sect typology to non-Christian complexes is whether one wishes to employ it culturally or socially. Culturally, that is to say, in terms of concrete religious beliefs and values, one cannot, of course, apply the Christian contrast between sect and church to, say, a Buddhist society. But on the other hand, as we shall see more fully in a moment, if we abstract from the actual cultural content of the church-sect distinction (and typological elaborations of it), we may, in so doing, focus simply on the relations between religious collectivities and their environment in a purely *social manner*. In cultural terms, however, it *is* still possible at least to extend the range of application of the church-sect distinction, if we are prepared to examine the *logic* of the major world-religious doctrinal systems.

Christianity gives rise to the church-sect distinction through its inherent tension between, on the one hand, conservation, conformity and range of impact, and, on the other hand, change, withdrawal and purity of religious commitment. But, as Martin points out, Confucianism in its great emphasis upon conservation of, and adaptation to, the socio-cultural order also implied 'churchliness', even though there was no institution which could meaningfully be described as a church in the heyday of Confucianism. 'Just because Confucianism is the extreme case of simple conservation the "church" is merged in the social pattern and becomes invisible.'[30] Martin points out that 'the ready propriety of Confucianism to the ecclesiastical idea is the reverse side of its inability to imply another category beside it'.[31] That is, the logic of Confucianism implies the church or the ecclesia, but not the sect. Thus, in cultural terms, the ecclesia or church concepts could be applied to Confucianism; but, as Martin notes, we could only include reference to sects by supposing that in the Chinese case Buddhism and Taosim, i.e. *other religions*, were sectarian with respect to Confucianism.

In such terms as *these* it is possible to argue that church and sect, and even other types, can be applied to Islam and, rather less easily, to Buddhism. Hinduism as a general religio-cultural complex is an interesting case, since its basic underlying principle is that of syncretism. It possesses no basic or fundamental norm and is made up of a series of different religious orientations. It can, therefore, 'include all sociological categories.'[32] In noting this *cultural* form of usage we cannot emphasize too strongly, however, that, of the religions which we have mentioned, it is only Islam which has manifested the degree of organization necessary to treatment in terms of a typology of religious *organizations*—as opposed simply to a typology of collective religious orientations—and in the case of Islam religion has historically been *organized but not differentiated*.[33]

In saying that we may well be able to apply the church-sect typology very widely in social terms, we mean that the typology should be formulated in such a way as to concentrate mainly upon social-relational aspects of the problem and not upon doctrinal ones. If this is a viable proposition, the only limitation upon the application of the typology would be that it be used in reference to organized collectivities, to collectivities which manifest a system of institutionalized roles and procedures regulating man's religiosity.[34] This is the common baseline for elaborating contrasting types. In these terms we suggest the following typology of religious organizations, based upon two main criteria: first, the bases of religious legitimacy as perceived by the effective leaders of the organization and, second, the operative principle of membership.

SELF-CONCEIVED BASIS OF LEGITIMACY

		Pluralistically legitimate	Uniquely legitimate
Membership principle	Exclusive	Institutionalized sect	Sect
	Inclusive	Denomination	Church

This typology stands within the Troeltschian tradition to the extent that its point of departure is the relationship between the organization and its environment, as defined on a religious basis. A number of typologists have sought to distinguish between religious organizations on a much wider variety of characteristics, including their internal organizational characteristics and their social constituencies. Yinger's inclusion of the criterion of contribution to the integration of society is one end of an alternative-extreme in this matter, which extends at the other to Johnson's argument that it is the purely *internal* doctrinal characteristics of a religious collectivity which should furnish the basis of typological explication. Yinger's stance diverts our attention from religious organizations *qua* religious organizations towards the general problem of societal integration and continuity, a common predilection of purely functional approaches. Johnson's argument is unconvincing. He argues that 'the attitude toward the secular culture is at best a derivative of other beliefs that provide the actual rallying point for adherents and furnish the basis for the precipitation of a social system'.[35] Such a view assumes that somehow individuals 'take to' a particular set of religious beliefs and that upon this choice or socialization process are contingent all other religious beliefs and the organizational means erected to maintain those beliefs. The impact of contextual features of the environment is thus reduced to zero and organization is totally determined by doctrine—neither of which propositions are borne out by the large amount of available evidence. The typology which we have depicted above steers a path between the religio-centric preference of Johnson and the societo-centric stance of Yinger.[36]

It should be emphasized that the present typology is adumbrated in reference to a *societal context*. That is, it is intended that we speak only of American *or* British Congregationalism and not of Congregationalism in general, of the Church of Christ of Latter Day Saints (Mormons) in Britain *or* America, or wherever, and not the Church of Christ of Latter Day Saints internationally. Thus, with the second example we would probably decide on the empirical evidence that whereas in Britain the Mormons are sectarian in character, in the U.S.A. they constitute an institutionalized sect. In Britain they are not generally accepted as part and parcel of the religious scene and to this extent they reciprocally propagate their doctrine in a relatively elitist manner, emphasizing their unique religious significance. In America more than a century's activity has yielded a *modus vivendi* situation *vis-à-vis* the wider society and other religious collectivities: Mormonism's sectarianism has become institutionalized. It is precisely this possibility of institutionalized sectarianism which is allowed for in the present typology—in line with the earlier work of Yinger and Wilson.[37]

In speaking of *legitimacy* we refer to whether the effective leaders of the collectivity regard the collectivity as one of a set of acceptable religious vehicles (the pluralistic case) or whether, on the other hand, the collectivity is regarded as the only valid religious vehicle (the unique case). (It should be established that we refer here to what is accepted *in practice*. Leaders of institutionalized sects probably continue to adhere to the uniqueness position in theoretical-doctrinal terms.) The dimension of *membership principle* refers to the extent that relatively demanding standards of admission and/or religious performance are exacted from members (exclusivism) or whether low standards are accepted (inclusivism). So long as we use these dimensions of the relationship between 'religion and society' in purely social terms and not with reference to concrete aspects of doctrine then the range of application seems rather wide.

The present typology differs from that of Yinger both in its choice of dimensions and in its greater parsimony in the matter of type-range. The main intention is to cater for the principal forms of religious organization as they are to be discovered in the most complex situations, which effectively means those obtaining in the U.S.A., Britain and West European societies, such as West Germany, which manifest numerous organizations and which are not dominated by Roman Catholicism. The factor of non-domination by Roman Catholicism is crucial. Typically, European Catholic societies have manifested a high degree of polarization of the kind implied by the original Troeltschian formula. The kind of sect which Troeltsch had in mind in elaborating his distinction was the diffuse protest movement, exampled by the Anabaptists and Hussites. In the centuries which followed the Protestant Reformation, societies such as France, Italy, Spain, Portugal and, less typically, Belgium and Holland came to be typified by social-structural situations in which opposition to Catholic hegemony was expressed in anti-religious terms. In a sense the logic of the structural situation in such societies has conformed broadly to Troeltsch's depiction, save for the important development that Communist and socialist movements have in large part taken the place of religious sectarian protest movements.[38] It is precisely the claim to universalism and diffuse control within Catholicism which has yielded this 'either/or', polarized situation. Thus anti-clericalism has been a major spurring factor in such societies. In contrast, the fact that the Protestant confrontation with Catholicism in the sixteenth century was a pluralistic one, involving various wings, notably Calvinism, Lutheranism, Zwinglianism, Anglicanism, Anabaptism and the Free Spirit, mystical, tendency, has allowed for a more flexible and inter-organizationally more complex situation in predominantly Protestant societies.[39]

Troeltsch tended to see in these 'protest' movements a generalized element of militancy which is now regarded as inaccurate—at least in terms of his church-sect schema. Thus he had some difficulty in coping with the Calvinists—mainly because of their established, 'societal' wide position in Calvin's Geneva and their mainstream position in some other societies, such as Scotland. In the case of sixteenth- and, more particularly, seventeenth-century England, Troeltsch was on even weaker ground, given the wide spectrum between the Anglican Church and the radical sects such as the Fifth Monarchy Men, the Levellers and the Diggers. There are good grounds for arguing that both in terms of our typology and the more comprehensive set of attributes applied to the concept of the denomination that such collectivities as the English Congregationalists and the General Baptists were denominational in form even at their earliest stages of development.[40]

Beyond the Reformation and the English Civil War period the empirical range of religious collectivities became even wider. With the advent of Methodism in England in the late eighteenth century we see the precipitation of a societal-religious situation characterized above all by its fluidity. Many commentators have indicated the intimate relation between the development of Methodism in its various forms and the increasing differentiation of British society attendant upon the rapidity of industrialization.[41] In terms of the typological range of relations between religious collectivities and the wider society, Methodism as it developed and fissured during the first half of the nineteenth century is a crucial phenomenon. Originating as an offshoot of the Church of England, Methodism split into numerous branches. The grounds for schism included at various points during the last few years of the eighteenth century up to the middle of the nineteenth century: internal organization; doctrine and practice; relationship to other religious bodies; relationship to particular types of social clientele; and relationship to the wider society generally.[42]

Such a state of flux, both in the relations between religious collectivities themselves and between the collectivity and the wider society, was generally even more typical of the United States during the nineteenth century.[43] When we consider the modern situation, notably in the United States, Canada, Britain and majority-Protestant European societies, we see the need for a typology which above all allows for changes and shifts in the societal stance of the religious collectivity. Particularly we need to cater for collectivities which, on the one hand, espouse a religious message which is out of line with the dominant religious and secular culture but which is also regarded

as an acceptable or perhaps even necessary part of the religious scene
—in Britain one thinks of the Salvation Army and of the Plymouth
Brethren, in America of the Mormons and Christian Science.

This emphasis upon dynamism brings us to a crucial aspect of the
church-sect theme. Nothing in our present typological formulation
enables us to state the conditions under which a particular religious
collectivity will shift from one typological position to another.
Since Niebuhr's statement on the process of denominalization, however, this has been a vital ingredient of the analysis of religious
organizations. In conformity with our basic analytic schema,
specified in chapter two, four sets of factors operate to constrain
the position of the collectivity in relation to the wider society: the
prevailing environmental culture; the wider social structure and the
social constituency upon which the collectivity draws; the culture
(doctrinal system) of the collectivity; and the collectivity's own
internal organization—its polity.[44]

We can briefly illustrate this mode of analysis with reference to
the history of the Salvation Army in Britain.[45] The Army has been
regarded by some as (of now) being a denomination and by others
as a sect. However it seems much more appropriate to regard the
Army as an established or institutionalized sect. It has retained a
sufficient number of its key pristine sectarian characteristics still to
qualify in one sense as a sect, but has yet achieved a firm *modus
vivendi* with the wider society.[46] In skeletal form, we may indicate
that in general-cultural terms British society has become more
tolerant of religious (and political) deviance since the crystallization
of the Army as a collectivity in the 1880s;[47] that in social-structural
terms the Army's clientele has become more 'respectable', more
definitely lower-middle class since that time; and that doctrinally
the Army has attenuated its militant stance towards modern industrial society—a tendency actually built into its pristine evangelism,
subscription to a belief in salvation-for-all, and its social reformism.
Organizationally, on the other hand, its authoritarian 'military'
structure has been relatively successful in maintaining the fairly
tight-knit *epistemic communalism* of a religious sect.[48] In sum, the
Salvation Army has established for itself an 'institutional slot' within
British society and the one critical factor which has saved it from

dissolution or absorption into another body has been its relatively complex bureaucratic structure. By adapting our typology we may trace the sequence of changes which have occurred, along the following diagrammatic lines:[49]

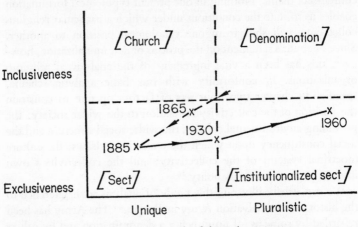

The Path of the Salvation Army

Sectarianism

Of all the themes entailed by the church-sect discussion it is that of religious sectarianism which has probably been the most avidly pursued and which appears to be still its most significant aspect. Sectarianism poses the problem of the relationship between religious and non-religious commitments in the most acute form. It has been proposed that religious sectarianism is the most religious form of sociation.[50] This proposition has to do not so much with religious sects as collectivities as with *processual* aspects of sectarianism. In these terms we may speak of sectarianism or the sectarian spirit *within* denominations and churches, as does Berger in his analysis of German Lutheran churches; the guiding principle of sectarianism being the inner meaning of the religious phenomena concerned. Thus the sect, as Berger defines it, is a religious grouping based on the belief that the spirit is immediately present. The most interesting sociological question which follows from this idea is that concerning the social-structural means through which the sectarian's allegiance is fostered and maintained. This problem is manifested in particularly acute form in modern industrial societies.

In the historical past of contemporary industrial societies—certainly in the period of Catholic hegemony in Europe—the problem did not arise so acutely. There were, of course, many significant religious-sectarian developments. The medieval period was replete with heretical movements—Waldenses, Brethren of the Free Spirit, Lollards, Albanenses, Manicheans, Cathars and so on; while the Reformation both embodied and precipitated a further proliferation of religious sects. Indeed, in one sense, the problem of fostering and maintaining sectarian allegiance might seem superficially much more formidable in medieval European society than in modern society. Knox writes of medieval sectarians that 'theirs was a furtive existence, most of the time, in most parts of Europe; the men and women who so pertinaciously detested the Catholic system went to Church, made the sign of the Cross, lived outwardly as normal subjects of . . . Christendom . . .'[51] Some sects did develop specific forms of organization; but, typically, institutional forms of organization were either eschewed on doctrinal grounds or impossible to erect in practice.[52] Medieval heretical sects constituted a 'congeries of scattered Christianities' confronted in theory with the dilemma of being 'a leaven within the lump . . . , an enclave of holiness within the corrupt body of Christendom', or, on the other hand, an open and separated 'true Church of Christ . . .'[53] In practice the geographical separation and dispersion of medieval sects and the fact that they were forced to operate in an underground, 'resistance' manner precluded the probability of serious organization.[54] It should also be stressed that medieval Europe was a period in which religious culture was pre-eminent, a period when the Christian-religious mode of thought and expression was paramount. The sect had no problem of protecting itself against a challenging *non-religiosity* or anti-religiosity, as does the modern sect. Thus the religio-political domination of the Catholic Church operated to prevent organization, whilst the pervasiveness of religious modes of thought left the sectarians free at least to be religious. The modern sectarian, while free of the first constraint in many societies (the exceptions are primarily Communist and authoritarian Catholic

K

societies such as Spain and Colombia), faces the second acutely. The religious sect in modern societies has to protect both its religiosity and its sectarianism—both its general and its specific *raisons d'être*. Religious sects in the modern period are thus of considerable interest in so far as they provide especially good case-studies for the analysis of the nature of religious commitment and religious control.

Religious sects have been sociologically endowed with the following main attributes: they are formally voluntary associations; there is membership by proof of some claim to personal merit; there is a self-conception of eliteness; and personal perfection is the expected standard of aspiration, accompanied by the ideal of the priesthood of all believers.[55] How, given these attributes, are sect leaders able to sustain the commitments of their members? As we have already indicated, one salient set of factors has to do with the kind of organizational structure which the religious doctrine calls for or permits. For example, in the case of the Quakers, a religious doctrine which emphasizes above all the 'free' availability of 'the spirit' is very congruent with a participatory-democratic mode of organization. But this is one of a relatively few cases where a mode of organization follows almost logically from a mode of doctrine. Most religious sects have manifested a more precarious interlocking of doctrine and organization. Much of the explanation in the sphere of religious commitment does of course relate directly to the connection between the social-structural 'catchment area' of the sect and the doctrine of the sect: there is, in Weber's term, an elective affinity between, for example, lower-middle-class groups and religious ethics of compensation. But here we are concerned with commitment to religious organizations in general terms. In the typology of participation in religious organizations adumbrated in the second chapter we noted four major types of participatory orientation. Sectarian participation or involvement embraces both of the consummatory types—the cultural and the social. Indeed it is an imperative of most types of sect that this should be the case.[56]

Parsons has distinguished between the sect and the denomination by stating that in the latter the religious role is differentiated from other roles (such as the economic or familial), whereas in the sect there is relatively no such differentiation.[57] In the sect the religious role is the master role—upon which other role definitions and role behaviours ideally depend. Thus in terms of our typology of participatory orientations, the member's orientation to the sect is primarily a cultural-consummatory one—but the scope and generality of the commitment attendant upon this orientation require that the sect as a collectivity becomes the dominant social priority in the life of the member (social-consummatory).[58] In view of this double commitment, a primary task of the sect elite is to maintain explicitly a system of 'incentives' embracing both the 'purely religious' sphere and the sphere of social participation in the collectivity.[59]

Such a problem is of course relatively small where there is spatial (or vicinal) seclusion of the sect—where socio-cultural boundaries are co-terminous with an ecological boundary. Historically, many sects within non-Christian religions have possessed the advantage of spatial seclusion—such as Islamic and Buddhist sects. There are examples of spatial seclusion in modern societies, notably North America: for example, Mennonites, Hutterites and Dukhabors. The Amish Mennonites, more particularly the Old Order Amish of Pennsylvania and other parts of the U.S.A., probably constitute the best-known case of spatial seclusion.[60] As Wilson points out, such sects which have arisen in rural communities 'tend to subsume religious organization in community structure, employing religious sanctions merely as boundary-maintaining devices. Religious practice and procedures are continuities of community practice and procedures.' Thus there is a 'relatively low level of distinctively *religious* organization'.[61] This is not to say that spatially secluded sectarian communities are safe from the problems of maintaining boundaries and the allegiance of their members. Relative to those sects which operate *directly* within the context of industrial societies, spatially secluded sects do of course have a considerable advantage in maintaining a distinctive and tightly knit epistemic community. They have a high degree of control over at least the early part of the socialization process of the child, they can fairly easily maintain the speaking of different language (if such obtains) from that of the wider society—as is the case with the Old Order Amish—and can maintain a coherence and interconnectedness as between the various aspects of an individual's life-style. On the other hand there may well be a lack of preparedness with respect to the possible impact of the wider society; the spatially isolated communal sect does not manifest a very high degree of *self-conscious deviance* from the wider culture. Its deviance is frequently passive, rather than active. Wilson has invoked the useful distinction between isolation and insulation of the sect from the wider society. Insulation of the sect represents an active, 'on guard', relationship to the wider society. An isolated, sectarian community, such as the Amish, may in fact learn to insulate itself, if the penetration of the wider society is not too abrupt. Thus the Amish have in this sense learned a certain degree of 'flexible insularity'. The (relatively long-drawn-out) impact of such wider-societal penetrations as modern farming technology, the legal pressure for Amish children to attend public schools, and, what was of tremendous symbolic significance, the introduction of the auto-mobile, has facilitated this learning process.[62]

By way of considerable contrast we may point to the abrupt, apocalyptic impact of a totally alien culture on another—probably best exampled by that kind of contact between Western, nominally Christian, culture and a primitive culture, which has yielded cargo cults and millennial movements. Quite clearly, in such cases the primitive socio-cultural system is totally unprepared for such a contingency. That is, the isolation of the society is so complete that it is virtually without mechanisms of insulation. The upshot is a movement or cult which is, in social terms, very fragile; and which, in cultural terms, *is* insulated in the sense that it is frequently a very closely articulated doctrine, but which is so counterposed to the alien culture, so inflexible and utopian, that it is subject to traumatic destruction. In social terms the indigents lack any practice in social organization in protection of a religious collectivity. On the other hand, some cargo-cult movements in Melanesia have learned over a period of time to establish social-organizational mechanisms of insulation. This has usually been attendant upon entry into an urban context, and has been regarded by some analysts, notably Worsley, as a concrete manifestation of the primarily political (as opposed to purely religious) significance of cargo cults in Melanesia.[63] Worsley traces the progression through which an *audience* becomes a *following*, then a *movement*, and finally an *organization*.

The main characteristic of spatially secluded collectivities in the present context is the relatively *coherent diffuseness* of commitment—religious commitment being, although perhaps the most salient mode of commitment, only one of a series of coherent and interconnected commitments. Twentieth-century industrial societies are characterized by a differentiated series of competing and sometimes conflicting commitments. The major problem of the sect in its attempt to maintain an epistemic community of religion-based commitment is to offset the divided attentions of the potential recruit, so as to close and narrow his perspectives into the sectarian 'channel'.

In examining this problem more closely we have to hold the doctrinal variable constant—that is to leave out of the *immediate* reckoning the actual content of the sectarian culture. Probably the most important aspect of the problem concerns the emphasis which has been laid upon the *voluntariness* of the sect. This emphasis derives in historical-intellectual terms from Troeltsch's observation that the individual was born into the church, he was in it unless he took a calculated decision to *leave* it; whereas he was not 'in' the sect unless he took a definite decision to *enter* it. Now in a rather restricted, legalistic sense it is indeed true that membership of the sect is voluntary, but two major reservations must be entered against the emphasis upon sectarian voluntariness. First, use of the term implies that individuals are, generally speaking, free to enter the sect; whereas in a number of societies the individual has to face a generalized opprobrium in order to accomplish this. In fact, legal or quasi-legal constraints may be put upon such entrance. Second, and more important, the emphasis upon voluntariness tends to divert attention from the factors of childhood socialization into the thoughtways of the sect and the various mechanisms of control of a coercive kind utilized by the leaders of some sects.

Wilson, in stressing the factor of sectarian voluntariness, argues that 'direct coercion can occur only within the tolerance of the individual's own belief . . . and [a sect] never has at its disposal physical means of exacting compliance. The sanctions applied must themselves be part of the belief system; if they are too severe the adherent may cease to believe, since he will usually have recourse to alternative standards of values.'[64] It is indeed true that the sanctions must be part of the belief system. But they are not necessarily inherent in the doctrine in its pristine state, nor are the sanctions which any particular individual encounters always justifiable in terms of the belief system as it was at the time of his entry into the sect. That is, specific negative sanctions may be applied and *then* incorporated into the belief system. Prone as sects are to schism, a frequent response to the prognosis of schism or actual schism is to introduce new sanctions which require either justification in terms of the existing belief system or, as often happens, a modification in the belief system. Some sects have become 'totalitarian' by virtue of systematically relating the sanction and reward systems to the doctrinal system in such a way as to justify a variety of coercive methods. Perhaps the best example of this is provided by the Salvation Army during the earlier years of its development in Britain. By putting the movement on a 'war footing', that is by claiming that an extraordinary crisis was at hand in the wider society, the leaders were able to amalgamate the themes of intense missionary effort, loyalty, total involvement and the religious need to 'sacralize' the Salvation Army as an organization. The Army was an instrument of God—He had called it into being.[65] The leaders of the Jehovah's Witnesses have also managed to erect a totalitarian form of organization, even though its doctrine does not *inherently* prescribe such a condition. In this case a different kind of crisis and sense of urgency is used as the rationale—namely, the millennial expectation of the end of the world in its 'normal', terrestrial sense within the present century. Unlike the Salvation Army, the Witnesses have not engaged in the activity of sacralizing their organizational form. The elitism within the organization rests primarily on the complex literalness (as opposed to the simple and selective literalness of the Army) of the belief system.[66] Another candidate for the label of 'totalitarian' is the collectivity of the Exclusive Brethren. Unlike the Salvation Army or the Jehovah's Witnesses, the Exclusive Brethren do not possess a strong centralized and concentrated leadership structure: 'The movement has always been disposed to accept a strong figure, whose position remains unlegitimated and informal.'[67] But on the other hand the hierarchy of leadership is informal, vague and shifting. 'The acknowledgment of leadership is

... always uncertain, and the esteem which a man enjoys depends very largely on his ability to initiate, and to win acceptance for, new truths of doctrine and liturgy.'[68] Moreover, there is no professional or regularly paid ministry. And yet the Exclusives manage to maintain a very high regulation of the details of everyday living amongst adherents, holding aloof from nearly all secularly accepted activities (political, recreational and so on), being on the available evidence much more thorough in this than the Witnesses (and certainly more so than the Army); although in recent years this thoroughness *has* resulted in numerous defections.

In such cases there is a need to pinpoint the social and social-psychological factors at work. In general terms we may state that there are two crucial sets of factors involved in the problem of sectarian commitment: the nature of the organization's system of compliance and the socio-cultural base upon which the organization draws its membership.[69] To this we may add the proposition that there are degrees of 'fit' as between this base and the organization's system of compliance. This depends particularly on the social location and experience of the individual, whether he or she may easily be recruited to, and 'imprisoned' in, an epistemic community.

The methods of control *are basically* those of persuasion. Leaders try to activate, and to sustain the activation, of the lower participants' moral commitments, and to foster and maintain an other-directedness, a commitment to the peer group and to the organization's leaders.[70] Given a strong commitment along these lines it is easy to see how the leaders of a sect may then be able to exercise other modes of control such as the coercive and the utilitarian. Thus although the initial basis of conversion is almost certainly normative, the leaders of the more centralized sects do in fact attempt to *fuse* and combine a wide range of control devices—normative (and social), utilitarian and coercive, but always attempting to legitimate these in normative terms.[71] It is in this sense that some sects are totalitarian in a rather thoroughgoing respect. What facilitates such totalitarianism is the circumstance in which there is a particular category of people who are both disposed to accept the sectarian doctrine *and* who are *socially isolated*, who in a sense comprise a captive audience. By social isolation (in comparison to spatial isolation, which almost certainly entails social isolation), we mean a condition of social uniqueness relative to the broad societal context. We are concerned with individuals who are deprived in specific ways which cut them off from others. Social isolation is regarded here as a very general analytic category. It covers a variety of deprivations of status—absolute and relative. Individuals who are absolutely deprived of basic material necessities—the poverty-stricken 'underclass'—are highly disposable for mobilization. S. D. Clark has graphically described the condition of the Salvationist in Canada around the turn of the present century, in terms of the extent to which the individual Salvationist was socially dependent upon the Salvation Army. Property rights were surrendered to the organization, which clothed and fed him, and earnings were turned over to the Army. 'The financial dependency of the worker assured obedience to Army orders and conformity to Army principles. On the other hand, the financial security provided by such an arrangement made enlistment ... highly attractive. ... The discipline of the soldier and the devoutness of the ascetic combined to build up among workers a strong feeling of group loyalty and attachment to leaders.'[72] In mid-twentieth century conditions of this kind of dependency arising from absolute material deprivation are much less likely to arise, and contemporary circumstances yielding social isolation of particular categories of people are more frequently based on relative deprivation, that is deprivation subjectively perceived *relative* to other people.

In speaking of subjectively perceived deprivation relative to other individuals and groups we must distinguish between general and partial deprivation. General relative deprivation is best exemplified by the individual who belongs to a lower-class group in which he is low on most, or all, relevant dimensions of status—such as the educational, the economic, the occupational and so on. Partial relative deprivation obtains when he is *relatively* high on one or more status or rank dimensions which he regards as significant to his own situation, but *relatively* low on one or more of his other significant dimensions. This second (partial) type of deprivation is especially productive of so-called *marginal men*.[73] It is obvious that individuals who perceive themselves as being marginal, 'out of the mainstream', are potentially more mobilizable for sect allegiance than those who are central, those individuals whose social attributes *are* of the 'mainstream' and who do not typically encounter the strains of being accorded an ambiguous status in the wider social system. This kind of reasoning has been applied frequently in the analysis of political radicalism—where the focus is usually upon the actual beliefs which the political 'deviants' adhere to.[74] Here, it should be stressed, we are only interested in the social circumstances which 'hive off' individuals in such a way that they are, relatively speaking, at the disposal of sect leaders. (We deal more fully with the type of doctrine which various categories of deprived individuals are attracted to in the next chapter.) Individuals who are marginal to the societal context are, all other things being equal, more likely to make themselves available for a wide range of organizational strategies than others more firmly and securely located in the social structure. While our sociological knowledge in this problem area is rather limited, we do have some evidence to suggest, for example, that individuals who are relatively and absolutely deprived are more likely to adopt sectarian postures in relation to religious organizations, as Demerath has shown in reference to some American Protestant denominations.[75] Sectarian postures in this connection have been identified in such terms as the tendency to view the organization diffusely, finding one's friends in the collectivity, and seeing one's life-style as closely bound up with the culture of the collectivity. Such findings and associated suggestions all tend to tie in with the notion of sectarianism as a condition of detachment from the wider society and a psychological investment in a distinctive epistemic community. Individuals are most ripe for sect commitment, then, when they are constrained to seek radical modes of self-fulfilment as alternatives to those normally accepted in the wider society. (As we have noted, such commitment need not necessarily be religious.) Having been constrained to involve themselves in a diffuse manner in one major direction, namely the sect in question, such individuals tend to manifest a larger 'zone of indifference'[76] to the controlling actions of sect leaders than do individuals who are less constrained and who typically in modern societies distribute their spans of attention and activity across a series of organizational and informal involvements.

By virtue of the specific religious ideology it *may* be that the 'totalism' of the sect is democratic, in the sense of decision-making and leadership being subjected to the collectivized dispositions of the membership at large—as with the Christadelphians. Even so the 'democratic' demands which can thereby be imposed upon the individual member are both intensive and extensive. In contrast, as we have seen, some religious collectivities exercise a highly authoritarian type of total control over their members.[77]

Some General Features of Religious Organizations

Much more attention is paid to religious sects than to denominations and churches when sociological problems of religious collectivities as such are being discussed precisely because many of the characteristics of denominations and churches are shared with other non-religious organizations—political parties, trade unions and so on. In comparison with sects, denominations, such as the Methodists and Congregationalists in England, tend to rely much less for their operation on high degrees of intensiveness or extensiveness in respect either of power or commitments.

In our discussion of sectarianism it was suggested that, in a limited sense at least, coercive methods of control are sometimes utilized. While religious denominations, like sects, are indeed primarily normative in modern societies, *they* frequently tend towards the utilitarian type, involving the exercise of, in the broadest sense, remunerative power: the manipulation of rewards and sanctions, including not only money but also status and prestige. (This is almost certainly less true of Britain than the U.S.A.) Correspondingly one finds in such cases the mode of orientation to the denomination to be that of a calculative kind: individuals, especially in the middle echelons of the organization, seeking to gain or maintain wider-societal prestige from membership and participation. One should also note that the manipulation of status and prestige is often an important feature of sects. But in the latter it would appear that status achievement is seen as valuable in *intra*-organizational terms. Achievement of a high rank within the organization may, then, be seen as a compensation for relatively low status in the wider society. The member of the denomination may also be motivated by the desire for high status within the organization as such. Thus we have three separate possibilities: (a) the use of the organization to enhance status mobility in the wider society (characteristic of the denomination); (b) seeking status mobility within the organization as valuable in itself (true both of the sect and denomination); (c) seeking to maximize status within the organization as a compensation for low status in the wider society (more typical of the sect than the denomination). Of these possibilities (b) is problematic in so far as there are two ways of interpreting it. Mobility may be sought because of the satisfactions gained from achieving high status *per se*, which empirically shades into (c), or because status achievement is regarded as subsumed by religious achievement. In the first type the commitment or orientation is, in Etzioni's terms, calculative, in the second it is moral.[78]

O'Dea has aptly labelled what we have identified as the relationship between calculative and moral involvement 'the dilemma of mixed motives'.[79] All religious organizations face the problem of motivating individuals to participate in such a way both as to contribute to organizational effectiveness as such and to internalize and uphold the religious culture of the collectivity. Particularly subtle attempts to create religious ambitiousness of this kind are made in the training of Roman Catholic priests.[80] Roman Catholicism is like religious sectarianism to the extent that there is a high degree of elaborateness about doctrinal substance; which means that the dilemma of mixed motives is particularly acute. In contrast many denominations lay little stress on the significance of doctrinal minutiae.[81] In these terms contemporary denominations are more open to the free play of purely secular status aspirations within the organization. A complicating factor here is that Roman Catholicism, and some sects such as the Salvation Army, have developed elaborate bureaucratic apparatuses which appear to be particularly productive of status motivations *per se*, almost as a direct consequence of the administrative difficulties involved.[82] But, even so, doctrine has, as we have seen, been invoked to infuse the *structure* itself with religious significance.

Secular status considerations are frequently used to account for the motivation of church and denomination leaders to engage in ecumenical ventures. In Britain the decline in prestige of the minister of religion may have been an important factor here (an indicator of the general process of secularization, which we discuss at length later). [83] By strengthening religion institutionally through rationalized procedures of administration and amalgamation, it is argued, ministers may think that they stand a good chance of restoring some of their lost prestige in the wider society. The plausibility of this argument as an account of the motivations at work depends very much on the degree of emphasis placed upon it. In the absence of satisfactory evidence it would seem more convincing to subsume this factor under the more general one of what might be called 'bureaucratic egotism'. Most denominations and churches, and quite a few sects, have gradually established quite extensive bureaucratic structures in precisely the same historical period in which their cultural *raisons d'être* have been called into question. Changes in the sphere of secular or non-religious culture have affected both religious culture and the social vehicles of religiosity. Religious culture has been undermined particularly in the sense that 'religion' has become less pervasively significant and taken-for-granted; religious organizations have been infused with secular-cultural notions of rational administration.

These two processes have by no means been independent. It is in large part in response to the decline in the pervasiveness of religious culture that religious organizations have become increasingly pre-occupied with considerations of efficiency; which in turn has led to the calling into question of the 'consumability' of their religious doctrines. So has come about the frequently noted situation in which many religious organizations in the U.S.A. and Britain appear to be primarily concerned with organizational self-preservation. Higher participants are obviously constrained to act in such a way as to preserve their own positions—which means either sustaining their own organization as such or helping to facilitate organizational amalgamations. [84]

It was a major feature of Weber's sociology of religion that, in spite of his stress on the independent significance of religious culture, he acknowledged the importance of the social vehicles through and by which the impact of religious culture was effected. Mainly because he was concerned with the historical sources of the modern cultural condition, he said relatively little about religious organizations in the respects which we have indicated in this chapter. He is, however, usually credited with first having put the sect-church distinction into focus—Troeltsch having taken over the usage and worked thoroughly with it. It should be noted that there is a link between the sect-church distinction and the distinction between ethical and exemplary prophecy which Weber used to such good effect in his historical studies. These considerations highlight the crucial importance of religious leadership as a vehicle of religiosity and religious change in the historical past, in comparison to the significance of religious organization in the modern period. This is, of course, not to deny that religious organizations have leaders. But in the study of religious organizations a focus on leadership tends to involve little more than the application of sociological and social-psychological principles of a very general kind. That is to say, the study of religious leadership in industrial societies rarely gets attention in terms of specifically religious-cultural themes.[85] In one sense this may be construed as a criticism of those sociologists of religion who specialize in such matters. But, on the other hand, the more important point is that religious leadership itself has in fact relatively little religious-cultural significance in modern societies. The study of religious leadership in these contexts typically involves, first, the analysis of the patterns of personnel recruitment and their socialization into the ministerial or priestly role and, second, the various segments of these roles—pastor, administrator, preacher, counsellor and so on. Such analytic themes reflect the phenomenon of organizational constraint upon the exercise of religious leadership. In fact, of the range of leadership types elaborated by Joachim Wach only one, the 'priest', is genuinely relevant to modern societies.[86] The others which Wach lists are: the founder; the reformer; the prophet; the seer; the magician; the diviner; the saint; and the 'religiosus'. Of these the prophet, the founder, the reformer and the saint (in decreasing order of significance) have been historically very important in a preservatory respect. The decline in significance of such leadership types in the modern period relates closely to Weber's emphasis upon the supplanting of charismatic authority (in its origin an essentially religious notion) by so-called rational-legal (or organizational) authority.[87] (Of forms of leadership in the modern period there is one type which both Weber and Wach neglect, but which may nevertheless be of considerable importance in direct relationship to religious culture—namely the religious intellectual, which we deal with in the final chapter.)

Our basic concern in this chapter has been to illuminate the characteristics of the social organization of religion and the social vehicles through which religious culture is expressed and transmitted—with particular reference to the problems involved in maintaining distinctive religious belief systems.

Notes to Chapter 5

1. Above, p. 69
2. These of course rested on the work of Glock and Stark.
3. Neil J. Smelser, *Theory of Collective Behavior*, London, New York, 1962. See the application of Smelser's work in Roland Robertson, 'The Salvation Army . . .', op. cit., esp. pp. 50 ff.
4. On the importance of literacy in relation to the development of organizations, see Arthur L. Stinchcombe, 'Social Structure and Organizations', in James G. March (ed.), *Handbook of Organizations*, Chicago, 1965, pp. 150–1.
5. Ibid., p. 149.
6. Ibid.
7. Ernst Troeltsch, *The Social Teachings of the Christian Churches*, op. cit., Vol. I, ch. 11, esp. pp. 328–82.
8. Troeltsch had difficulty in classifying Calvinistic collectivities. For an analysis which points up some of the problems, see Michael Walzer, *The Revolution of the Saints*, Cambridge, Mass., London, 1966. See below, p. 176.
9. For a survey, in addition to those cited in chapter three, including discussions of state-church *tendencies* in the modern period, see F. H. Littell, *From State Church to Pluralism*, New York, 1962.

10. H. Richard Niebuhr, *The Social Sources of Denominationalism*, New York, 1929.

11. The method of exposition in respect of the church-sect theme is to trace through some of the major sociological contributions and in so doing to point up empirical phenomena. Thus we are not simply concerned with stating what particular analysts have said. We are equally concerned with the empirical problems with which they have tried to cope.

12. *The Social Teachings*, op. cit., p. 337.

13. Ibid., p. 339.

14. Ibid., p. 331.

15. Ibid., p. 332.

16. Troeltsch did speak of an additional, third type, that of mysticism. Mysticism is unproductive of collective continuity. See below, p. 243, n. 14.

17. See Troeltsch, *The Social Teachings of the Christian Churches*, Vol. II, p. 725.

18. Niebuhr, op. cit., p. 25.

19. Ibid., p. 19.

20. For an analysis of this aspect of Methodism, see W. J. Warner, *The Wesleyan Movement in the Industrial Revolution*, London, 1954.

21. See B. R. Wilson, 'An Analysis of Sect Development', in Wilson (ed.), *Patterns of Sectarianism*, op. cit., pp. 22–45. More specifically, for Christian Science see Wilson, *Sects and Society*, op. cit.

22. Howard Becker, *Systematic Sociology on the Basis of the Bezeitungslehre and Gebidelehre of Leopold von Wiese*, New York, 1932.

23. J. M. Yinger, *Religion in the Struggle for Power*, op. cit., and *Religion, Society and the Individual*, op. cit., pp. 142–55. Only the second contribution is dealt with here.

24. Such a condition manifests a high degree of 'fit' as between the 'official' objective religious culture and subjective religious experience. See Luckmann, *The Invisible Religion*, op. cit.

25. See *Journal for the Scientific Study of Religion*, VI (Spring, 1967), pp. 64–90.

26. Paul Gustafson, 'UO–US–PS–PO: A Restatement of Troeltsch's Church-Sect Typology', in ibid., pp. 64–8.

27. See, for example, Benton Johnson, 'On Church and Sect', *American Sociological Review*, XXVIII (August, 1963), pp. 539–49; and David O. Moberg, 'Potential Uses of Church-Sect Typology in Comparative Religious Research', *International Journal of Comparative Sociology*, 2 (1961), pp. 47–58; Bryan R. Wilson, 'Typologie des sectes dans une

perspective dynamique et comparative', *Archives de Sociologie des Religions*, 16 (1963), pp. 49–63.

28. Allan W. Eister, 'Toward a Radical Critique of Church-Sect Typologizing', *Journal for the Scientific Study of Religion*, VI (Spring, 1967), pp. 88–9.

29. For an historical perspective on denominationalism in America, see Sidney E. Mead, 'Denominationalism: The Shape of Protestantism in America', *Church History*, XXIII (December, 1954), pp. 291–320.

30. Martin, *Pacifism*, op. cit., p. 7.

31. Ibid.

32. Ibid., p. 9.

33. Hinduism has been by far the least organized of the orientations discussed in this chapter.

34. See Bryan R. Wilson, 'Religious Organization' in David Sills (ed.), *Encyclopedia of the Social Sciences*, New York, 1968.

35. Benton Johnson, 'A Critical Appraisal of the Church-Sect Typology', *American Sociological Review*, XXII (February, 1957), pp. 88–92.

36. Compare the presently delineated typology with that produced in Gustafson, op. cit.

37. Yinger, *Religion, Society and the Individual*, loc. cit., Wilson, 'An Analysis of Sect Development', op. cit. (cf. David A. Martin, 'The Denomination', *British Journal of Sociology*, XIII (March, 1962), pp. 1–14). The term *institutionalized* sect is preferred here to established sect. The former is a more genuinely sociological term, denoting in the present context the *modus vivendi* situation. It has previously been employed by Harold W. Pfautz, 'The Sociology of Secularization: Religious Groups', *American Journal of Sociology*, 61 (September, 1955), pp. 121–8. For further discussion see Robertson, 'The Salvation Army: the Persistence of Sectarianism', op. cit., pp. 49–58. See also David O. Moberg, *The Church as a Social Institution*, Englewood Cliffs, 1962, ch. 4.

38. This is not only a phenomenon of Catholic societies, although it has been most marked there. See, *inter alia*, Rodney W. Stark, 'Class, Radicalism and Religious Involvement', *American Sociological Review*, 29 (October, 1964), pp. 698–706; and Demerath, op. cit., pp. 24–5. See also Glock and Stark, *Religion and Society in Tension*, op. cit., ch. 11.

39. For an excellent summary of these Reformation tendencies, see Roland Bainton, *The Reformation of the Sixteenth Century*, London, 1953. See also Swanson, *Religion and Regime*, op. cit.

40. See Martin, 'The Denomination', op. cit.

41. For two contrasting analyses converging on this point, see Neil J. Smelser, *Social Change in the Industrial Revolution*, London, Chicago, 1959; and Edward Thompson, *The Making of the English Working Class*, London, New York, 1964.

42. For a good discussion, see Robert Currie, *Methodism Divided*, London, 1968.

43. For a good, brief summary of major aspects of this situation, see Richard Hofstadter, *Anti-Intellectualism in American Life*, New York, 1962, pp. 55–141. More extensively, see William G. McLoughlin, Jr., *Modern Revivalism*, New York, 1959. For Canada see S. D. Clark, *Church and Sect in Canada*, Toronto, 1948.

44. Above, pp. 65–7.

45. The comments which follow are based on Roland Robertson, 'Salvationism's Century', *New Society*, No. 144 (July 1, 1965), pp. 11–13, and Robertson, 'The Salvation Army: the Persistence of Sectarianism', op. cit. (Wilson's analysis is the major general statement on sect transformation. See 'An Analysis of Sect Development', op. cit.)

46. The *modus vivendi* circumstance points up the special attributes of the institutionalized sect. It constitutes an exception to the following generalization: 'Regarding the degree of conflict with or dependence on the environment, if, like a religious or political sect, the organization is totally at war with its environment, it will not be moved to hire specialists in accommodative techniques. . . . If it has a monopoly of the relevant resources it has no need for information about rivals' (Harold W. Wilensky, *Organizational Intelligence*, New York, 1967, pp. 39–40). The Army being highly conversion-oriented, has from very early on been concerned with 'environmental specialists'.

47. Religious and political deviance have become more *institutionalized*. See Seymour Martin Lipset, *The First New Nation*, London, New York, 1964, esp. p. 269.

48. I am indebted to Burkart Holzner for the term *epistemic community*, although he is in no way responsible for the way in which it is used here. In the present context an epistemic community is a closely integrated group which sustains a deviant belief system. It is not necessarily a *community* in the literal sense—but the maintenance of a deviant belief system requires a relative high degree of communalism, i.e. patterns of *diffuse* interaction. It is no accident that the communalism of the Salvation Army has declined as it has become less distinctive in cultural terms in relation to the wider society. (See Robertson, 'The Salvation Army . . .', op. cit., pp. 104–5.) The fact that the Army has never

L

maintained an *acute* hostility to the wider society like many sects, makes its preservation of a distinctive belief system *more*, rather than less, interesting—since this characteristic points to the great importance of the organizational structure. *It must be emphasized very strongly that in speaking of communalism and community in this chapter we are not using the terms as Lenski (The Religious Factor, op. cit.) does.* We are referring to a relatively high degree of diffuseness of interaction. This theme is developed in the following pages.

49. There are two extreme alternatives in interpreting this sequence. We can either view the Army as changing within a constant environment or the environment changing whilst the Salvation Army has 'stood still'. Empirically the sequence is a complex outcome of the interplay between the two factors. This general problem of analysis is a relatively uncharted, but also highly, important one. Cf. E. D. C. Brewer, 'Sect and Church in Methodism', *Social Forces*, 30 (May, 1952), pp. 400–8. See also, Liston Pope, *Millhands and Preachers*, New Haven, 1942; Pfautz, op. cit., and Oliver R. Whitley, 'The Sect to Denomination Process in an American Religious Movement: The Disciples of Christ', *Southwestern Social Science Quarterly*, 36 (December, 1955), pp. 275–82. (On the Disciples, cf. Demerath, op. cit., pp. 121–3.)

50. Peter L. Berger, 'Sectarianism and Religious Sociation', *American Journal of Sociology*, 64 (1958–9), pp. 41–4. (See also Berger, 'The Sociological Study of Sectarianism', *Social Research*, 21 (Winter, 1954), pp. 467–85; *The Noise of Solemn Assemblies*, New York, 1961; and *The Precarious Vision*, New York, 1954. For an opposing view see Fallding, op. cit., p. 361.) (This does of course raise *theological* and *religious* problems, some of which are taken up in the final chapter.) In most elaborate form, see Demerath, *Social Class in American Protestantism*, op. cit., *passim*. See also Russell R. Dynes, 'The Church-Sect Typology and Socio-Economic Status', *American Sociological Review*, XX (October, 1955), pp. 555–60.

51. R. A. Knox, *Enthusiasm*, Oxford, 1950, p. 71.

52. See above, p. 115.

53. Knox, op. cit., p. 109.

54. The maintaining of secret religious commitment has historically been legitimized amongst Moslems in environments hostile to Islam.

55. See, *inter alia*, Wilson, 'An Analysis of Sect Development', op. cit., and *Sect and Society*, op. cit. For a detailed listing of the characteristics of churches, sects and denominations, see David A. Martin, *A Sociology of English Religion*, London, New York, 1967, pp. 79–80.

(See above, pp. 54–5.) This does *not* mean that we would find no elements of instrumental orientations in religious sects.

57. In Talcott Parsons, Edward Shils, Kaspar D. Naegele and Jesse R. Pitts, *Theories of Society*, Glencoe (Illinois), Vol. I, p. 251.

58. These two aspects of sectarian commitment broadly correspond to those which Etzioni distinguishes within his category of normative organizations—*pure normative* and *social*. Amitai Etzioni, *A Comparative Analysis of Complex Organizations*, Glencoe (Illinois), 1961, pp. 10–11. Compare the distinction with Demerath's statements: Demerath, op. cit., pp. 70–2.

59. For the idea of an economy of incentives see Chester I. Barnard, *The Functions of the Executive*, Cambridge, Mass., 1938 *passim.;* and James D. Thompson, *Organizations in Action*, New York, 1967, pp. 105 ff. Thompson notes that the significance of the inducements/contributions 'contract' lies mainly in its reduction of 'the expression of heterogeneity' by members. 'The contract, explicitly or by implication also provides limits on the organization; it can call on a limited array of the individual's total repertoire of possible behavior. There remains, however, a "zone of indifference" . . . which indicates that within the confines of the contract, the organization may specify any of several modes of behavior and the individual member is indifferent as to which.' (Ibid., pp. 105–6.) It is a characteristic of 'pure' sect involvement that the zone of indifference is very large.

60. A particularly interesting phenomenon is represented by the history of the Mormons. In their long westward trek across the U.S.A. in the middle years of the nineteenth century they were in one sense isolated, but their frequent encounters with mid-western and western communities intermittently eclipsed this isolation. Their eventual ensconcement in Salt Lake City led to a more complete isolation lasting for a number of years, until Mormonism began to disperse and spread across the United States. For a good sociological study of Mormonism, see Thomas F. O'Dea, *The Mormons*, Chicago, 1957.

61. Wilson, 'Introduction', *Patterns of Sectarianism*, op. cit., p. 12.

62. On the Amish, see particularly John A. Hostetler, *Amish Society*, Baltimore, 1963. (For system learning, see Karl W. Deutsch, *The Nerves of Government*, Glencoe, 1963.)

63. Peter Worsley, *The Trumpet Shall Sound*, op. cit. See also the perceptive discussion of Yonina Talmon, 'The Pursuit of the Millennium', *European Journal of Sociology*, III (1962), pp. 125–48; and Bryan Wilson, 'Millennialism in Comparative Perspective', op. cit. For discussion, see below, pp. 163–7.

64. Wilson, 'Introduction', op. cit., p. 8.

65. Robertson, 'The Salvation Army . . .', op. cit., esp. pp. 75–89.

66. On the Jehovah's Witnesses, see, *inter alia*, Werner Cohn, 'Jehovah's Witnesses as a Proletarian Movement', *The American Scholar*, 24 (Summer, 1955), pp. 281–98; H. H. Stroup, *Jehovah's Witnesses*, New York, 1945; E. Royston Pike, *Jehovah's Witnesses*, London, 1954. Witnesses *themselves* deny that they are a religious organization—they are simply students accepting the truth as God presents it. But they do acknowledge that they have a *publishing* organization. In fact they have a dual structure—an apparently 'leaderless' movement and a tightly organized publishing agency.

67. Wilson, 'The Exclusive Brethren: A Case Study in the Evolution of a Sectarian Ideology', in *Patterns of Sectarianism*, op. cit., p. 321.

68. Ibid., pp. 321–2.

69. With more theoretical sophistication it should be stated that the variable described here as the social base is but part of a wider set of variables pertaining to the environment in which the collectivity operates. Generally the environmental factor has been ignored in the history of the sociological analysis of organizations. See the discussion in Thompson, *Organizations in Action*, op. cit., pp. 3–10. The study of specific religious organizations has tended to ignore the problem of the relationship between the collectivity and its social base—at least in the terms used here.

70. See Etzioni's discussion of normative organizations in his *An Analysis o, Complex Organizations*, op. cit., pp. 40–67.

71. For these three main modes of control see ibid. (The term identitive has been substituted for normative in Etzioni's more recent work.)

72. S. D. Clark, *Church and Sect in Canada*, op. cit., p. 420.

73. For the origins of the concept of the marginal man see Robert E. Park, 'Human Migration and the Marginal Man', *American Journal of Sociology*, 33 (May, 1928), pp. 881–93; Everett Stonequist, *The Marginal Man*, New York, 1937. For some associated conceptions see, *inter alia*, James A. Davis, 'A Formal Interpretation of the Theory of Relative Deprivation', *Sociometry*, 22 (December, 1959), 280–96; Ralph Turner, *The Social Context of Ambition*, San Francisco, 1964. With special reference to religious sects, see Charles Y. Glock, 'The Role of Deprivation in the Origin and Evolution of Religious Groups', in Robert Lee and Martin E. Marty (eds.), *Religion and Social Conflict*, New York, 1964. pp. 24–36.

74. See particularly Daniel Bell (ed.), *The Radical Right*, New York, 1963.

Less has been done on religious radicalism in this vein; but see, for example, Robertson, 'The Salvation Army . . .', op. cit., pp. 98 ff.

75. N. J. Demerath III, *Social Class in American Protestantism*, Chicago, 1965.

76. See above, p. 147, n. 59

77. It should be made clear that in seeking to modify the orthodox emphasis upon the *voluntariness* of sect membership we have interpreted that term in essentially legal terms. Our point has been to underscore the *social constraints* which channel the individual's sectarian allegiance. But this is not to be interpreted as a *deterministic* argument. In philosophical terms the author is committed to the voluntaristic stance.

78. Etzioni, op. cit.

79. O'Dea, 'Sociological Dilemmas: Five Paradoxes of Institutionalization', op. cit., pp. 75–8.

80. See Fichter, *Religion as an Occupation*, op. cit.

81. For an illuminating case study of this and related themes, see P. M. Harrison, *Authority and Power in the Free Church Tradition*, Princeton, 1959.

82. For the ways in which power struggles develop in complex organizations see especially Michel Crozier, *The Bureauenetic Phenomenon*, London, 1964.

83. There is confusion amongst analysts as to the extent of this decline. See Robert Towler, 'The Changing Status of the Ministry?', in Roland Robertson (ed.), *The Sociology of Religion*, Harmondsworth, 1969. Surveys tend to show in fact that the clergy are maintaining their high 'prestige' in Britain—in spite of a relative drop in incomes. Yet it seems agreed on the non-quantitative evidence that there *has* been a decline. It may well be that *esteem* has been retained, rather than prestige or status.

84. We return to this problem briefly below, p. 239.

85. For a bibliographical survey, see R. J. Menges and J. E. Dittes, *Psychological Studies of Clergymen*, New York, 1965. (In respect of organizational issues raised in this chapter, see especially Luke Smith, 'The Clergy: Authority Structure, Ideology, Migration', *American Sociological Review*, XV (June, 1953), pp. 31–8; Bryan R. Wilson, 'The Pentecostal Minister: Role Conflicts and Status Contradictions', *American Journal of Sociology*, 64 (March, 1959), pp. 494–504.)

86. Wach, *Sociology of Religion*, op. cit., pp. 341–70.

87. See, however, Etzioni's adaptation of the concept of charisma; *An Analysis of Complex Organizations*, op. cit., pp. 201–62.

6

Religious Culture: Sources and Consequences

In this chapter we turn to some themes which have been discussed at great length by many sociologists and social anthropologists. Basically, what is at issue is the interplay between, on the one hand, religious ideas, beliefs, values and symbols and, on the other hand, the experience of social structure. In the first half of the chapter we consider the influence of social structure upon religious culture in two major respects: first, the impact of the general morphology or configuration of social structure; second, the social sources of religious culture in terms of the experiences of individuals located in specific positions within the society. In the second half of the chapter we discuss the other side of the coin, religious culture as a determinant of social relations; taking as our main example the Weberian thesis about the significance of Protestantism in the development of industrial capitalism. Clearly, the very structure of the overall discussion suggests that we do not hold to the view that it is either desirable or possible to establish a definite pattern of priorities with respect to the culture/social-structure relationship. The approach is in a loose sense 'dialectical'—paying particular attention to the role of acting, perceiving, comprehending and reflecting individuals and groups.[1*]

I

Religious Culture as Derivative of Structural Configuration

Durkheim's theory of religion was in large part based upon the tenet that categories of thought are not inherent in man's nature as such. Man's cognitive mechanisms and processes of categorizing 'objects' hinged upon the group structure of the particular society.[2] Durkheim's most direct and unique contribution to the sociology of religion was of course his emphatic insistence that individual man

* Notes for this chapter begin on page 185.

experienced social life as awesome and oppressive. But the full significance and potential of his approach cannot be fully realized without relating this view to his theory of knowledge. The two are complementary: collective social life was the primary reality and man thought in terms supplied by that reality which subjugated him. These 'terms' were the ways in which aboriginal society was divided into clans, marriage classes and so on. Totemism was the most elemental form of religion because it displayed a relatively straight forward example of the members of a society thinking in terms of the group structure, the morphology, of that society. As we have seen, there is now much doubt about whether totemism as such may usefully be regarded as a religious phenomenon.[3] But for Durkheim it had to be regarded in this way—it was the most clear-cut example of man regarding as sacred that which (i.e., the totemic object) represented the group structure. (Durkheim felt constrained to supplement this kind of reasoning by emphasizing the importance of ceremonial and other 'crowd' situations in inducing individual sentiments of dependent involvement in the social group. It is these experiences which, according to Durkheim, particularly contribute to man's conception of supernature.[4])

Criticisms of Durkheim's thesis have been numerous.[5] But here our main concern is to sift that which appears to be most valuable for modern sociological analysis. What is particularly fruitful in Durkheim's work is the suggestion that experience of social-structural contingencies generates certain types of feelings of dependence on the social condition. But if this is indeed the line of inquiry we cannot be committed *a priori* to the Durkheimian claim that religion is 'really' the worshipping of society by man ('God is society'). Particularly in considering more complex societies than aboriginal Australia, we have to entertain virtually the opposite hypothesis—that man lacks confidence in his participation in society, that he needs and wants 'something else'.[6] This position is, it should be noted, very much in line with the preferred definition of religious culture which we stipulated in the second and third chapters; that is, religion as belief in and orientation to extra-empirical 'otherness'.

In recent years Swanson has persisted most elaborately and successfully with the basic thrust of Durkheim's theory; and we will use his work as an example of the problems involved. Swanson takes from Durkheim the assumption 'that some experiences with other people generate the concept of supernature and its two forms—mana and spirit'.[7] (It must be emphasized here that in *the present context* the phrase 'the concept of supernature' will be taken to mean *the sociologist's* conception of supernature; for, as we have seen, supernature, like 'religion' or 'religious', has been very much a Western cultural notion. We as sociologists or anthropologists largely identify what is supernatural—Australian aborigines or Trobrianders do not.) Of Swanson's objections to Durkheim's work, the most important has to do with the question: 'What is the society that is venerated?' Swanson asks: 'Is it the composite of all the effects which contacts with one another have on people's conduct? Is it the pattern of such contacts? Is it but one special kind of social relationship to which people may belong? If there are gods of the winds or sea or the heavenly bodies, how can these somehow be the society in other guise when human actions do not exert obvious control over these natural forces? Is it all of the society which is venerated or just some of its aspects?'[8]

Thus Swanson embarks on an inquiry into the kinds of social relationships and experiences which give rise to a variety of supernatural beliefs—monotheism, polytheism, ancestral spirits, reincarnation, immanence of the soul and witchcraft. Basically, Swanson's argument is that individuals experience (what we call) supernatural properties in social life not merely, as Durkheim suggests, because they are 'unwittingly controlled by social norms which they learn, but because social relationships inherently possess the characteristics we identify as supernatural'.[9]

In what sense do social relationships manifest 'supernatural' qualities? According to Swanson spiritual beings are conceptualizations of the constitutional structures of social life. Constitutional structures or arrangements define the purposes, sphere of competence and appropriate procedures of a social group. More specifically, it is groups which have 'sovereignty' that are crucial in shaping beliefs in supernatural beings. Sovereign groups are defined principally by their 'original and independent jurisdiction over some sphere of social life',[10] such as nuclear families and local communities. In

contrast to belief in spirits or supernatural beings, Swanson hypothesized that belief in mana arises in response to the recognition of
'primordial links among men'—vague, undisclosed links, 'possessing
unsuspected potentialities'.[11]

Swanson's theoretical approach is important for a number of
reasons. Its most general attraction lies in its distinctively sociological
nature. It contrasts with the early anthropological accounts of the
forces making for supernatural beliefs in its attempt to identify
definite social sources of religious beliefs—the impact which experience of social relations have upon individuals.[12] Swanson also places
primary emphasis upon political factors as affecting the nature of
religious beliefs—in the broad sense that there is a determinate
relationship between the extent to which the members of a society
feel they have control of their social affairs and their propensity to
posit entities or agencies as having affected, or as actually affecting,
social life.

The most important of Swanson's findings is that high gods
'appear in those societies in which a . . . society's central government
. . . provides political co-ordination for the activities of at least two
other types of organization, the latter being arranged hierarchically
and each having some sphere of autonomy in making decisions'.[13]
There is much variation in primitive and ancient societies in respect
of the degree of activity attributed to gods. For example, the Lengua
of Gran Chaco believe simply that a beetle created all things, but that
he takes no interest in his creation; the Nuer believe in a god who
created everything and now 'governs' them; while, in full monotheistic terms, the ancient Israelites believed that Yahweh created
everything and that He governed actively and morally. What seems
to effect the variation is, Swanson claims, the degree to which there
are specific groups that implement the decisions of a central political
agency. In his discussion of polytheism Swanson discovered that the
number of superior deities is closely related to the degree that a
society has social-class divisions and is differentiated on the basis of
division of labour. (Comparing this finding with the data on monotheism brings about the peculiar conclusion that more 'advanced'
societies are more likely to be polytheistic.) In line with other
suggestions, Swanson found that witchcraft tends to obtain where

people interact with each other on important issues 'in the absence of legitimated social controls and arrangements'.[14] Another important finding was that supernatural moral sanctions occur most frequently in societies with inequality in wealth.[15]

Swanson readily agrees that constitutional structures are features of all human associations, in modern as well as pre-modern societies. Thus if the supernatural is believed in as a consequence of the experience of the sovereign demands of associations, then why is it that supernatural beliefs are on the decline? According to Swanson, disbelief is promoted by one or more of the following conditions: (a) lack of contact with constitutional structures; (b) alienation from those structures; (c) *the assumption that all, or the most significant, features of those structures are knowable and controllable* by human effort'[16] (my italics). The third of these introduces a completely new factor. Rather than speaking of the direct impact of structural constraint upon belief, Swanson now allows for *reflection upon* structural constraint, reflection also, indeed, upon beliefs and their serviceability in any given society.[17] As we shall see this is a very important variable, one which severely mitigates attempts to establish models of one-way structural determinism.

Religious Symbols and Beliefs

Durkheim's famous statement that it was through religion that man first became able to think about society, that religion is a means of expressing what society and social life consist in, has in one form or another been remarkably influential. The influence is manifest in the work of anthropologists and sociologists; but one can trace a more indirect influence in many other areas as well. On the contemporary theological scene one frequently encounters the idea that 'really' religious notions, particularly that of 'God', *refer* to a feature of the human condition. The most sophisticated statements of this kind have emerged in the writings of Paul Tillich. For Tillich, God is the name of, the *symbol* which conveys, man's ultimate concern: 'Symbols are not signs. They participate in the power of what they symbolize. They are not true or false in the sense of cognitive judgments. But they are authentic or inauthentic with respect to their rise; they are adequate or inadequate with respect to their expressive power; they are divine or demonic with respect to the ultimate power of being.'[18] This approach thus removes the substantive content of the notion of God.[19] What Tillich and other theologians particularly reject is what Parsons calls 'intermediary symbolism'—cognitive references such as God as 'an old man with a long white beard'.[20] Science as well as religion involves 'intermediate symbolism', which makes it possible to have a concrete image 'to fill an essential place in the cognitive orientation system'. Parsons argues, indeed, that the psychological functions of the old man with a beard are similar to believing that an electron is a spherical solid particle of 'matter', 'a little round ball'.[21] He notes that scientists do actually *believe in* their intermediate symbolism—although theirs is subject to more frequent revision than in the religious case.

There has developed in theology and the philosophy of religion an impatience and dissatisfaction with elaborate intermediate symbolism. This has resulted in a vogue for regarding all the contents of religious culture as *symbolic of* features of the human condition. (This vogue goes well beyond the domain of theology and the philosophy of religion.[22]) Much of this can be related to Durkheim's insistence that the sacredness of totemic objects derived not from their intrinsic properties—a crocodile was not sacred because of its crocodileness—but that sacred meaning was 'super-added' to its intrinsic properties. Totemic objects were sacred because of their connection with the group structure of the society. Thus, within social anthropology an impressive line of analysts, notably Radcliffe-Brown, have seen religious beliefs in broadly functional terms—as either simply a mode of group coherence or as facilitating the individual's relations with groups and categories of his fellow men.[23] In the structuralism of Lévi-Strauss we see an emphasis upon religious beliefs as a mode of ordering relations between nature and culture. More strictly, they become for Lévi-Strauss a symbolic *code* for conveying such relations.[24] The dangers in these kinds of approaches are numerous. The fundamental problem has to do with the frequent failure to distinguish between *the conditions which promote religious beliefs and symbols of certain kinds*

(Swanson's approach) and *the phenomena to which symbols may actually refer*. The two are by no means the same. When we speak of conditions which promote religious beliefs, we, as sociologists or anthropologists, speak of the social experiences which constrain individuals to believe in religious phenomena; but this is not to say that the phenomena themselves therefore refer to the experiences. They may, but frequently they do not. To take a simple example: if we can show that monotheistic beliefs developed in a society following the development of a system of omnipotent kingship we are not entitled to say that the god symbolizes the king, especially since many religious belief systems actually stipulate a cosmological *relation between* god and king.[25]

Another danger is pointed out by Worsley, in the course of which he actually damns most existing approaches. Religion, he says, is 'a cluster of beliefs which are *used* in day-to-day activities, with (variously) some of one's fellow men (not some abstract fellow man) in the context of changing situations focused on a diveristy of social activities'. Religion is neither 'an ideal operation in the soul, heart, or intellect' nor 'the ritual dance of puppets determined by the morphology of their social structure'.[26] The import of this critique (which undoubtedly overstates its case) is that people 'do things' with religious beliefs. In the sense employed by Geertz, they are symbols *for* social action and communication in the context of social and other exigencies and circumstances.[27]

Wilson points to another complicating factor on the basis of his analysis of the Exclusive Brethren. Having discovered that the Brethren *do* perceive in some degree that elements in their doctrine symbolize and allegorize their community, Wilson observes that they 'do not know it from Durkheim, or in the way in which he knew it, but they know it in a way in which sociologists do not always care for latent functions to be evident to those who benefit from them'.[28] This raises in a new context the old question of the degree to which deliberate allegorizing and symbolizing takes place in primitive societies, the theme of the 'poetic' nature of expression in primitive societies.[29]

We cannot hope to resolve such problems here. But we may draw attention to some of the more salient analytic issues. First, the tendency to construe the elements and themes in religious cultures as always symbolic *of* social, psychological or other circumstances in the society detracts attention from the problem of the conditions under which such elements and themes appear and are sustained. Second, and conversely, concentration upon sociological accounts of how beliefs and symbols appear and survive may ignore the creativeness, reflectiveness and expressiveness of human agents; that is, we have to pay attention to *conscious* religious symbolizations of social experience and social structure. The first point is directed as a warning at those who would dissolve all aspects of religious culture into 'symbols' and see them inevitably as 'ways of talking about society', so ignoring questions not only having to do with the factors giving rise to these 'symbols' but also the *values* implicated in religious culture. The second point is directed at those who do not recognize that once acquired religious culture is *utilized*.[30]

In diversified, pluralistic societies the point of finding some straightforward connection between a system of beliefs and the structure of society becomes in large part redundant. In these societies, religious beliefs are frequently expressions of particular groups within the society; and religious *traditions* compete with each other for adherence. We may in any case seriously question the degree to which religious beliefs are in fact systematized in primitive societies. Frequently the appearance of system in religious beliefs in such societies is a construction of the anthropologist: the *anthropologist*, not the primitive, interlocks the various elements in the belief 'system'. Worsley reports that he has discovered cases where individuals are aware only of practices and beliefs of local significance and very ignorant of the 'official', general cosmological beliefs.[31] Such findings suggest that even in primitive societies there may be much less synchronization of beliefs than is often depicted.

Even more important, we may contrast the kind of approach manifested in Swanson's work with that of Weber. In attempting to account for the failure of monotheism to develop in certain cultures, Weber draws attention not to features of the general social structure, but to 'the pressure of the powerful material and ideological interests vested in the priests, who resided in the cultic centres and regulated the cults of particular gods'.[32] Weber also mentions the 'religious need of the laity for an accessible and tangible familiar object which could be brought into relationship with concrete life situations or with definite groups of people to the exclusion of outsiders, an object which would above all be accessible to magical influences'.[33] Here we clearly have a pointer to the problem of the variations in religious beliefs attendant upon social-structural differentiation—most particularly vertical differentiation, in terms of class and status distinctions. It is to this problem we now turn.

Religious Culture as Derivative of Difference in Social Experience

This perspective finds one of its most piquant expressions in Marx's view that '*religious* suffering is at the same time an expression of real suffering and a *protest* against real suffering. Religion is the sigh of the oppressed creature, the sentiment of a heartless world, and the soul of soulless conditions. It is the *opium* of the people.'[34] And yet it is in the work of Weber that we discover the most elaborate and comprehensive analyses of the differential religiosities (and the nature of those religiosities) of specific social strata and social classes. In one sense we may see the Weberian analysis of religion as a response to the Marxist tendency to place major emphasis upon the lower class as the most significant agent of historical change. Both Weber and his friend Troeltsch criticized the Marxist view, manifested most rigidly in the work of Karl Kautsky, that Christianity had been the initial product of a 'proletarian' class—a severely underprivileged class. Weber argued that lower-middle-class groups were particularly productive of new religious traditions. The most underprivileged individuals in a society were typically more likely to concern themselves with immediate issues of worldly significance, while upper-class individuals were especially concerned with religious legitimations of their position, exhibiting a detached kind of religiosity or subscribing frequently to what Weber called *theodicies of good fortune*.[35] In contrast it was those strata whose circumstances exhibited much less consistency and stability which were prone to be intensely religious and, of primary concern to Weber, to activate themselves to rationalize and systematize a coherent religious ethic.

These were primarily middle strata, especially the lower-middle class.

Weber underscored the point that the lower-middle or artisan class was not susceptible to economic determination of its characteristic religious tendencies. Individuals located in such positions in a society are particularly disposed to propagate and embrace congregational religions of salvation, with a strong rational-ethical emphasis. What Weber called 'the sense of honour' of such disprivileged strata 'rests on some concealed promise for the future which implies the assignment of some function, mission, or vocation to them. What they cannot claim to *be*, they replace by the worth of that which they will one day *become* ...'[36] In Weber's brief, but brilliant, analysis of the religious situation in industrial societies he crystallizes his view of lower-middle-class religiosity, in a way which is consonant with modern insights into the phenomenon of relative deprivation. The established industrial middle class (and this would include in mid-twentieth-century societies those dependent economically on bureaucratic positions) and the working class are both committed to the industrial order in a way which contrasts with the lower-middle class. Weber notes that dependence on one's own achievement is supplanted in the case of the worker by 'a consciousness of dependence on purely societal factors, economic conjunctures and relationships guaranteed by law'.[37] While the most prosperous and economically secure individual feels less at the 'mercy' of such factors, he shares with the worker an involvement in the pivotal structural circumstances of the existing society. These are the individuals who largely shape the society. In contrast those in between, sharing some attributes with one class and some attributes with another, tend to be more marginal to the forces which determine the major features of the society. This very marginality (relative deprivation with respect to the 'topdog' and relative advantage with respect to the 'underdog') produces the perception of a disproportion between effort and reward. It is in these terms that an ethic of compensation—of reward in an after-life—has historically been the special predilection of the lower-middle class.

To argue that in societies manifesting salient distinctions in terms of social stratification it is those who are located between a dominant class or stratum and a lower class or stratum who are most prone to religious innovation and intense religiosity, can be misleading. We must remember that Weber's special interest was in salvation religions with strong *rational* and *ethical* components. Thus religious rationality for Weber was marked above all by the absence of magical elements (in his interpretation of magic the emphasis was on the way in which material ends were gained through ritualistic forms of manipulation). In terms of the preference in this book not to make a clear-cut distinction between religion and magic it is obviously the case that the great stress on this kind of activity in rural-peasant populations qualifies the peasantry as being highly 'religious'. Indeed most of the evidence we have on the subject shows that rural populations in general tend to be more religious in this sense than urban ones. This applies both within and between societies of all types.

Underlying the general problem of the religious beliefs and values generated by differences of location within a society is the finding that societies are more prone to possess religiously-based ethical systems if there are marked inequalities, especially economic inequalities.[38] It appears that those most sensitive to inequalities in a society will be those most likely to develop and adhere to strongly ethical religious doctrines. But, as we have suggested, it is not those who are most severely deprived in objective terms who typically perceive such inequalities in acute form. In a society manifesting a caste or a feudal system of social stratification there is a high degree of consistency in the experience and expectations of individuals located in different positions with the system. These are relatively 'tight' systems with a series of well-defined, vertically-separated social layers. In these types of society, like feudal Western Europe or caste India, there tend to be systems of religious culture which provide an overall ethico-religious rationale for the given state of affairs—as did the Great-Chain-of-Being motif in medieval Europe. In contrast, it is societies which have 'looser', more open stratification systems—*class* systems of stratification—which promote greater 'opportunity' for the *moral appraisal* of the society.[39] (As we will see in looking more comprehensively at Weber's arguments in connection with the economic consequences of Calvinism, 'moral appraisal' includes such notions as moral justification for one's own actions. It is a hypersensitivity to moral and ethical matters which is at issue here.[40])

In emphasizing the religious creativity of those who are relatively deprived we must bear carefully in mind three major points. First, we must establish that such creativity occurs only in societal contexts which are generally religious in the broadest sense—where super-empirical or supernatural referents are highly salient cultural phenomena. Second, to emphasize the religious fecundity of a particular stratum or class does not mean that we find no examples of other strata or classes being religiously productive. Third, we have to take into account that the concept of relative deprivation is open to a much wider range of application than to the artisan or lower-middle-class individual. The last two points deserve special consideration; they will be treated together.

In his classic essay on the social psychology of the major religions, Weber maintained that each of the world religions had been decisively developed by specific strata: Confucianism by the Chinese literati; Buddhism by contemplative, mendicant monks; Hinduism by a hereditary caste of cultured literati; Islam by warriors; Christianity by itinerant artisan journeymen.[41] Clearly, with the exception of the journeymen, we see little sign of an obviously deprived condition as such being particularly important. Thus we need to specify that while major religious traditions have been established as general 'world-views' by dominant strata in the historic past, it is deprived strata who are primarily responsible for producing the major variations within those traditions and for providing resurgences of 'religious energy'. We should also note that the 'world' religions are all characterized by a relatively high degree of *intellectualism*—they have been, as a matter of degree, conceived and re-conceived; although this characteristic has had very different implications among the major religious traditions. Christianity stands out in respect of the crucial nature of *doctrine*. Historically, within Christianity an effective power hierarchy has made true doctrine and precise forms of interpretation the determinants of in-groups and out-groups.

But in spite of the tremendous historical importance of mainly

M

privileged intellectuals—priests, nobles and so on—Weber convincingly observes that often a more important kind of intellectualism has been that of what he, perhaps misleadingly, calls the 'proletarian' intellectual. Here he refers to 'small officials . . . , elementary school teachers . . . ; wandering poets; narrators; reciters . . .'[42] It is these to whom a *religious need* is particularly strong; that is, the need for salvation. (The concept of religious need must be given prominence in any evaluation of Weber's work. For it was largely in these terms that Weber can be seen to have sought to avoid the view that religious culture is socially, economically or politically determined. He accorded considerable autonomy to religious needs. Probably the best way of interpreting this emphasis is to say that Weber wished to refute the essentially Marxist argument that religious beliefs, values and symbols were direct 'translations' of social experience: there was no automatic one-to-one relationship to be discovered by the sociologist between the economic, social or political circumstances of the individual and the religious ideas which he adhered to. The emphasis upon religious intellectualism in Weber's work thus deliberately, and surely correctly, points to the great significance of reflection and self-conscious elaboration of religious ideas, which very frequently has gone well beyond the mere articulation of the interests of the individual, group, stratum or class.)

Weber's discussions of religious intellectualism in themselves enable us to generalize the importance of relative deprivation. In a minimal sense intellectuals themselves are typically open to the perception of relative deprivation. It has in modern history been a prominent characteristic of intellectuals that they are marginal to the mainstream of the society or societies in which they operate. To be sure, priestly intellectualism has frequently been closely tied to a dominant social stratum. But even so intellectual reflection nearly always involves the frustrations attendant upon 'knowing how things work', and yet being unable to directly affect those 'things'. As Bendix demonstrates, one of Weber's most important generalizations was that great religious leaders had been active in urban areas, but not in 'the great cultural centers'. Individuals in the latter centres were not constrained to ask profound religious questions, 'because they had become enmeshed in the techniques of civilization'. 'Only men who

were not so enmeshed but whose central interests were affected by
the culture centers retained the capacity to be astonished by events
and to question their meaning.'[43]

In slightly broadening the idea of relative deprivation to include,
quite deliberately, individuals who are located in situations which
constrain them to compare acutely their own situations with other
situations we are able to cope with many of the religious-cultural
innovations and variations which have not in fact derived from
lower-middle-class, artisan or similar sources. As we shall see,
there is much evidence to suggest that marginality and social
insecurity were influential factors in promoting the elaboration of
Puritan doctrines amongst displaced nobles. To take an example
from a different context, Jansenism in seventeenth-century France
was largely the product of *officiers* made marginal by the steps taken
towards royal absolutism.[44] Another example of the importance of
marginality and social insecurity in the generation of new religious
ideas is provided by the significance of women in many medieval
millennial movements.[45] (Weber noted that the religious 'enfran-
chisement' of women was a common feature of many new middle-
class religious doctrines within Protestantism.[46]) Here again we have
an example of a category of people whose position in the social
structure was made uncertain during periods of rapid social and/or
cultural change. In fact in periods of rapid change many sections of
the population are exposed to precisely this experience; and this in
turn allows us to focus on a favourite religious phenomenon of
early Marxist sociologists, the European, especially German, millennial movements of the sixteenth century.

Millennial Movements

It is extremely interesting that Weber said relatively little about
millennial movements in any concentrated fashion. Whether he
uneasily acknowledged that the plebeian and peasant movements of
the sixteenth century, such as the Anabaptists, were genuine examples of religious beliefs arising as a direct consequence of material
deprivation and material interest we do not know. Certainly the
views expressed by Marxists on this point are difficult to deny,

although they need qualification. Mannheim notes that the inter-mittently reviving millennial ideas of Europe became, with the Hussites 'and then in Thomas Munzer and the Anabaptists ... transformed into the activist movements of specific social strata. Longings which up to that time had been either unattached to a specific goal or concentrated upon other-worldly objectives suddenly took on a mundane complexion. They were now felt to be realizable —here and now—and infused social conduct with a singular zeal.'[47] Mannheim, like Engels, speaks of the starting-point of proletarian self-consciousness in these movements; and he characterizes the period as one of the 'spiritualization of politics'. But perhaps a more accurate description would be the 'politicization of religion'. Inter-estingly, these points bear closely on the idea that the Protestant Reformation was basically significant for its secularization of West-ern cultures.[48] In numerous respects the peasantry and much of the urban lower class was, during the sixteenth century, increasingly displaced from the 'security' of consistent subordination in a 'tight' system of stratification. This led to breaks in the plausibility of received religious culture in such a way that concrete, 'mundane' interests and demands could be and were expressed—although couched in religious language.

Considerable controversy has surrounded the topic of millennial movements; one of the main issues of contention being precisely that of the political significance of millennialism.[49] In one sense the debate is a false one; for one of the main tasks in the analysis of millennial movements is to determine why *some* become explicitly political movements and *some* do not.[50] Moreover, we have to distinguish between movements which, over a period of time, themselves become expressly involved in the political affairs of the dominant stratum or strata and those which did not. There is a difference between identifying one and the same cargo cult becom-ing, in the space of a few years, embroiled in trade union and political affairs in an urban context and viewing a *series* of millennial 'outbursts' over a number of centuries of European history as becoming increasingly political and secular.

Wilson characterizes the goals of millennial movements, as they have appeared in Europe, Melanesia, Africa and North America, as:

the awakening and preparation of men and women to the 'fact' that the world is to be transformed and that the transformation will be sudden and soon. Two general aspects of such movements relate closely to this—that millennial movements are collectivist and that they are oriented to this world, to effecting or sometimes just anticipating here-and-now terrestrial change.[51] Few would now deny the similarities exhibited between millennial movements and secular revolutionary movements—although we should note that some millennial movements are *restorative* and some *innovatory*. Furthermore, the very characterization of millennial movements as this-worldly and collective gives them, by definition, a political colouring. But the critical factors relating to whether millennial inclinations become more definitely political—concerned with problems of terrestrial achievement and the generation of power— would appear to be, first, the extent to which there is elaboration of an organizational complex and, second, the nature of the response of the movement's opponents. Obviously these variables are empirically interdependent, but they warrant separate analytic treatment. In the first case, as Worsley notes, the 'simple fact of organization . . . carries with it the built-in inevitability of political action, in so far as any organization . . . must stand in relationship to the world and ask of it something, even if it is only to be left alone in peace to worship God . . .'[52] The response factor is equally important. If the superordinate group uses force, for example, or is thought likely to use force, then clearly some political considerations become implicated in the millennial tendency. But the clearest case of the inducing of politicization in the millennial tendency is where the dominant group couches its response in secular, political terms. The use of brute force may lead to an accentuation of the religious elements in the millennial movement, whereas if the colonial power seeks to interpret the concrete elements in the millennial doctrine or to translate the religious elements into concrete terms, then the likelihood of the movement itself becoming politicized is strong. Such considerations apply notably to these examples of millennialism in Melanesia and Africa.[53]

The fact that movements conforming to usual definitions of millennialism have occurred almost entirely in either Judeo-Christian or Islamic contexts, or largely as a consequence of confrontation with Christian culture, has an interesting bearing on the Weberian conceptions of inner- and other-worldliness. In characterizing millennial doctrines, sociologists have been constrained to contrast the this-worldliness of millennialism with the *other*-worldliness of more mainstream forms of Christianity, including Christian sects of a non-millennial kind. It may be, then, that millennialism represents a much more genuine form of religious this-worldliness, the fusion of religious beliefs and concrete goals, than does the mainstream of Protestantism; although such an idea would have to be tempered by the fact that millennial collectivities in industrial societies, such as the Seventh Day Adventists and Jehovah's Witnesses, manifest somewhat less immediately-concrete terrestrial beliefs. This may, in fact, be, somewhat paradoxically, a matter of political judgment on their part—a judgment to avoid too dramatic a confrontation with the wider society. Religious sects in modern societies would appear to be sensitive to such political considerations; aware, for example, that religious power may be lost through failure of a millennial claim to withstand empirical test.[54] And, of course, millennial doctrines by definition do make empirical claims—in contrast to the super-empirical claims of, for example, holiness doctrines.

In dealing with the social determinants of millennialism, sociologists and anthropologists have drawn implicitly or explicitly on conceptions of deprivation and isolation. The data suggest on the whole that millennialism is the religion of those who are persecuted or depressed to the point of being marginal or pariah groups with respect to another group which is seen to enjoy a wide range of privileges. (This observation covers therefore both stratification within a society and the perception of a stratification *of* societies.) In summing-up the literature, Talmon argues that, given the conditions of marginality or pariah status, millennial movements are most likely to occur in periods of transition from a relatively stable social condition, involving the disruption of traditional ties and norms; where there has been a cumulative deterioration of life conditions, involving a marked incongruence between expectations and the means of their satisfaction; and where there has occurred a sudden dramatic crisis which crystallizes discontent and precipitates action to overcome it.[55]

Thus in the present context the major significance of millennialism lies: (a) in its relation to Weber's conceptions of the social sources of religious innovation; (b) in the fact that it is the most important example of rapid, comprehensive religious change; (c) in that study of it helps to highlight some of the more salient problems having to do with the relationship between religious and non-religious factors. However, we should stress that as interesting and important as millennialism may be in these terms, millennial movements are, largely by virtue of their short duration, unlikely to have profound long-run social effects (unlike secular revolutionary movements). Even when millennialism survives continuously in one collectivity, for example the Jehovah's Witnesses, their social and cultural effects are not conspicuous. The numerous millennial movements of nine-teenth-century England, such as the Southcottians and the Mormons, have had singularly little impact on the nature of British society, whereas Methodism quite clearly has had a vital impact. Perhaps only when millennialism arises as a generalized societal response to alien intrusion, as in Melanesia, does it have critical long-run consequences.

Social Sources of Religious Variation in Modern Societies

In the last chapter we pinpointed some of the conditions which facilitated the development of deviant religious doctrines in modern societies. There we were concerned with the social circumstances that are conducive to men being drawn into sectarian collectivities. Here we are concerned, correspondingly, with the types of circum-stance which tend to yield sectarian *doctrines*. In modern societies the general tendency in the direction of one or another form of seculari-zation (continued in Britain from the early part of the nineteenth century, but interrupted by occasional religious reawakenings) makes the sect a particularly intense object of sociological discus-sion.[56] What has emerged from this has been a repeated rejection of older notions that sectarian doctrines are invariably the product of those who are economically 'disinherited', or that sectarian doctrines are necessarily forms of socio-economic protest. In the first case, there are numerous sectarian doctrines which are not the province of the economically deprived, such as Christian Science, Open Brethren and Exclusive Brethren. In the second case, there are sects, notably conversionist and holiness sects, which, far from being protests against societal values, are sometimes agencies of upward social mobility and agencies for the acquisition of dominant values.[57]

Any one doctrinal tendency is adhered to on the basis of a manifold set of individual circumstances. Personality factors, features of individuals' life-experience; familial influences; exposure to particular religious contexts and so on, each play their part. Nevertheless, at the sociological level, it is possible to delineate some of the more general circumstances which are productive of religious sectarianism. Noting that the conditions he specifies may lead either to religious or secular beliefs, Glock has indicated four types of deprivation other than the economic. (In fact he argues that responses to the deprivation are more likely to be secular in modern societies where the diagnosed cause of the deprivation can be attacked more or less directly.[58]) Thus we have *economic, social, organismic, ethical* and *psychic* deprivations.[59] Social deprivation relates mainly to issues of prestige and acceptance; organismic to deprivation in respect of physical and mental well-being; ethical deprivation arises when an individual feels the need for values which will inform him in a situation of high status, when he has become satiated with rewards; psychic deprivation is close to ethical deprivation, but here the concern is with a general sense of meaning in life, not simply a concern with ethical guidelines.

This delineation tells us nothing directly about the type of religious belief which particular deprivations lead to. Indeed it would be wrong to think that there could be a one-to-one relationship between a particular form of deprivation and a particular doctrinal preference. Besides which, the doctrines of religious sects tend to be totalistic, involving numerous beliefs, values and symbols covering a very large number of social, cultural and cosmological issues. Thus the range of motivations for adhering to any one sectarian doctrine is probably very large. The major attempts to establish a typology of sectarian doctrines have been those of Wilson.[60] He has distinguished between *adventist, conversionist, gnostic* and *introversionist* sects. Adventist sects are characterized by millennial forms of belief; conversionist sects by an emphasis upon individual salvation on the basis of a fairly simple doctrine; gnostic sects by an emphasis upon happiness, health and well-being, in terms of an esoteric teaching which replaces secular scientific explanations and offers new religious accounts of psychological, cosmological and biological processes. Finally, introversionist sects emphasize the members' possession of the Spirit and tend to direct attention away from the wider society. With the warnings about looking for direct correspondences between form of deprivation and form of belief in mind, we may nevertheless suggest some possible links. One would expect that ethical and psychic deprivations would tend to attract individuals to gnostic types of belief and perhaps introversionist ones; although as Glock describes ethical deprivation, he comes close to Weber's theodicy of good fortune. Social deprivations, in so far as they lead to sectarian commitments, would probably relate most closely to conversionist beliefs—emphasizing the need to moralize the world religiously. Organismic deprivations might also find some resolution in this context, in so far as some sects of the conversionist type, like the Salvation Army in its early years, have subscribed to faith-healing beliefs. (There are also many physical cripples in Christian Science and in Pentecostal sects.[61]) Finally, economic deprivations would probably be distributed in terms of their resolution across both adventist and conversionist beliefs. However, such suggestions are not intended as genuine hypotheses; since, to take but one complicating example, it is perfectly conceivable that a lower-middle-class housewife would join the adventist Jehovah's Witnesses on the basis of what Glock calls psychic deprivation. Of particular importance in this connection is the factor of the conspicuousness and 'availability' of religious sects.

II

The Influence of Religious Culture upon Social Action and Social Structure

As we have noted, discussions as to the overall and general priority of religious-cultural or social-structural factors are ultimately fruitless. Structural arrangements and rearrangements come about because people act on the basis of beliefs and values and through culturally provided means of communication. On the other hand, the structural arrangements themselves create problems and tensions calling for resolution and dispose individuals to believe and act in specific ways. But there are two major respects in which it becomes not only fruitful, but sociologically necessary, to inquire directly into the influence of religious culture upon social structure and the dispositions and actions of individuals and groups. First, in periods of social transformation when it is clear that religious ideas have been an important part of the cultural system we must try to ascertain the significance of religion in the changes involved. Second, in societies manifesting a number of different religious-cultural patterns, especially where the general importance of religious culture is obvious, it is necessary to inquire into the differences which may be wrought socially by the coexistence of these patterns. In both of these cases the problem of assigning relatively dependent or independent status to religious culture is brought into focus precisely because religious and seemingly non-religious factors are much more visible to the sociological observer than they are in relatively static societies or societies with little religious heterogeneity.

Weber has most clearly posed a sociological thesis connecting a prior religious-cultural change with a subsequent social-structural one. We shall argue here broadly in favour of Weber's most general thesis—that which stresses the vital contribution made to the proclivity for social-structural change in the Occidental as opposed to the Oriental world; but tend to be more critical of the specific thesis concerning the causal connection between Protestantism and the development of the spirit of capitalism.[62] We will deal most fully with the latter proposition. (For Weber, of course, these were not really distinct theses at all. The development of Protestantism was seen as a crystallization of inherent tendencies in the Western religious tradition. But, as we have noted, there are problems connected with this contention.)

Weber argued that although there had been capitalists in archaic, medieval and post-medieval societies there was something distinctive about nineteenth-century capitalists. The entrepreneur of the modern period was unique in his *ethical* orientation to commercial and industrial activity. The 'spirit' which characterized the modern entrepreneur consisted primarily in an emphasis upon the inherent worthwhileness of the activity itself and a willingness to forgo immediate gratifications in order to achieve long-run rewards. Thus, entrepreneurial activity in late nineteenth-century industrial societies was marked by its dedication, asceticism, propensity to work out the best means for achieving desired economic rewards (economic rationality), and to save and invest accordingly.

Having pinpointed what he regarded as the central attitudinal characteristic of industrial capitalism, Weber sought an explanation in the content of the Protestant Reformation. The most vital ethical dimension had been provided, argued Weber, by Calvinistic Protestantism. The key general features of Protestantism which propelled and, for Weber, largely initiated the entrepreneurial ethos were its ideas of the individual standing in a stark confrontation with God, unmediated by priestly communication, notably in Biblical interpretation. The notion of individual salvation is critical here. For while Protestantism generally stressed individual responsibility in respect of salvation, there was a differentiation within Protestantism as to whether there was salvational democracy or salvational elitism. Calvinism was highly elitist in its doctrine of salvation. As Parsons notes, Weber saw Calvinism as a fully consistent philosophy of moral meaning: it maintained that ultimate resolution of the problem of meaning 'depends upon relations between an absolute, all powerful God, whose "motives" are in principle inaccessible to finite human understanding, and a creation, including man, which is absolutely and completely dependent on his will'.[63] At the core of this conception lies the notion of God's inscrutability and omnipotence. Weber saw the most effective keys to the demonstration of the link between Calvinism and entrepreneurial capitalism in the Calvinistic conception of 'the calling' and its doctrine of predestined salvation (what we have styled salvational elitism). While Puritanism, generally, emphasized the religious importance of faithful, ascetic performance of one's earthly roles, Calvinism contained an especially demanding religious expectation in this respect. The doctrine of predestination introduced, according to Weber, a constraint to discover whether one was of the religious elite or 'elect' or whether one had been denied salvation. There was no *religious* prescription upon discovering worldly indications of religious success.[64] But Weber maintained that there was a *social-situational* constraint upon so doing. Thus there was an (unintended) pressure upon the individual to conceive of success in one's social roles as an indication of religious status. Since endeavour was to the Calvinist primarily of religious significance, monetary and social status rewards were not thereby valued as ends in themselves. Functionally, this was precisely the kind of orientation which was required in order that capitalist entrepreneurs might be adventurous in a disciplined fashion.

It must be emphasized that the evaluation of Weber's sociology of religion hinges very much upon the fact that *The Protestant Ethic and the Spirit of Capitalism* was written before he embarked systematically upon his analyses of the major distinguishing characteristics of the 'world' religions. It is in this sense that we may speak of two Weberian theses. The first, very specific thesis was concerned with a fairly narrowly circumscribed phenomenon—the rise of entrepreneurial capitalism. The second, regarded by Weber as corroborating the first, tried to delve into the historical points of divergence between Eastern and Western cultural traditions and trace the culmination of Christianity in Calvinism. We have already noted the pressures within Weber's sociological perspective to see Calvinism as the ultimate rationalization of the Christian tradition. In evaluating the Protestant-ethic thesis we have here to attend to two main issues: first the logic of Weber's argument; second, the question whether Weber correctly diagnosed the relationships between religion and social structure in the industrial transformation of Western societies. As we shall see the first of these leads directly to the second.

One of the most obvious objections that can be, and has been made against the structure of Weber's argument is that Calvinism in particular, and Puritanism in general, are so defined as to make their relationship with 'the spirit of capitalism' tautologous. That is, the independent and the dependent variables are each defined in such a way as to make empirical testing of the hypothesis fruitless. Much of Weber's work on this problem does indeed read as if one can only say of an entrepreneur that he was a 'calvinist' or a 'puritan', regardless of the degree to which this was true in the sense of a definite religious commitment. But on the other hand, Weber did not claim in producing substantiating evidence of his thesis that one had to identify clear proof of a Calvinistic or even a Puritan commitment. At one time Weber would point merely to Protestants manifesting a greater degree of economic activism than Catholics, at another he would merely speak of the impact of Calvinism or Puritanism. Thus there is an incongruence in his argument as between what he had to say about the *plausibility of the idea* of a connection between Calvinism and capitalism and what he produced by way of evidence. The plausibility of the idea does stem in large part from the very close proximity of his definitions of the spirit of capitalism and of Calvinism. In fact so close are these definitions that at least one critic has been led to assume that Weber considered Calvinism actually to advocate the type of economic behaviour associated with the 'spirit of capitalism'. But although such an interpretation is undoubtedly very misleading, Weber himself did vacillate between saying that it was inherent in the logic of the Calvinist's situation that he should see good works as an indispensable sign of election and saying Calvinists actually believed in practical terms that God helps those who help themselves.[65] Thus *purely in terms of the presentation of his argument*, Weber's thesis is exposed as placing far too much stress on Calvinism.[66]

There have also been numerous criticisms in historical, empirical terms about both the emphasis upon Calvinism and more generally the significance attributed to Protestantism. We may delineate four main positions among those who do see vital connections between religious change and social-structural change: (a) Weber had made out an important case, but that he overstressed the autonomy of religious beliefs in effecting new forms of social action and social structure; (b) that although Weber was correct in attributing great significance to religious factors he had misconstrued the ways in which religious beliefs affected the rise of capitalism; (c) that Protestantism was an important epiphenomenon of the transition to capitalism; (d) that the major importance of Weber's thesis is to draw attention to the *transformative* capacities of

Protestantism. (As we shall see, there is overlap between these views.[67])

(a) The man most closely associated with this view is Tawney, who underlined the importance of some pre-Reformation forms of capitalism, and emphasized the interpenetration of religious and secular economic beliefs. In this latter respect Tawney attributed as much if not more significance to Calvinism than Weber.[68] More recently, Hudson has, on the one hand, denied the importance of the Puritan conception of the calling and, on the other hand, accorded special emphasis to the Calvinist conception of man's relationship to God—man as steward, God as 'Owner'.[69] Hill has argued that the Puritans tried to spiritualize economic processes; showing how some of them thought that God had instituted economic market processes. He also points out that the appeal to inner conviction, 'the motives of the heart', undermined the obstacles to economic progress inherent in Catholic society.[70]

(b) What Weber claimed for Calvinism and Puritanism has been at various times attributed to other religious doctrines as such—for example, to Judaism and to particular doctrinal tendencies within Christianity, including aspects of Catholicism such as Jesuitism.[71] Many of these have been variants on the theme which we have already raised in the second and third chapters: that it is not so much the inherent beliefs and values of a doctrine which are crucial in bringing about an innovative orientation to social life, but rather the structural position in the society of the adherents to the doctrine. Thus the marginal status of Protestants (for example, in France), emigrant Protestant groups or, indeed, deviant Catholic groups have been given the accolade of having instigated the 'spirit of capitalism'. Weber himself discounted this sort of view—pointing to the counter-examples of minority Catholics in England, the Netherlands and Germany (as contrasted with the confirmative examples of Huguenots in France, Quakers and Nonconformists in England, and Poles in Russia): Weber argued strongly that it was in 'the permanent intrinsic character of their religious beliefs, and not only in their temporary external-historio-political situation' that an explanation for the Catholic/Protestant differential must be sought.[72] In fact much evidence has been produced to show that subordinate

Protestants in particular, but also other religious groups, have been especially innovative and economically successful. Excluded from traditional professions and occupations, they asserted themselves in economic activities. Undoubtedly, as Weber maintained, the religious individualism of Protestantism, particularly in its Puritanist and Calvinist forms, *was* positively functional in this respect; although the very clear-cut case of Calvinists being in a majority—namely Calvin's Geneva—belies Weber's implication that it made no difference whether Protestants were in a majority or a minority; for there economic activity was quite severely circumscribed.

Enthused as he was with the autonomous significance of religious factors in this period of history, Weber never fully explored the full implications of what he called the 'temporary external historio-political situation'. Trevor-Roper, in examining this problem, has drawn attention to the ways in which religious minorities were economically innovative on the basis of the marginal positions in which they were placed through the migrations attendant upon the Catholic Counter-Reformation; although there is still counter-evidence from certain contexts.[73] As Andreski notes, in Holland Catholics were placed in 'a politically subordinate position but with ample opportunities for business activities'—but were generally unsuccessful in economic terms.[74] In a more recent period, the same observation applies to Canadian Catholics—in contrast to the U.S.A., where clearly Catholics went as poor immigrants into a context of unbridled economic activity. Recent research into the social characteristics of recruits to Protestantism in the sixteenth and seventeenth centuries throws further light on the problem by showing that it was social groups and classes who were displaced from their traditional 'safety' that took particularly keenly to Protestantism.

(c) The view that Protestantism was in large part determined by features of the transition to capitalism and functioned to legitimate capitalism in Western Europe has a number of variants. The most rigid is the Marxist position which tends to regard middle-class Protestantism as an ideology of capitalists, and the left-wing Protestant sects as responses of protest to the conditions of nascent capitalism and religious expressions of deprivation. For example, Engels drew attention to the fact that Protestant heresy first appeared among the Albigenses of Southern France at a time when 'the cities reached the highest point of their florescence' and the burghers had become very active.[75] Calvinism's doctrine of predestination is seen as a religious expression of 'the fact' that in economic matters success was unrelated to a man's activity or thrust, but upon circumstances uncontrollable by him. Much more perceptively, Kautsky thoroughly worked through the thesis that Calvinism developed in cities where commerce and early industry prospered. But, as Andreski notes, the epiphenomality position is counter-evidenced by the Calvinistic conversion of pre-industrial Scotland and of major sections of the Hungarian nobility.[76]

This reversal of the Weberian priorities is not so complete in others who see the significance of Puritanist Protestantism as an 'ideology of transition'.[77] We may briefly mention two such theses —one having to do with the microsocial level, the individual, the other with the macrosocial level, the structure of societies.

Walzer argues that individuals became Calvinists and Puritans primarily because they felt the need for security, for a new mode of self-control and identity in a period of social instability.[78] These individuals belonged both to displaced social groups (notably intellectuals and gentry) and to emergent groups, such as middle-class businessmen. Their Protestantism was part of an attempt to legitimate and justify their new positions within the social order. In this connection the break-up of the 'Great-Chain-of-Being' conception of the cosmos was especially important. Displacement and emergence of new social groups made this conception redundant. Protestant conceptions of 'the calling' contributed in turn to the dissolution of this religious theme. (The idea that faithful devotion to one's calling was a contribution to the common good was an important mode of transition to the secular, classical-economic dogma that social welfare was maximized through the pursuit of individual self-interest.)

Swanson's analysis of the Reformation provides a macrosociological variant of this thesis.[79] His claim is that the clue to an explanation of why certain societies remained Catholic and others took to one variety or another of Protestantism lies in the political structure of those societies. Those manifesting immanentist tendencies—those with one main centre or source of decision-making—tending to remain Catholic, while the pressures towards Protestantism came from societies where there was a plurality of decision-making sources. (Within Protestantism immanentism was most foreign to Calvinism—much less to Anglicanism and Lutheranism.) It follows from this view that Weber's argument is misconceived. Protestantism, on Swanson's thesis, developed in societies which relatively speaking manifested what he calls balanced heterarchic or limited-centralist regimes. In these societies merchants and artisans were frequently bearers of interests and powers external to the central governmental agency.[80] Thus Protestantism functioned as a form of legitimation of entrepreneurial enterprise. Swanson's view differs from the Marxist position—in that it focuses not on economic factors *per se*; but on the general 'loosening' of the social structure, of which the growth of economic individualism was only one, if a very important, aspect.

(d) The view that the major significance of Protestantism lay in its *transformative* significance is in many ways a compound of the three previous standpoints.[81] As a consequence of continuing re-appraisal of Weber's thesis and recent developments in the fields of political and comparative sociology, attention has shifted particularly to the *political* significance of Protestantism, including Calvinism. We have already seen earlier in this chapter the political significance of lower-class millennial movements in the sixteenth century. Recent research, including that of Walzer and Swanson, has been concerned very much with the contribution of Protestantism to the growth of stable, political democracies. This interest has been partly fostered by an increasing recognition that political factors have been seriously underestimated in accounting for societal differentials with respect to economic growth. Thus there is now emerging a much more complex analytic stance—not so much concerned with ascertaining definite independent, causal priorities, but with isolating the relevant factors and illuminating the interdependencies between them. For example, a recent study concludes that the critical factor affecting differential rates of economic growth between France, England, Japan and China in the sixteenth, seventeenth and eighteenth centuries was the degree to which the state

N

managed and allocated economic resources.[82] The lower the centralization in these respects the more likely a society was to achieve 'take-off' into sustained economic growth. The study itself makes little or no mention of religious factors; but we can readily see the links between this and Swanson's conclusions about high centralization being productive of Catholicism and low centralization producing Protestantism. To take the two European examples of Holt and Turner, namely France and England, we see that France was centralized, Catholic and slow in economic growth in the centuries following the Reformation; while England was *relatively* decentralized, Protestant and rapid in economic growth. This very briefly stated perspective indicates the lines of inquiry which are now being pursued. In terms of the three variables mentioned here there are several possibilities as far as direction of influence is concerned: (a) religion → economics → politics; (b) politics → religion → economics; (c) economics → religion → politics; (d) economics → politics → religion; (e) politics → economics → religion; (f) religion and politics acting independently on economics; (g) economics and politics acting independently on religion; (h) economics and religion acting independently on politics; (i) politics producing both economic and religious changes; (j) economics producing both political and religious changes; (k) religious changes producing both economic and political changes.

But it is more than likely that no solution to the 'Weber problem' would be forthcoming even if a large-scale historical analysis were undertaken along these relatively sophisticated lines. For there are other factors which have been adduced, as being central to the debate, including not only those having to do with the historical-structural experience of innovative groups, but also child-rearing practices, cultural phenomena other than purely religious ones, and variation in personality types.[83] Generally speaking, the major problem, apart from the sheer complexity and, we suggest, the ultimate unanswerability of the Weber hypothesis or of the counter-hypotheses, is that variables like religious culture and economic growth or economic motivation vary in their nature of association from societal context to societal context. This problem of contextual uniqueness is undoubtedly the most confounding one in the general problem area.[84]

One of the major arguments about the political consequences of Protestantism hinges upon the idea that it promoted what Andreski calls 'civic virtues'. By making the individual responsible to religious conscience Protestantism freed the individual from the demands of and dependency upon a corporate church, i.e. the Catholic church, and instilled the principle that honesty is the best policy. This argument in fact is couched in terms of an indirect link between Protestantism and capitalism; that is, via a political factor—the orientation of the individual to public life in the community. The Puritans regarded themselves as chosen men in a time of rapid change and social instability, men committed to a new order of discipline requiring that they relinquish 'older loyalties not founded upon opinion and will—loyalties to family, guild, locality, and also to lord and king'.[85] We should, however, remember that the original impulse of Calvinism was a 'totalistic' one, one oriented towards the *religious community* seeking to establish a new, closely stipulated system of religious rules for the old Catholic one. (Lutheranism differed from Calvinism in that the impulse was more simply in the direction of the individual as such.) Thus argues Eisenstadt: 'The transformative capacities of the Protestant groups were smallest in those cases where they attained full powers—when their more totalistic restrictive orientations could become dominant—or in situations where they were downtrodden minorities.'[86]

What is strongly implied by this line of analysis is that the actual circumstances upon which Protestantism 'acted' is of great importance in determining whether it was transformative in the direction of political citizenship and civic responsibility. Calvin's Geneva is the classic case of a Protestant impulse taken to its limits—that is, taken 'too far'. But in those societies where Protestants had to press for new arrangements in the sphere of church-state relations, where they had to think through the correct stance towards the state (as in Britain, Scandinavia and later America), there was ample opportunity for the forging of *differentiated* conceptions of societal life, of attaining the kind of pluralistic posture which is essential to the development of any form of democracy. This emphasis upon pluralism is the core of Luethy's transposition of the Weber thesis to the political field, Luethy arguing that direct reference to the Bible was of prime importance in providing a basis for innovatory legitimations of authority.[87]

These arguments about Protestantism's importance in the transition to liberal democratic societies are attractive. We have evidence from various sources about the ways in which religious commitments of various non-Protestant kinds inhibit democratic developments—notably in freezing the attachments of individuals in the spheres of the family, locality or, as in Catholic societies, in the Roman Catholic Church. Eckstein has shown how societies with large proportions of Catholics tend, relative to those with large proportions of Protestants, to be either non-democratic or unstable democracies.[88] Outside of the Christian sphere, Pye's study of Burmese politics illustrates very well the constraints exerted by Buddhism in preventing the development of political citizenship.[89] However, we must guard against accepting these theses too readily. We have to contend with, for example, the frequently stated argument that Lutheranism in Germany helped to facilitate the eventual rise of Fascism through its tendency to allow the state full powers of social control. We might also mention that American Protestantism in many ways directly assisted the development of *populism*, which has inherent anti-democratic tendencies.

The trend of much recent discussion of Weber's argument has been very much in line with what has been described as the second phase of the Weber thesis: the view expressed by Bellah that it is the fact of *reformation* which is important, not *particular* doctrines or ideologies. There is a sense in which such a view can easily degenerate into tautology: 'the determinant of change is the determinant of change'. But, more constructively, the emphasis upon the significance of reformation in values and beliefs, leading to social-structural changes, links the work done specifically on the Weber thesis as such with that concerned with change in non-Christian societies. However, in speaking of functional equivalents of the Protestant ethic, such as Marcuse's emphasis upon the transformative significance of Soviet Marxism in these terms,[90] or treatments of nationalism in developing societies, we must be careful not to conceive of these as by definition 'religious' factors.[91]

We said earlier that the view favoured here was that Weber was on the whole wrong about the Protestant ethic, but right about the general contribution of Judaism and Christianity to the forms taken economically and politically by Western societies. Here the major difference between ascetic activism and Oriental mysticism is of course crucial. We would agree with Bendix that the forward-looking, eschatological orientation of Christianity (including the greater perceptual differentiation of culture from actual social relationships) is crucial and that the 'Reformation added a last, all-important synthesis of this orientation with the mundane interest of the believers'.[92] In any case, Weber's subsequent writings very much bear out this kind of interpretation; in so far as he there allowed much more for the operation of 'interests' other than purely religious ones. Bendix is undoubtedly correct too in asserting that Weber 'overestimated the importance of religious ideas whenever he moved more or less unwittingly from analysing the direction of religious influence to assertions concerning the degree to which religious ideas became internalized'.[93] This is the crucial factor. The intensity with which religious beliefs are held is only now being studied adequately; and we will of course never know in any remotely accurate way the intensity of religious beliefs held in the past. Certainly Weber never even demonstrated that those who became Puritans really believed in predestination or lived through the 'salvation panic',[94] let alone that these same people became capitalist entrepreneurs. It is precisely the problem of degree of internalization and intensity which lies at the heart not only of the Weber controversy, but also of any evaluation of many more recent studies of the relationship between religious commitment and other orientations such as the economic, the political and the scientific.[95]

The Impact of Religious Culture in the Modern World

The basic problem, then, in estimating the significance of religious commitment in moulding political, economic and other forms of social behaviour lies in the degree to which that culture is actually internalized. The work of Lenski, and more particularly of Glock and Stark, bears very closely on this problem; in so far as their dimensional schemata are important steps in the direction of establishing whether to be, say, a Roman Catholic in a particular society is more a matter of self-identification or communal attachment than a positive commitment to the tenets of Roman Catholicism. Many of the studies which seek to show that there is a pattern of voting in a given society—Catholics tending to vote for one political party and Protestants for another—do not allow for this type of highly important discrimination.[96] For example, finding that in an English town working-class members of the Church of England voted nearly two-to-one for the Conservative Party, while individuals of the same class, but with no religious affiliation, voted nearly two-to-one for the Labour Party tells us relatively little of the actual influence of a religious factor.[97] In the United States there is a tendency for individuals *within Protestantism and Judaism* to change their denominational attachment as they move upward in social mobility terms—a pattern which suggests again a relatively low degree of internalization and intensity of commitment along a cultural dimension of religiosity. In fact this kind of 'distance' from religion, even though a religious attachment is declared, points to the fact that religious behaviour has come increasingly in some societies, notably the U.S.A., to be a response to a diffuse expectation that *membership* of a religious collectivity is culturally appropriate. This is the kind of consideration necessary in evaluating studies showing significant links between religious activity or commitment and political or economic behaviour.

In spite of these reservations, it has to be freely acknowledged, as Lipset maintains, that as an institution that generates values religion explains much of the variation in political diversity in electoral democracies as well as 'such nonpolitical aspects of behaviour as work habits, achievement aspirations, and parent-child-relations'.[98]

Britain is something of an exception here, but in many other liberal democratic societies the relationship between political and religious allegiance is strong.[99] In America by the end of the nineteenth century a definite pattern had been established of Catholics identifying with the Democratic Party and Protestants with the Republicans—the former association resting upon the Democrats' relative sympathy with new immigrants and greater disposition to use political procedures to cope with economic problems and the inequalities attendant thereon. (Once again, however, we must draw attention to the ecological and social-structural variables: Catholics were, and still are, overwhelmingly urban-dwellers in the U.S.A.—which undoubtedly accounts for much in the establishment of this pattern.) On the other hand, the low status of the more fundamentalist and ascetic Protestant groups disposes their members to vote disproportionately for the Democratic Party; and yet Republican voting is still higher in these contexts than would be suggested by a mere consideration of their low economic status. In one important study Johnson shows the ways in which the variation in Protestant beliefs reduces the relations between social class and political allegiance.[100] Summing-up the evidence in the light of Johnson's contribution, Lipset concludes that, in America, religion affects political choice in two independent ways: as a source of political beliefs and as a determinant of status. These two variables operate at cross-purposes among Protestants. 'Active membership in a liberal high-status church pulls one toward political liberalism; nominal adherence primarily serves as a source of status and hence strengthens the political conservatism associated with high position. And the opposite pattern operates among the inactive and active adherents of the more fundamentalist low-status groupings.'[101]

It will be noted that Lipset's generalizations do invoke the factor of intensity of commitment (although only in a unidimensional dichotomous manner, i.e., active versus nominal commitment). Much research needs to be done in other societies along similar lines, in order that we may generalize more confidently. In terms of the general analytic posture adopted in this book, mere demonstration that religious affiliation (in the sense of declared attachment to a religious collectivity or tradition) affects party preference is insufficient to conclude that a religious factor is significantly at work in an independent manner. On the other hand, there is no doubt that in many societies religious beliefs and values emphatically do affect political (and economic) behaviour.[102] Religious political parties, although clearly secularized in some places, are highly conspicuous in a number of Catholic, Calvinist and Moslem societies, and also in India, Israel and those societies in Asia where Buddhism is prominent.

Where, as in the case of Roman Catholicism, belief is maintained in the unique, God-ordained significance of the religious collectivity, then religious culture is a highly potent determinant of political behaviour, since it claims a source of authority lying outside the national society: the Pope.[103]

In another respect religious culture may be *renewed* through the perception of external threat to a people's survival in its preferred condition—and then become bound up with the life of that people.[104] Such renewal may lead to religious culture becoming a quasi-independent source of social behaviour. We think here of the religious legitimation given to *apartheid* by the Dutch Reformed Church in South Africa; the growth of the Black Muslims in the U.S.A.;[105] the white Southern Baptist response to black militancy in the U.S.A. Resistance to nationalistic and socialistic tendencies in new nations has led in some cases to a reassertion of indigenous religious culture by conservatives. In some societies one particular religion, such as Islam in Pakistan, has become a substantive focal point of politics. In a rather different respect, the significance of Islam in West Africa may well be further heightened as a consequence of the Nigerian civil war.[106]

In this chapter we have dealt with religious culture from two principal vantage points: first, the social forces which produce and sustain such culture; second, the respects in which internalization of religious culture exercises constraints upon behaviour in such fields as politics and economic interaction. In noting the various pitfalls involved in making facile assumptions about the direction of impact, we have tried to draw attention to the complex interrelatedness of religious culture and patterns of social relations. In general terms, the sociological attempt to estimate the significance of religious factors in the social and cultural life of a society must rest as much upon a consideration of issues discussed in chapters four (religious systems) and five (religious collectivities) as upon the analysis of the sources and consequences of religious culture. Finally, we should re-emphasize the importance of two themes discussed in the present chapter. First, in our discussion of religious symbolism we argued against the tendency to view the contents of religious culture as either a direct outcome of structural features of the society *and* against the tendency to view such contents as always symbolic of such features. We suggested a more probative approach, allowing not only for either possibility but also the operation of individual and group reflection, and creativity. Second, in our discussion of the Weber thesis and outgrowths of this, we referred on a number of occasions to the problem of the degree to which religious culture is internalized. It should be repeated, however, that we have not maintained that if the degree of individual internalization is low we may not speak of religion *per se* being a significant factor in the operation of the society in question. There are important macro-sociological considerations in this connection, which we discussed in chapter four, notably patterns of commitment at the societal level.

Notes to Chapter 6

1. Cf. Berger, *The Sacred Canopy*, op. cit., p. 127.
2. See the early part of *The Elementary Forms of the Religious Life*, op. cit., and Emile Durkheim and Marcel Mauss, *Primitive Classification* (trans. and ed. by R. Needham), London, 1963.
3. Above, p. 17.
4. This is discussed very well by Parsons in *The Structure of Social Action*, op. cit., esp. ch. XI.
5. For a presentation of many of these, see Imogen Seger, *Durkheim and His Critics on the Sociology of Religion*, Bureau of Applied Social Research, Columbia University, 1957. For a partial bibliography of Durkheimian writing on religion, see Paul Honigsheim, 'The Influence of Durkheim and His School on the Study of Religion', in Emile Durkheim *et al.* (ed. Kurt H. Wolff), *Essays on Sociology and Philosophy*, New York, 1960, pp. 233–46. It needs to be stressed here that Durkheim has frequently been accused of resting much of his sociology on an anti-Catholic stance. (For a religious critique, see H. H. Farmer, *Towards Belief in God*, London, 1942, ch. 9.)
6. Cf. Ludwig Feuerbach, *The Essence of Christianity*, New York, 1925. This was in many ways the beginning of the Marxist theory of religion.

Durkheim was adamant in his rejection of materialist theories of religion.

7. *The Birth of the Gods*, op. cit., pp. 17–18.

8. Ibid., p. 17.

9. Ibid., p. 22.

10. Ibid., p. 42.

11. Ibid., p. 26.

12. See Evans-Pritchard, *Theories of Primitive Religion*, op. cit.

13. Swanson, *Religion and Regime*, op. cit., p. 22.

14. *The Birth of the Gods*, op. cit., ch. 8. Cf. Mary Douglas, *Purity and Danger*, London, New York, 1966. As in other respects a number of Swanson's findings can and have been challenged by anthropologists. For example, some Middle Eastern semi-nomadic tribes have relationships which lack institutional social controls, but do *not* practise witchcraft. It must be stressed that our paying particular attention to Swanson's work derives from the distinctiveness and ambitiousness of his approach and also from his work being a very clear-cut example of structural determinism. There are profound methodological and procedural difficulties implicated in *The Birth of the Gods*.

15. See below, p. 160.

16. *The Birth of the Gods*, p. 188. Swanson applies the same conditions to the relationship between mana and *primordial* structures.

17. This obviously bears very much on the development of secular social contract theories of societal origins and societal cohesion during the three centuries following the Protestant Reformation. This point, in turn, relates closely to the discussion of Swanson's analysis of the Reformation below, pp. 176–7. (It is interesting to note that the sociological critique of secular contract theories and of notions like sovereignty involves a *resurrection* of the significance of ideal and moral factors, notably in the work of Durkheim and Parsons. See particularly Talcott Parsons, 'Durkheim's Contribution to the Theory of Integration of Social Systems', in Durkheim *et al.*, op. cit., pp. 118–53. See also below, p. 223.)

18. Paul Tillich, 'Existential Analysis and Religious Symbols', in Will Herberg (ed.), *Four Existential Theologians*, Garden City, New York, 1958, p. 291. Cf. the analyses of Mircea Eliade, cited p. 73, n. 40.

19. Cf. Alasdair MacIntyre, *Secularization and Moral Change*, London, New York, 1967, p. 69.

20. Talcott Parsons, *The Social System*, op. cit., p. 377.

21. Ibid.

22. Cf. Bellah, 'Religious Evolution', op. cit. See also Bellah's review of John Robinson's *Honest to God*, in *Christianity and Crisis*, XXIII (November 11, 1963), pp. 200–1.

23. Worsley, *The Trumpet Shall Sound*, op. cit., p. xxix. (See, for example, A. R. Radcliffe-Brown, 'Religion and Society', in *Structure and Function in Primitive Societies*, Glencoe, 1952.)

24. See particularly Claude Lévi-Strauss, *The Savage Mind*, op. cit., and *Structural Anthropology*, New York, 1963, London, 1967, esp. chs. XI and XV. Cf. Douglas, *Purity and Danger*, op. cit.

25. All societies, to some degree, have bodies of ideas relating directly to social institutions and activities. See Charles Madge, *Society in the Mind*, London, New York, 1964.

26. Worsley, *The Trumpet Shall Sound*, loc. cit.

27. Geertz, 'Religion as a Cultural System', op. cit.

28. Bryan Wilson, 'The Exclusive Brethren: A Case Study in the Evolution of a Sectarian Ideology', in Wilson (ed.), *Patterns of Sectarianism*, op. cit., p. 337.

29. Durkheim acknowledged this poetic quality. Some like Lévy-Bruhl have seen it as a form of *pre-logical* thought. (L. Lévy-Bruhl, *How Natives Think* (trans. L. Clare), London, 1926.) This position is of course now rejected, notably in the work of Lévi-Strauss. For a brilliant analysis of allegoric thinking, see Evans-Pritchard, *Nuer Religion*, op. cit., esp. p. 231.

30. Bellah's 'Religious Evolution' (op. cit.) is one of the best illustrations of the problems discussed here.

31. *The Trumpet Shall Sound*, op. cit. See also Worsley, 'Groote Eylandt Totemism and *Le Totemisme aujourd'hui*', in Leach (ed.), *The Structural Study of Myth and Totemism*, op. cit., pp. 141–59.

32. Weber, *The Sociology of Religion*, op. cit., pp. 24–5. However, Weber *does* at various points briefly explore the impact of structural morphology on conceptions of the cosmos. But he does not see this as affecting the general population. See his emphasis upon the characteristics of mass religion (*Alltagsreligion*) (ibid.). (Conversely, in *Religion and Regime*, Swanson acknowledges the significance of competing conceptions of religious traditions.)

33. *The Sociology of Religion*, p. 25.

34. T. B. Bottomore (ed.), *Karl Marx: Early Writings*, op. cit., pp. 43–4.

35. 'The Social Psychology of the World Religions', in Gerth and Mills, op. cit., p. 271.

36. Weber, *The Sociology of Religion*, op. cit., p. 106.

37. Ibid., p. 100.

38. See above, p. 154; Talcott Parsons, 'Evolutionary Universals in Society', *American Sociological Review*, XXIX (June, 1964), pp. 339–57. See also Alvin W. Gouldner and Richard A. Peterson, *Technology and the Moral Order*, New York, 1962, esp. pp. 50–1.

39. Underlying these observations are Johan Galtung's various analyses of systems of stratification—notably 'A Structural Theory of Aggression', *Journal of Peace Research* (1964), pp. 95–119; and 'International Relations and International Conflicts', International Sociological Association, Proceedings of Plenary Session, Sixth World Congress, 1966.

40. Victorian England provides an excellent example of the consolidation of a middle-class *conservative* religious moralism, involving a great ostensible stress on sexual propriety. See Peter L. Cominos, 'Late Victorian Respectability and the Social System', *International Review of Social History*, VIII, Pt. 1 (1963). Lower middle-class moralism in modern societies often takes the form of heavily emphasizing the moral evils of tobacco and alcohol. For an American study, see Joseph R. Gusfield, *Symbolic Crusade*, Urbana, 1963.

41. 'The Social Psychology of the World Religions', op. cit.

42. Weber, *Sociology of Religion*, op. cit., p. 125.

43. Bendix, *Max Weber*, op. cit., p. 276. There is a sense in which urban areas which are not great cultural centres also have populations who appear to feel relatively deprived, or 'culturally retarded'. This may in small part help to explain some of the cases where religious fecundity has been notable in 'non-mainstream' cities. Bryan Wilson has drawn my attention to Leicestershire in this connection: this area being significant for the vitality at various points in history of the Quakers; the Baptist revival in the mid-eighteenth century; the Countess of Huntingdon's Connexion; and, in the modern period, the large numbers of Christadelphians and members of the Churches of Christ.

44. Lucien Goldmann, *The Hidden God* (trans. Philip Thody), London, New York, 1964, esp. ch. VI.

45. See Norman Cohn, 'Medieval Millenarism: its bearing on the Comparative Study of Millenarian Movements', in Sylvia Thrupp (ed.), *Millennial Dreams in Action*, The Hague, 1962, esp. p. 37. (See also Norman Cohn, *The Pursuit of the Millennium*, London, New York, 1962.)

46. Although it was an age of female emancipation (but only incipiently so), many religious movements and organizations during the second half of the nineteenth century and early part of the twentieth century

made special play of the role of women; e.g. Holiness religion in America, the Salvation Army, Seventh Day Adventists, Christian Science, Theosophy and some of the New Thought movements.

47. Karl Mannheim, *Ideology and Utopia*, 1936, pp. 190–1.

48. See below, pp. 169 ff.

49. The major contemporary advocates of the political significance of millennial phenomena are Worsley (*The Trumpet Shall Sound*, op. cit.) and Eric Hobsbawm (*Primitive Rebels*, London, New York, 1959).

50. Most, if not all, of the movements in Europe from the eleventh to the fourteenth century did not become political in any meaningful sense. In *The Trumpet Shall Sound*, Worsley does attempt to delineate those Melanesian cargo cults which had explicit political significance from those which did not.

51. Bryan Wilson, 'Millennialism in Comparative Perspective', op. cit.

52. *The Trumpet Shall Sound*, op. cit., p. xxxvi.

53. For analyses of the different types of African religious and political movements, see Fernandez, 'African Religious Movements . . .', op. cit., and F. B. Welbourn, *East African Rebels*, London, 1961.

54. Although 'millennial failure' may in fact lead to heightened millennial commitment. See L. Festinger *et al.*, *When Prophecy Fails*, New York, 1964.

55. Yonina Talmon, 'Millenarian Movements', *European Journal of Sociology*, VII (1966), pp. 159–200, esp. pp. 181 ff.; and the same author's excellent 'The Pursuit of the Millennium: the Relation Between Religion and Social Change', op. cit. See also Howard Kaminsky, 'A Note on Relative Deprivation Theory as Applied to Millenarian and other Cult Movements', in Thrupp (ed.), op. cit., pp. 209–17; and Wilson, 'Millennialism in Comparative Perspective', op. cit.

56. For different forms of secularization see below, ch. 8.

57. See Benton Johnson, 'Do Holiness Sects Socialize in Dominant Values?', *Social Forces*, 39 (May, 1961), pp. 309–16.

58. Cf. Smelser, *Theory of Collective Behaviour*, op. cit., esp. ch. 10. See also the remarks above on surrogate religiosity and Luckmann, *The Invisible Religion*, op. cit.

59. Charles Y. Glock, 'The Role of Deprivation in the Origin and Evolution of Religious Groups', in Robert Lee and Martin E. Marty (eds.), *Religion and Social Conflict*, New York, 1964, pp. 24–36.

60. See particularly Wilson, 'An Analysis of Sect Development', op. cit.

61. See Wilson, *Sects and Society*, op. cit.

62. Weber, *The Protestant Ethic and the Spirit of Capitalism*, op. cit. It seems

often to be assumed that Weber originated the Protestant Ethic thesis. Certainly there was a great uniqueness about his own contribution; but there were important intellectual antecedents. For example, see Philip Shasko, 'Nikolai Alexandrovich Mel'gunov on the Reformation and the Work Ethic', *Comparative Studies in Society and History*, IX (1966–1967), pp. 256–65; Reinhard Bendix, 'The Protestant Ethic—Revisited', in ibid., pp. 266–73. In any case, the work-disciplining virtues of Protestantism were frequently stated by economic and political elites in the nineteenth century.

63. Parsons, 'Introduction' to Weber, *Sociology of Religion*, op. cit., p. xlviii.

64. Nevertheless, Weber was sometimes ambiguous on this point. See below, p. 173.

65. Kurt Samuelsson, *Religion and Economic Action* (trans. E. Geoffrey French), New York, 1961, esp. pp. 43–4.

66. For a different type of criticism of the logic of Weber's argument, see Alasdair MacIntyre, 'A Mistake about Causality in the Social Sciences', in Peter Laslett and W. G. Runciman (eds.), *Philosophy, Politics and Society*, II, Oxford, New York, 1962.

67. We do not deal here with those who have tended to deny any important connection between Protestantism and the political and economic changes which swept European societies in the seventeenth to nineteenth centuries, one of whom is Samuelsson, op. cit. The first chapter of his book summarizes part of the early debate. See also, Green (ed.), *Protestantism and Capitalism*, op. cit.; Ephraim Fischoff, 'The Protestant Ethic and the Spirit of Capitalism', *Social Research*, XI (1944), pp. 54–77; and R. F. Baerling, *Protestantisme en Kapitalisme*, Groningen-Batavia, 1946.

68. R. H. Tawney, *Religion and the Rise of Capitalism*, London, 1926.

69. Winthrop S. Hudson, 'Puritanism and the Spirit of Capitalism', in Green (ed.), op. cit., pp. 56–62.

70. Christopher Hill, 'Protestantism and the Rise of Capitalism', in F. J. Fisher (ed.), *Essays in the Economic and Social History of Tudor and Stuart England in Honour of R. H. Tawney*, Cambridge, 1961, pp. 15–39.

71. On the Jews see Sombart, op. cit. For the argument that Judaism does contain economic ethics appropriate to capitalism (which Weber denied), but that its pariah status prevented it from playing a decisive role, see Stanislav Andreski, *Elements of Comparative Sociology*, London, 1964, pp. 195–7.

72. Weber, *The Protestant Ethic . . .* , p. 40.

73. Trevor-Roper, op. cit.

74. Andreski, op. cit., p. 190.

75. Marx and Engels, *On Religion*, op. cit., p. 264.

76. For a very brief consideration of Kautsky's *Materialistiche Geschicht-sauffassung*, see Andreski, op. cit., pp. 191-3.

77. e.g. Norman Birnbaum, 'The Zwinglian Reformation in Zurich', *Past and Present* (April, 1959), pp. 27-47. See also *idem*, 'Conflicting Interpretations of the Rise of Capitalism: Marx and Weber', *British Journal of Sociology*, 4 (1953), pp. 125-41.

78. Walzer, *The Revolution of the Saints*, op. cit.

79. Swanson, *Religion and Regime*, op. cit.

80. It might be thought, then, that North Italian cities should have gone Calvinist. But Swanson counts these, such as Florence and Venice, as independent *commensal* regimes—regimes which are governed by precluding the exercise of power in the service of special groups. Florence is conceded by Swanson to be a difficult case to categorize. Commensal regimes, it is hypothesized, are likely to be associated with the persistence of Catholicism. (Ibid., esp. ch. VII.)

81. See especially S. N. Eisenstadt, 'The Protestant Ethic Thesis in Analytical and Comparative Context', *Diogenes* (Fall, 1967), pp. 25-46; Robert Bellah, 'Reflections on the Protestant Ethic Analogy in Asia', *Journal of Social Issues*, XIX (1963), pp. 52-60.

82. Robert T. Holt and John E. Turner, *The Political Basis of Economic Development*, Princeton, 1966.

83. See, *inter alia*, Everett E. Hagen, *On the Theory of Social Change*, Homewood, 1962; David C. McClelland, *The Achieving Society*, Princeton, London, 1961.

84. For such methodological problems, including a brief look at the Weber problem, see Hayward R. Alker, Jr., 'Regionalism and Universalism in Comparing Nations', in Bruce M. Russet *et al.* (eds.), *World Handbook of Political and Social Indicators*, New Haven, 1964.

85. Walzer, op. cit., p. 318.

86. Eisenstadt, op. cit., p. 44.

87. H. Luethy, 'Once Again: Calvinism and Capitalism', *Encounter*, XII (1964), pp. 18-45.

88. Harry Eckstein, *A Theory of Stable Democracy*, Princeton, 1961.

89. Lucian W. Pye, *Politics, Personality and Nation Building*, New Haven, 1962.

90. Herbert Marcuse, *Soviet Marxism*, New York, London, 1958.

91. Cf. Apter's emphasis upon political religions in new states: *The*

Politics of Modernization, op. cit. Clearly some nationalisms seem designed to crush 'those traditional systems which Weber himself found less permissive than Protestantism for economic activity'. (Neil J. Smelser, *The Sociology of Economic Life*, Englewood Cliffs, 1963, p. 42.) For the clear equation of nationalism with secularism, see Kingsley Davis, 'Social and Demographic Aspects of Economic Development in India', in Simon Kuznets *et al.* (eds.), *Economic Growth: Brazil, India, Japan*, Durham, 1955. Cf. Robert N. Bellah, 'Religious Aspects of Modernization in Turkey and Japan', *American Journal of Sociology*, 64 (July, 1958), pp. 1–5; *idem, Tokugawa Religion*, Glencoe, 1957.

92. Bendix, *Max Weber*, op. cit., p. 286.

93. Ibid., p. 282.

94. Walzer, op. cit., p. 306.

95. We have not dealt here with an important outgrowth of the Weber thesis—the relationship between religious commitment and scientific achievement. See, *inter alia*, R. K. Merton, 'Science, Technology and Society in Seventeenth Century England', *Osiris*, IV (1938); L. S. Feuer, *The Scientific Intellectual*, New York, 1963; H. F. Kearney, 'Puritanism, Capitalism and the Scientific Revolution', *Past and Present*, XXVIII (1964), pp. 81–101. See also Greeley, *Religion and Career*, op. cit. (For further references on the Weber thesis, see Morris I. Berkowitz and J. Edmund Johnson, *Social Scientific Studies of Religion*, Pittsburgh, 1967, pp. 203–4.)

96. See Lenski, *The Religious Factor*, op. cit.

97. See A. H. Birch, *Small-Town Politics*, London, New York, 1959, p. 112.

98. Seymour Martin Lipset, 'Political Sociology', in Smelser (ed.), *Sociology*, op. cit., p. 473.

99. See, *inter alia*, Alford, *Party and Society*, op. cit.

100. Benton Johnson, 'Ascetic Protestantism and Political Preference', *Public Opinion Quarterly*, 26 (Spring, 1962), pp. 34–46.

101. Seymour Martin Lipset, 'Religion and Politics', in Lee and Marty (eds.), *Religion and Social Conflict*, op. cit., p. 102.

102. From the point of view of political sociologists such strictures are not so applicable; for they are usually concerned simply with the sources of cleavage in social systems which lead to differences in party allegiance and voting behaviour. In one sense, there is nothing wrong with their labelling these religious cleavages in terms of *their* specific interests; but it makes for *general* sociological difficulties. See, *inter alia*, S. M. Lipset and Stein Rokkan (eds.), *Party Systems and Voter Alignments*, New York, 1967.

103. See Lipset's excellent discussions in Lee and Marty (eds.), op. cit., and Smelser (ed.), op. cit.
104. Cf. the discussion of millennialism, above, pp. 163–7.
105. See the good study, C. E. Lincoln, *The Black Muslims in America*, Boston, 1960.
106. For the background, see J. S. Trimingham, *Islam in West Africa*, Oxford, New York, 1959.

7

Attitudes towards the Modern World: Religion in Relation to Social Science

Throughout this book there runs almost continuously the thread of the interpenetration of religion and sociology. As we have hinted before, the situation could hardly be otherwise—the only difference in the present analysis being that the thread has been a highly visible one. A good case could be made out for the proposition that the sociological enterprise is essentially 'Christian' in character; a secularized issuance of religious Christianity, influenced very much also by Judaism. Such prescriptions as 'know thyself' and 'go forth into the world' and others which emphasize comprehension of the socio-cultural situation support this contention. It is not suggested, however, that sociology and adjacent pursuits be regarded as *religious* activities. In the theological sphere many of the most prominent issues in recent years have revolved around the so-called Death-of-God school. In sociology discussion of what religiosity is and, even more important, the resurgence of the long-dormant *theoretical* sociology of religion have gained increasing attention. We have already noted that there has been some direct confrontation between theology and sociology along these lines.[1*] But the confrontation has been a rather confused one. Theologians have not *comprehensively* followed through with their sociological interests; while most sociologists of religion have, unfortunately, been content only to 'raid' very selectively the works of established theologians or the more popularized manifestations of the trends in 'radical' theology, such as John Robinson's *Honest to God*. It is thus interesting to note that *some* theologians are saying almost the same things as *some* sociologists of religion. Even more intriguing is that we frequently have conflicting interpretations and prescriptions on the basis of initial agreement. We have already concluded that it is wrong simply to claim that the sociologist's and

* Notes for this chapter begin on page 224.

the theologian's ultimate purposes and intentions are different and therefore that they are not directly comparable. The fact that a theologian may utilize a sociological generalization in an approving way or invoke a sociological point in order to underscore or substantiate a theological proposition demonstrates the fallaciousness of this argument. As does the fact that some sociologists invoke theological definitions of religion (and thereby reject others) or argue that an activity is religious in spite of religious-intellectual disclaimers.[2] All of this makes the sociology of religion so much more difficult a discipline to engage in; and this closely relates to the fact that sociological orientations in themselves constitute world views.[3] Put in these terms the claim that the twentieth century has witnessed a significant degree of sociologization of human culture becomes even clearer. We do not wish to exaggerate this—but the relative 'openness' of modern societies alone has led to a greater, generalized tendency for individuals to reflect upon, for example, the causes of war, chances of social mobility, social determinants of delinquency and so on. This 'lay' sociology may be 'bad' sociology —but that is not the point.

The explanatory content of Christianity (with which we are primarily concerned) is rather low—whereas sociology has historically sought to *explain*, to account both for fundamental, universal features of socio-cultural life and for significant unique occurrences in social history.[4] Martin stresses, largely following Weber, that 'the higher religions' (in particular Judaism, Christianity, Islam and Buddhism) arise by way of answer to the problem of 'injustice, disharmony and sheer inexplicable misery'.[5] But they do not *explain* evil. A concept like *karma* may 'function as a partial explanation' but on the whole the belief systems involved here are 'fundamental attempts to find viable *Weltanschauungen*'.[6] Two points about the rivalry of sociology and theology follow from this. First, sociology stands as a rival to the religious perspective through the very fact that it does attempt to explain. Second, much of sociology has in fact been concerned with the establishment of paradigms and perspectives—usually on the grounds that the particular set of empirical problems in question cannot as yet be tackled in rigorous explanatory terms. Thus the rivalry takes two closely related forms.[7] In the first case sociology in a sense claims more for itself than does theology or religious intellectualism. In the second case it sets itself up as a provider of *Weltanschauungen*. Again, however, it cannot be stressed too strongly that many modern theologians would *not* see the situation as one of rivalry. This difficulty will require us subsequently to venture into the 'theological arena'—to see the degree to which the sociological or the religious perspective is winning out.

In this chapter we first survey some of the salient philosophic underpinnings of sociology and deliberately state a sociological perspective in counterposition to a theological one. This is followed by a brief discussion of modern theological trends which intertwine with sociological themes. Finally relations between religion and scientific world views are discussed.

The Claims of Sociology

We have encountered the claim that the classical sociologists were above all concerned with religious phenomena.[8] The latter were, it is argued, the cornerstone of the work of Weber and Durkheim. The same has even been claimed for Marx, while Comte's ambivalent commitment to a 'religious' position is well known. Now there is of course a difference between analysing religion in a comprehensive manner and adopting a religious perspective. All four sought to analyse religion—though this is less evident in the work of Marx and Comte than of Durkheim and Weber. But what about the second aspect—the adoption or promulgation of a religious perspective? The idea that the sociologists of this period dealt in *religious* issues arises because they sought to replace a conventional-Christian position by another position. In the case of Comte the replacement was a kind of sociological Catholicism. He sought to make sociology into a religion of humanity, embodying very similar principles of social organization to those of Roman Catholicism, and, incidentally, taking a very strong anti-Protestant-individualism form.[9] With Marx the situation is rather more complex. Dahrendorf has noted that the major German impulse towards the crystallization of sociology, taking both moral and scientific forms, can be seen in the period 1830 to 1850 when Marx, Engels, Feuerbach, Hess and others took two simultaneous steps—from criticizing religion to criticizing society and from emphasizing theory to emphasizing practice.[10] The important point here is that, as with Comte, there was a vital *symbiosis* as between the anti-religious stance and the innovative thrust. Marx having come to eschew religion in a (mainly Hegelian) religious context, remained preoccupied with the kinds of questions raised by a religious commitment.[11] The shift from theory to practice might also be seen in such terms. To come to believe in the capacity of men collectively to 'stand on their own', provided the thrust towards a practical, almost missionary attempt to realize man's human potential.[12]

Some sociologists of roughly the same period remained wedded to a fairly orthodox religious position. For example, Saint-Simon, regarded in many ways as Comte's sociological predecessor, was quite convinced of the vitality of Christian culture; notwithstanding the great attraction to him of the idea of the rationally administered and perfectible society. Thus Comte and Marx in their different ways marked an important step forward in the release from religious beliefs and symbols. But they were still encapsulated *in particular terms of reference* to a religious position. Certainly in Marx's early work, and in the view of many devotees of Marxism of the mid-twentieth century, a major emphasis is upon man's self-realization as an individual and the fulfilment of human potential generally. Embedded here is obviously a conception of man in relation to society, a conception of man's social nature. The emphasis in Marx's conception is, at philosophic base, quite clearly upon the integral individual human being: the communist society is the society where individuals are not hedged by constraints. The key word here is 'integral'. An individual is regarded as an autonomous, bounded agent; the individual is the primary reality. Conditions like those of capitalist societies blunt his capacity both to perceive this autonomy and to achieve it. Thus the whole context (other than the physical and chemical givens) must be changed in a direction where integrity (in the literal sense of the word) is possible.

Marx's concern with the liberation of man, indeed the 'salvation' of man, has been characterized from time to time as a religious preoccupation.[13] In terms of our own analysis, this would be an inappropriate interpretation. On our definition of religious culture we must agree with Marx's own statements as to his anti-religious position. But Marx did nevertheless find it necessary to parallel religious themes. Like so many social analysts of the nineteenth century he sought agents of social and cultural change which lay at least partially outside of the control of man—historical and dialectical materialism. (Later in the century Herbert Spencer was to talk in terms of a mysterious force or cause which propelled socio-cultural life in a specific evolutionary direction.) Marx's emphasis upon the potential integrity of the human individual contrasts strongly with much of modern sociology, which has found it necessary to postulate what Dahrendorf has called *homo sociologicus*—a conception of man which is susceptible to sociological analysis.[14] We will return to this important point in a moment. But of the nineteenth century we can say that the release from frames of reference derived from religion was very gradual. And when, at the end of the century, a more frontal attack or diagnosis of religious decline made its appearance we can still see the influence of religious terms of reference. The reaction against assumptions of inevitable human progress and the perfectibility of man and/or the socio-cultural order took a number of forms. Some social analysts, like Durkheim, did not subscribe to the general pessimism; while others, notably Weber, tended merely to declare their pessimism and leave it at that. But there were some, such as Pareto and Sorel, who acknowledged the importance for the functioning of societies of certain beliefs and symbols, and yet who at the same time obviously did not subscribe to such beliefs and symbols themselves.

Nothing of course is straightforwardly new.[15] Voltaire's famous dictum—to the effect that if there had not been a God it would have been necessary for man to invent one—foreshadowed the kind of disjunction, between what was regarded as necessary to the operation of society and what the analyst might actually believe in, that appeared so prominently in late nineteenth- and early twentieth-century social thought.[16] Two major themes contributed to the significance of this disjunction as it has manifested itself among many anthropologists and functional sociologists. Among anthropologists in particular the notion of relativism appeared in the 1930s—the principle that each society the anthropologist analysed should be 'respected', that there should not and could not be universally applicable criteria of what was good or bad, true or false. Among both social anthropologists and many sociologists also arose the great emphasis upon the *systemic* perspective—societies were looked at as functioning wholes, in each of which certain imperatives had to be met.[17] Amongst these imperatives was usually one specifying that members should be committed to a set of religious beliefs. Indeed, as we have already seen, some sociologists have come to regard the most basic sets of beliefs, symbols and values as religious by definition.

The emphasis upon *system* has had very important philosophic ramifications in sociology. In the present context the most important of these is that it has brought to the fore the postulation of a specific conception of man—sociological man. Much of sociology does not treat the individual as an individual *qua* individual. Now, it may be said that the sociologist proceeds in this way for analytical reasons— that he is not tied to the sociological perspective in a *sociologistic* sense. But this would appear to be a naïve interpretation—one which is not borne out by the actual practice of contemporary sociologists. The basic unit of analysis with which many 'system' sociologists typically deal is that of the social role. Individuals occupy positions (or rather series of positions) in social systems. Each position which they occupy entails an appropriate set of rights and obligations. Such is the mainline sociological perspective. And in these terms we find, for example, Parsons saying that, typically in the modern socio-cultural situation, the religious role is differentiated from other non-religious roles. This is, of course, to run very much against the grain of mainline theology and historical conceptions of religious commitment. Taken to its extreme, role analysis of this kind really maintains that there is no individual as such; but rather a *series* of 'individuals'. A 'person' is different from one situation to another. Thus the idea of integral man disappears.

Presumably a defence of this allegation would, amongst other things, point to the fact that the dominant sociological perspective acknowledges the importance of the analytically separate concept of the individual personality. This, it might be argued, is where the notion of the integral human being is applicable—but beyond the domain of sociological analysis. The main trouble here is that a great many psychologists also ignore the question of the integral human being. It may also be argued that there are other prominent sociological perspectives—clustering notably in the spheres of so-called symbolic interactionism and phenomenology—which take as their departure point the concern with the continuing interplay between the individual and other individuals, groups and institutions which he or she encounters. The emphasis here is upon the dialectical relationship between the individual and other objects in his environ-ment. While in many ways it is true that some sociologists and social psychologists within these schools focus upon problems of integral identity, the fact also remains that many of them present a con-ception of individual man which is at considerable odds with a Christian perspective. One of the best-known sociologists of the interactionist tradition is Erving Goffman, whose work is based on a dramaturgical conception of socio-cultural life; one in which the individual is for ever engaged in a series of 'plays'.[18]

By no means all recent sociologists of this broad tradition have taken this position. The phenomenological perspectives of Berger and Luckmann, deriving in part from the work of Alfred Schutz, come close to respecting the integralness and (within limits, of course) the autonomy of the individual.[19] Their work puts great stress on individuals constructing their own worlds and upon the dangers inherent in a sociological approach (like Parsons') which reifies or hypostasizes social groups, social institutions and societies. In these terms it is clearly apparent why Luckmann has put so much empha-sis upon the sociological enterprise having primarily to do with 'the fate of the individual' and why he regards the condition of mankind as a kind of religious condition. In stressing these features of Luck-mann's work once more we must also point up the fact that he himself emphasizes that man's religiosity is an anthropological feature of human society. This is important, as we shall see, since it is in response to the alleged dehumanizing of man that some have argued forcibly for a widening of the sociological base to the point of concentrating our intellectual resources upon *philosophical anthro-pology*, which, it might be additionally argued, is what a number of contemporary self-declared theologians are engaged in. But we must

note at this stage that although the work of both Berger and Luckmann starts from the individual and stresses the individual's social
and cultural creativity, the nature of the creativity or rather the
capacity for 'fulfilment' is basically (and this is truer of Berger than
of Luckmann) a pessimistic one. The kind of 'world' which the
individual creates is one which is largely tied to the multiple, everyday realities of an industrial society.[19a] What purports to be a perspective underlining individual autonomy and creativity thus
frequently turns out to be a philosophic commitment to the notion
that, in the modern world at least, individuals are constantly and
inevitably 'pulled back' to the mundane necessities and *status quo*
routines of everyday existence.[20]

Dahrendorf has explicitly raised the problem of the sociologist's
conception of man in relation to mainline American sociology with
its emphasis upon role analysis as being the elemental component of
social systems. He argues very persuasively that sociology which •
seeks to be explanatory and genuinely scientific does not and cannot
have a conception of *man as such*. Rather he postulates *homo sociologicus*—a fictional man like economic man—which serves his
explanatory purposes pretty well. But Dahrendorf is acutely
concerned about the disjunction between sociological man and real,
moral man—the integral human being. Three quotations from his
two essays on this theme will make clear Dahrendorf's position: 'In
sociological investigations . . . the person has no place, yet he must
never be forgotten. Awareness of the autonomous individual and
his claim to liberty must inform every sentence the sociologist speaks
and writes; society must constantly be present to him not only as a
fact, but as a vexation; the moral insufficiency of his discipline must
always appear as a passionate undertone in his work.'[21] 'Not only is
sociology improperly defined as a science of man, but it is fundamentally indifferent to man as such, since it can reach much further
with *homo sociologicus* than with statements that aim at an accurate
description of man's nature.'[22] 'The sociologist should make it clear
that for him human nature is not accurately described by the principle of role conformity, that indeed the difference between this
theoretically fruitful construct and his idea of human nature amounts
almost to a contradiction.'[23]

We need to note here the ambivalence of the sociologist's orientation to social life which Dahrendorf advocates. The major difficulty with his statement is that if sociology is supposed to be at the service of mankind, as Dahrendorf suggests it should be, what is the *route* from *homo sociologicus* to integral man? Dahrendorf in fact fails to provide a genuine linkage between sociological man and integral man. Moreover he apparently neglects the important consideration that sociologists often appear to manifest a vested interest in getting empirical reality to conform to their own *scientific* conceptions of it. It is a familiar enough occurrence for the sociologist to witness his colleagues arguing for a particular social policy which would help to confirm his theory. Herein lies the danger of too generalized a reliance on role analysis.[24]

Thus, praiseworthy as Dahrendorf's recommendations may be, it seems doubtful whether sociology can really serve the cause of the integral man or dampen the implications for integral man along the lines which he suggests. If this is the case, conceptions of integralness —more particularly the cause of integral man—are indeed seriously challenged by much of contemporary sociology; especially when one also acknowledges that although the sociologist may operate entirely at the role-analysis level—concentrating that is upon typical *relationships* between individuals in stipulated situations—he must always carry in the back of his mind certain assumptions about individual motivations and evaluations in role situations. Occasionally, sociologists have, so to speak, taken time off from their strictly sociological enterprises to state their position on the kind of issue which Dahrendorf has raised. In response to an article by William Kolb claiming that the mainline sociological conception of man was incongruent with the adequate analysis of religious phenomena,[25] Parsons argues that his own emphasis upon the cultural and social constraints under which man acts is far from being a freedom-restricting conception of man. It can, he suggests, be viewed as virtually the opposite.[26] Kolb objects, among other things, to Parsons' ideal-typical characterization of societies as involving a high degree of institutionalization—that is, a regularized patterning of social activities.[27] Parsons' reply is that it is 'precisely because some things have come to be socially determined, i.e., "institutionalized" that a new range of freedom is opened up'.[28] A precondition for 'freedom' is a patterning of norms and social organization which enables the individual to be free from arbitrariness and to enter into a wide range of voluntary agreements with others.

Very significantly, Parsons invokes the authority of Durkheim to back up his argument. Durkheim is a crucial figure in the present context because of his abiding concern with the individual. This aspect of Durkheim's work is frequently neglected, but all the evidence goes to show that Durkheim was above all interested in the socio-cultural conditions which were most productive of 'respect for the human person and fulfilment of personal autonomy'.[29] On the other hand, he also focused intently on the prerequisites of a stable society. Both Marx and Durkheim claimed to be concerned with promoting the full flowering of integral man; both also saw the social structure as of primary importance in establishing such a condition. But they had almost opposite recommendations as to the social-structural prerequisites of individual integralness. This, to the point that it must be concluded that they had different conceptions as to what integralness and individuality consisted in. Basically, Marx saw the division of labour as productive of a condition of alienation—man estranged 'from himself', from others and from his work. Durkheim on the other hand tended to see the division of labour as productive of the conditions under which men could be genuinely individualistic.[30] Man could only be completed as an individual through being involved in a reciprocal relation with another person, a relation which was productive and part of a wider series of relations. In essence, individuality is only meaningful in a situation which is in some sense cohesive; individuality only makes sense in the *relation* of one individual to another. Thus the key importance of Durkheim was that he conceived of the integral man as gaining his integralness through, and in specific kinds of, differentiated social situations.

Going rather beyond Durkheim we may say that integral man has the capacity to comprehend and cognitively to surmount the situations in which he finds himself. This is a rather different type of man from either of those posited by Dahrendorf. We are not saying that there is a real man so to speak behind the role situations in which he is involved. Rather, we are positing a man who has the capacity to understand the constraints under which he operates. Knowledge of these is essentially a freedom-enlarging circumstance, though the extent of the freedom depends crucially on the intersubjectivity of this knowledge. It must be strongly emphasized that the freedom spoken of here is not characterized by an escape from socio-cultural contingency. Rather, freedom lies in the capacity to comprehend it and to utilize it both for oneself and others. In these terms a major task of sociology is indeed to understand the relationship between objective, external circumstance and subjective, internal orientation.[31]

Thus the position advanced here is that the 'sociologization' of society in the sense of people becoming more 'sociological' in their orientations, is, potentially at the very least, a force making for integralness and human fulfilment. On the other hand we are not saying that such development has gone very far. Berger, Rieff and others have argued strongly that in American society it is *psychological man* who has come to the fore.[32] Psychological man is fundamentally concerned with his psychological well-being and his *adjustability* to 'normal' social situations rather than his capacity to comprehend and understand them. We have posited a relatively new conception of sociological man here for two major reasons: first, to indicate that Dahrendorf's disjunction between sociological man and integral man is unnecessary and that sociology need not (be it all reluctantly) contribute to the dehumanization of man; second, to fill out the range of social-scientific 'challenges' to religious conceptions of man. We do not deny the evidence presented by Berger and Rieff as to the present American situation—nor is it claimed that sociological man as we depict him is anywhere near so common as psychological man. But we do draw attention to the fact that even in order to be psychologically adjustable to social situations individuals do have to appreciate and comprehend those situations. In this respect psychological man is in a negative sense at least 'sociological'. In contrast sociological man is, in the present context, regarded as *active*, rather than passive—active in the sense that we view him as seeing himself positively *in relation* to social situations; understanding that he is what he is as a consequence of situations; that he is capable of reflecting upon what brought those situations about; that he can act positively in terms of cognizing the constraints in the situations, microscopic and macroscopic, which he encounters. Role analysis, upon which Dahrendorf predicates his conception of (fictional) man does not typically allow for such characteristics. It emphasizes one-sidedly the constraints upon the individual. We disagree with Dahrendorf in that we maintain that sociology should seek a basic social unit of analysis which is more faithful to Dahrendorf's own conception of 'real' as opposed to fictional man. (One candidate for such a unit would be that of *action premise*—the bases upon which individuals act. This *would* include constraints upon action, *including* role expectations; but also involved would be a range of assumptions and preferences which the individual would bring to any situation. Such a concept would not therefore deny the fundamental sociological point that individuals are socially constrained. It would refer both to this characteristic *and* the creativity of the individual.)

(A final point on this theme: There is *one* sense in which mainstream sociology is notably 'Christian'. In seeking sociological explanations of social behaviour, particularly deviant behaviour, the analyst does so in terms of the social and cultural factors which brought the behaviour about—objective factors 'pushing' or 'pulling' individuals in certain behavioural directions. One of the most conspicuous areas where such thinking has penetrated 'real' society is the legal system. Legal philosophy and those dealing with, for example, delinquency, have increasingly invoked the social and cultural circumstances of individuals acting in an illegal manner. The 'victim-of-circumstance' syndrome bears no small similarity to the injunction, 'Forgive them, for they know not what they do.' In this respect modern social science is, at least on the surface, 'compassionate'—but, unfortunately, neglectful of crucial philosophical and ethical issues.)

Intellectual Religiosity and Modern Theology

The warning against taking the interpretations of religious intellectuals as directly indicative of a specific type of religiosity or arelgiosity must be repeated. We cannot infer from theology to general religiosity. Yet the modern situation is so complex that we must bear in mind, on the other hand, that much modern, 'radical' theology takes as its departure point a *diagnosis*, or a set of diagnoses, of *what does in fact* characterize the 'popular' religious situation in Western industrial societies. So, whilst it is impermissible to generalize the stance of religious intellectuals beyond the intellectual stratum,[33] it is nevertheless the case that significant clues as to the characteristics of religiosity in general terms may be found in the writings of many religious intellectuals. In fact this discussion is primarily about diagnoses, sociological and theological, of the modern situation.[34]

We must also re-invoke Weber's observations upon the religiosity of intellectuals. Speaking of periods when there was a relatively high degree of synchronization as between 'official' religion and mass religion, Weber stated that 'once a religion has become a mass religion, the development of a salvation doctrine and its ethic by intellectuals usually results in either esotericism or a kind of aristocratic class ethic adjusted to the needs of the intellectually trained groups within the popularized official religion'.[35] More generally, Weber proposes that

> the salvation sought by the intellectual is always based on inner need, and hence it is at once more remote from life, more theoretical and more systematic than salvation from external distress, the quest for which is characteristic of non-privileged classes. The intellectual seeks in various ways, the casuistry of which extends into infinity, to endow his life with a pervasive meaning, and thus to find unity with himself, with his fellow men, and with the cosmos. It is the intellectual who transforms the concept of the world into the problem of meaning. As intellectualism suppresses belief in magic, the world's processes become disenchanted, lose their magical significance, and henceforth simply 'are' and 'happen' but no longer signify anything. As a consequence, there is a growing demand that the world and the total pattern of life be subject to an order that is significant and meaningful.[36]

Weber then goes on to note that there is a conflict between the empirical realities of the world and the intellectual requirement of meaningfulness. It is this incongruence which, Weber alleges, is responsible for 'the intellectual's characteristic flights from the world'. Historically, he maintains, the flight has been into 'absolute loneliness'; but in industrial societies he argues that men seek to escape into 'a nature unspoiled by human institutions'.[37] (The latter remark was almost certainly aimed at Marxists.)

Presumably, few would wish to quarrel with the general tenor of Weber's characterization of intellectual patterns of thought. But the writings of modern intellectuals in the field of religion reveal a rather more complex situation than that suggested by Weber. In one major sense 'radical' theologians depart considerably from the Weberian depiction. Far from trying to escape from the empirical realities of the modern world, a number of them have systematically argued for almost the opposite—an embracing of the world. While there is much variation, among even acknowledged radical Protestant theologians, a significant proportion in effect argue on empirical, worldly grounds that traditional Christian beliefs should be dispensed with altogether. They welcome many facets of the secularization process. In Weberian terms, they seek to cope with the disenchantment of the modern world, neither by fleeing to an inner loneliness nor by denying the significance of human institutions. To be sure they seek significance and meaningfulness—but these are to be accomplished by making a virtue of the modern situation. Such themes as the alleged maturity of man in the modern period, the capacity for mankind to stand on its own feet testify to this interpretation.

'Intellectuals' in the mid-twentieth century covers a rather more heterogeneous range of orientations and characteristics than at the time when Weber wrote. For one thing intellectualism is a more diffuse phenomenon in the mid-twentieth century. In the institutional-religious sphere theologians have been exposed to increasingly extensive ranges of educational and general, socio-cultural experience. They have also been confronted with many very visible groups of internationally-focused non-religious intellectuals. Add to this the fact that virtually all of the elites in institutional-religious spheres —theological, administrative, pastoral, ministerial and educative— have come to agree that religiosity in the modern world is being rapidly attenuated, and we have a situation in which there are great pressures on the religious intellectual or theologian not to flee from the world, but to *cope with* the phenomenon which Weber labels disenchantment. We should also emphasize that there is a very real sense in which industrial societies have been increasingly intellectualized in a much more general way.[38] Not only has the number of practising scholars, artists and writers increased very rapidly indeed, but also their audiences have increased probably at an even greater rate. This does not of course mean that the phenomenon of 'disenchantment' is unimportant. Far from it. But the breadth of interest in the theological issues presented by radical theologians has been much greater than is suggested by Weber's interpretation. What follows is by no means intended to be an adequate theological or philosophical discussion of modern radical theology—an exercise which the writer would not be qualified to undertake. The concern is to reveal the themes which overlap in the sociological analysis of religion and in the 'religious analysis of religion'.

Thomas Altizer, one of the most prominent members of the Death-of-God school, has recently argued that 'traditional theology must be challenged by a theology which encounters the world— even if such confrontation condemns theology to negation of itself'.[39] Of this group it is Altizer who appears to believe most literally that God is dead. The question has been raised over and over again whether it is worth taking seriously such views as theological or religious theses. The answer from a sociological standpoint must be a qualified yes. According to the definitional prescriptions advanced in this book, Altizer is, in his theological writing, only very marginally religious—a judgment which he would be only too glad to accept.[40] On the other hand, more significantly, he is writing within an ostensibly religious context, he is addressing himself to problems traditionally defined as religious problems in a very positive manner. But above all his work is interpreted as directly relevant to religious problems and themes. In this last respect, it may well be that Altizer and others of the Death-of-God school constitute a focus for the 'desocialization' of the religiously committed. Immersion in the Death-of-God theology is a kind of 'cooling-out' process, easing the break with long-held religious commitments. It is a self-conceived 'religious legitimization of non-religiosity'. Thus on this ground, and on the more general one that these theologians are being taken seriously, and that their works become best-sellers, we can learn a great deal *sociologically* about the modern religious situation. Robinson's *Honest to God*, Cox's *The Secular City* and Kavanaugh's *A Modern Priest Looks at his Outdated Church* are excellent examples of this phenomenon. It matters very little in a sociological discussion of theology and religious intellectualism whether the beliefs held and the prescriptions offered are intellectually respectable or not. What is at issue is the discernment of trends and, of particular significance in the present context, the implicit or explicit reliance of these beliefs and prescriptions upon sociological insights and perspectives.

Berger has argued that the most prominent theme of radical theology during the last thirty years has been the transition from 'transcendental ontology' to 'immanent anthropology'.[41] With this judgment we can readily agree, noting in addition that the thesis implies a mid-twentieth-century resurrection of philosophical anthropology among religionists, a consummation of Feuerbach's famous statement about reducing theology to anthropology. While the Death-of-God school is the contemporary phenomenon which most demands sociological attention its significance can only be fully understood by indicating the major intellectual developments in the religious sphere of the last one hundred and fifty years or so, and characterizing the modern religious situation in general.

In the first chapter we noted how the interest in non-Christian religions grew during the nineteenth century—with the full flowering of such interest in the discipline of comparative religion in the middle of that century. The fascination which Eastern societies exerted on late eighteenth-century French philosophers, the development of missionary work on a large scale and the encyclopaedism of early sociologists, notably Comte, all contributed to a very profound awareness of the significance of non-Christian religions. The upsurge in anthropological studies of primitive and non-Christian religions in the late nineteenth and early twentieth centuries added considerably to this theme. Internally to Western Christian societies the development and pervasiveness of scientific orientations—the institutionalization of science—during the present century has also stimulated

P

Protestant theologians in particular to rethink the bases of their belief systems. More generally the rise of Communism and Fascism and the impact of the First World War, the depression years and the widening of the global system of national societies, following the trauma of the Second World War, have all constrained religious intellectuals to seek a more universalistic and all-embracing set of religious principles which will both accommodate and at the same time transcend the diversity of religious orientations of the world. Within nominally Christian societies the diagnosis that there has been a long-term trend away from religious beliefs and principles has obviously been a major motivating factor in the erection of new theologies.

(Of the factors mentioned here the most neglected in general commentaries is that of the impact and repercussions of missionary experiences. These have stimulated and facilitated much 'liberalization' amongst Western theologians. Thus both sociological and theological conceptions of 'God' and religion have been modified through study of and involvement in non-Western societies.[42])

The theologians with which we are concerned are primarily Protestant and the principal cultural areas of their operation have been Germany and the United States, with Britain an important secondary centre of discussion and dissemination.[43] Each of these societies has had a Protestant majority in its population. There have, of course, been 'radical' Catholic intellectuals. But the two most widely known, Chardin and Maritain, lived much of their lives outside of their native France and neither they nor another French Catholic, Marcel, were in any real sense Catholic intellectuals or philosophers of religion. As Hughes notes of Maritain and Marcel, they were philosophers who were also Catholics. Catholicism has been generally more immune from radical theologizing for two closely related reasons, one cultural, the other social-structural. Culturally Catholicism has been less susceptible to cataclysmic upset through scientific innovation—as is demonstrated in its reception of the Copernican revolution and the Darwinian theory of natural selection. Catholicism has been less dependent on 'natural theology' as an argument for the existence of God; and Catholic intellectuals have been 'inclined to keep their religion in one compartment of their minds and their scientific work in another'.[44] Conversely, as we have often noted, Protestants more eagerly confront secular activity. At the social level the very structure of the Catholic Church has served as a buttress against engagement with the intellectual issues posed by intellectual innovation. To be sure, Papal declarations since the end of the nineteenth century have been more or less continuously responsive to secular affairs, culminating in the Second Vatican Council. But relative to the Protestant intellectual the Catholic intellectual has been quiescent.[45] (French Catholicism has however had a negatively indirect impact on modern Protestant theology. One of the major twentieth-century reactions to Catholicism in France has been the emphasis upon *subjectivism* by French existentialists and phenomenologists. Some American radicals have in turn been influenced by the subjectivism of Frenchmen such as Sartre and Camus.[46])

It is the internal pluralism of Protestantism in the United States which has obviously played a large part in inspiring the religious-intellectual attempt to discover universal principles of faith and religiosity and which has made radical theology much less anathematic to church and denomination leaders than it might otherwise have been. Another more basic factor is the greater 'rawness' of American religious beliefs. American religion has manifested a greater vernacular form than the more historically rooted Christianity of European societies. There is therefore an important symbiosis between the 'primitivism', inspirationalism and anti-intellectualism of popular American Protestantism and the 'radicalness' of many contemporary American theologians. There is in fact a tradition of *flexible* adaptation of Christian beliefs and symbols in American Protestantism. The relative unimportance of theology in American church life has also been important in stimulating theologians to be 'popular'.

In the United States Unitarian Universalism is undoubtedly more widespread as an ethos than mere perusal of membership figures of the formal body would suggest. However this statement applies much more to the leaders of, and intellectuals within, American religious denominations than to the rank and file. There is significant evidence that there is a high degree of particularism amongst the 'ordinary' rank and file members of such movements—who wish to retain the distinctive features of the organizations to which they belong.[47] The leaders and intellectuals realizing that there are considerable costs and inefficiencies in competing with rivals on an 'all-out' basis are motivated to join in ecumenical and 'cartel' ventures in order to preserve some kind of religiosity in American society. The ecumenical choice obviously involves the merging of religious organizations; while the cartel choice involves the maintenance of at least a semblance of denominational distinctiveness—in terms of agreements among religious organizations to restrict themselves to certain geographical areas and types of social constituency.[48] Thus the American National Council of Churches promulgates very general religious principles to which none of its member organizations will have much difficulty in subscribing; while in recent years seminaries have been established on a federated basis—members of a wide range of organizations participating, including, very significantly, Roman Catholics.

Through the nineteenth century until the 1920s the dominant theological orientation within Protestantism had been that of liberalism—which put considerable emphasis upon religious experience and 'feeling for the infinite'. As Berger points out, the period of Protestant liberalism is also the period of liberal-capitalist optimism,[49] which crumbled rapidly after the events of the First World War. In Protestant liberalism, dogmatic doctrinal stances are *relativized* on the basis of the subjective experience. The so-called neo-orthodox reaction to liberalism was led by Karl Barth in Germany during the 1920s: the major point of departure was the reassertion of *objectivity* —the Christian tradition and message were external to and independent of any relativizing conceptions. The theological school known as Barthian neo-orthodoxy is very closely related to the attempt to maintain the Christian perspective and tradition in the face of the rise of Fascism. The so-called rediscovery of the corporate church took the form of the 'Confessing Church'. Many of today's advocates of church reunification refer to this period as the baseline for the hoped-for ecumenical achievements during the second half of the twentieth century. This is an important phenomenon, because the period of neo-orthodoxy marked a synchronization of both theology and attempts by church leaders to institute specific kinds of religious organization. For although neo-orthodoxy stressed the objective validity of Christian doctrine and concomitantly rejected the validity of autonomous subjective relativizations of it, it also safeguarded the mainline Protestant churches from the divisive effects of independent interpretations of the Christian gospel: 'Put a little crudely, the objectivity of the tradition having been defined as independent of all . . . contingencies, "nothing can really happen" to the theologian.'[50] It is not difficult to see how this theological position could appear as a reliable rock on which to stand against the shifting tides of an age in turmoil. Wherever this kind of objectivity can be plausibly asserted, to this day it serves as an 'Archimedean point from which, in turn, all contradictory definitions of reality may be relativized'.[51]

It is in this light that we may view such ecumenical ventures as the Consultation on Church Union in the U.S.A.,[52] where the operating principle appears to be 'Doctrine divides, service unites'. A derivative of this is the idea of 'getting on with the job while the theologians talk'. Such views are manifestations of the differentiation of church leadership from theological reflection. The relationship between the two is a kind of virtuous circle. Ecumenical moves give more leeway to radical theology; the latter's emphases upon universalism and generality serve to dampen down doctrinal differences (at least within Protestantism); while the organizational preoccupations of church leaders provide the universalistic setting necessary for the adumbration of radical perspectives. There are, of course, denominations and churches which seek to retain a rather more clear-cut orthodox stance, even when engaged in ecumenical ventures. (In fact ecumenical consultation *may* promote the sharpening of doctrinal differences.[53]) In this case the emphasis upon any kind of orthodoxy will entail a particularism unconducive to radical theologizing. There is obviously a strong group within the Roman Catholic hierarchy committed to this position.

The rallying symbols of radical theology are fairly well known—de-mythologization; religionless Christianity; death of God; and so on. The key figures either symbolically or intellectually have been Bonhoeffer and Bultman (in Germany), the Niebuhr brothers,

Tillich and the Death-of-God school (in the U.S.A.) and John Robinson (Britain). Barthian neo-orthodoxy has been vitally important in the development of the radical perspectives, through its emphasis upon the 'Archimedean point'. Many of the radicals have been highly critical of religion. Theology to them is not about religion, but about God (dead or alive). 'Religion' in these terms has to do with forms of organization and worship which are at odds with the fundamental issue of man's relationship to God and/or his acting responsibly and in accord with Christian perspectives. Religion is distinguished from faith and from Christianity. The radicals can thus be accommodated to the emphasis upon transcendence and objectivity. To put the matter more precisely, the neo-orthodox movement opened up the field for radical re-casting; emphasizing the objective continuity of the Christian tradition over and beyond particularistic interpretations, and distancing God from man by making Him less easily accessible on subjective terms. In a sense then God and the Christian tradition were 'lifted' from immediate socio-cultural contexts. This lifting or raising has had the consequence of laying bare the whole of Christianity for perusal. The fact that the crisis in Christianity as perceived by the radical theologians has involved a reappraisal of the religious component in that tradition is of course the crucial point of linkage between theology and sociology. Both are interested in the conditions which produce institutional religion and the characteristics of religious forms. Rarely have such interests merged so explicitly as in Richard Niebuhr's *The Social Sources of Denominationalism*, but the same theme is present in Bonhoeffer's dismissal of 'gap religion', as we have already noted. Conventional religious orientations are instruments for accommodating men to such conditions and occurrences as sickness, death and tribulation.[54] This theme of arguing against 'religion' and in favour of 'religionless Christianity' is probably the most common denominator in the writings of the radical theologians.[55] To be free of religion in this sense is to acknowledge 'the fact' that in Bonhoeffer's terms man has 'become of age'—which, as we have already noted, is a keynote of the sociological perspective which we depicted earlier on the basis of Durkheim's work. But if this is a very common element in the writings of radical theologians the meanings ascribed to it vary considerably. Basically the axis of variation concerns the extent to which the theologian in question views socio-cultural life as manifesting the quality of *sacred imma-nence*.

Shiner has usefully analysed modern theology in terms of a polar continuum, varying between an emphasis upon dialectical theology and historical theology.[56] Those emphasizing dialectical processes regard 'the sacred' as richly concrete and immanent. The two most notable figures here are Eliade and Tillich.[57] At the other end of the continuum are those, like Bonhoeffer and Van Buren, who, taking a historical-developmental view of Christianity, ascribe relatively little or no significance to sacredness.[58] In the middle, between the dialecticians and the historicists lie theologians, such as Reinhold Niebuhr and Maritain, who see the sacred in a transcendental form. Thus at one extreme we have Eliade emphasizing the dialectical interplay between the sacred cosmos and the chaos of everyday experience: 'The sacred cosmos emerges out of chaos and continues to confront the latter as its terrible contrary.'[59] At the other extreme, there is van Buren, utilizing the methods of analytical philosophy to reduce Christianity to its ethical and historical dimensions. Another, slightly less 'extreme' position at the historicist end of the continuum is that of Bonhoeffer and his close adherents, who stress the historical maturation of man along the lines of Christian precepts.

But it is by no means easy to locate some of the American radicals in this schema. Altizer and Hamilton, particularly the latter, diag-nosing the death of God and maintaining contact with convention-ally accepted Christian religiosity only through a *Christological* emphasis—that is, viewing Christ as a great man whose precepts should be followed—do have definite views on the operation of the *sacred* in modern life.[60] Altizer argues that the 'radical profane' may emerge '*as* the sacred. In certain modern literary experiences of ecstasy in the midst of profanity there is a clue for developing a concept of an incarnation from within history.'[61] In another essay specifically devoted to theology in relation to American society, Altizer argues for the discovery of a meaning of America which should be 'both redemptive and apocalyptic, redemptive in the sense of America's original promise of a liberation of a universal historical liberation of humanity, and apocalyptic in the sense of the Christian hope in a new and final victory of the Kingdom of God'. Only the death of God 'can make possible the advent of a new humanity'.[62] What is quite remarkable about this kind of statement is that it is so similar to the views expressed by the sociologists Parsons and Bellah. Neither of these appears to be interested in sacredness in the sense in which Altizer is. But both stress a theme consonant with the idea of 'incarnation'. As we have noted, Parsons sees Christian values as coming to be most fully institutionalized in modern American society; while Bellah comes even closer to the Altizer statement in his analysis of American 'civil religion'.[63] Civil religion he sees as distinct from institutional religion, its central theme being 'American Israel'—Americans as the new Chosen People. Extensive immigration from Europe was analogous to the Jewish Exodus, the Civil War was a rebirth through bloodshed, death and an expiation of old sins. The third great event is now taking place. America is assuming responsibility in a revolutionary world, which can only be met either by internationalizing American civil religion or joining the latter to a new world civil religion. To pursue the former course would be Procrustean and could lead to more Vietnam-type situations. (Altizer, Parsons and Bellah all see the 'religious' promise of America as *presently* 'blotted'.)

It is apparent that the relationships between sociology and society, theology and society and between sociology and theology are very different in the American context from what they are in European and British societies. The major contrast in the first respect, the sociology/society relationship, is that whereas sociologists in Europe have tended to be alienated from their socio-cultural context and critics of it, American sociologists have occupied a more central position—a precariously institutionalized detachment, with a great emphasis upon professionalism. The theology/society relationship in American society has shown a closer involvement in, and direct concern with, the fate of the society, in contrast with the greater intellectualism of European theology. (A crucial exception to this generalization arises in connection with the theological response to the First World War and particularly the 'resistance theologies' adumbrated by some German Protestants during the Nazi period—

which as we have seen has had an impact on modern American theology.) In sum, the theological tradition has been more autonomous in Europe, partly because it has been so largely Catholic. The consequences of these relationships, and the fact that America, unlike Europe, has had no really significant tradition of anti-religion, are a greater popularization of theology and an intellectual interpenetration of theology and sociology in the American setting. Thus the following statement of Parsons is one which is, in terms of the above considerations, typical of an American posture:

> ... social sciences must soon in some sense assume the position, among the secular discipline groups, which has, in relation to theology, been historically occupied by the humanities. It is here that 'spirit' (almost in the German sense of *Geist*) and 'world' with its connotations even of the physical world, most intimately meet. For theologians to center their worldly cognitive attention only on the humanities is too easy, since they are basically 'religious' anyway. To be completely preoccupied with their relation to natural science on the other hand bypasses the critical 'human' problems. It is in the social sciences that the intellectual battles concerning the meaning of the relation between the ordered 'creation' which is independent of man, his interests, and his will and the process of 'creative action' in which man is the divinely appointed responsible agent will have to be worked out.[64]

There is then a strong immanentist theme common to some radical theologians and some sociologists. On the sociological front it is no accident or coincidence that those like Parsons and Bellah who, with reservations, favour the emergent civil religion, also hold to a sociological position, one combining functionalist and evolutionary orientations, which has frequently been charged with manifesting immanentist attributes.[65] In the functionalist emphasis immanentism appears in the view that there is a general tendency for societies to move automatically to a state of equilibrium following a disturbance in that society's 'normal condition'; and in the belief that societies call forth certain social processes and institutions—talking generally in the language of *necessity*. In its evolutionary focus the structural-functional position often tends also to speak in the language of necessity as if there were inbuilt directing agencies in human societies, and to see societies *unfolding* along particular lines of evolution or development according to some preformed programme of change.[66] The immanentism which has permeated not only the writings of radical theologians, but also many aspects of intellectualist American Protestantism is basically secular. In terms of the definition of religion utilized in this book it is not in any strict sense religious. There is no *otherness* about the operative forces, little indication of a deeper or higher reality to be attained. (It should be emphasized that some contemporary theologians stand out strongly against the immanentist type of thinking. Vahanian argues that the conception of an immanentist world has involved *the reduction* of Christianity to the status of a civic religion.[67])

Religion in Relation to Psychiatry and Psychology

Klausner has extensively analysed the relationship between religion and science at the level of the practitioner—specifically the relationship between the ministerial role and the psychiatric role.[68] In early classical society there was no specialized differentiation of scientific healing and religious healing. But gradually science became autonomous in this domain, with medicine eventually emerging as an independent branch of applied science. Psychiatry itself is a relative newcomer as a specialism within medicine. 'Religion, for its part, underwent a parallel differentiation. For centuries pastoral, sacerdotal and educational activities were intertwined. Gradually, different churches or, within a church, different orders or roles occupied themselves more with one of these activities than with the others. The pastorate has but recently emerged as a specialized ministerial role.'[69] The nineteenth-century clash between science and theology obscured the common concerns of psychiatry and pastoral care, in spite of their contemporaneous crystallization.

> Yet each constituted the world in which the other lived. Theologians were surrounded by a spreading scientific hegemony. Some accepted the new scientific revelation of the

physical universe and awaited archeological authentication of Holy history and philological insights in Holy Writ. Many scientists had grown up in a church atmosphere and some were ministers' sons. Even those who had abandoned religion were faced with patients speaking in religious tongues. At the dawn of the twentieth century, religion and psychiatry were related like the tree tops of a jungle rain forest. Branches of the tallest trees might intertwine above separate trunks, but there was scant awareness of the roots knotted around one another.[70]

The relationship between science and religion, at all levels, from the practical to the philosophical and theoretical, was extremely complex during the second half of the nineteenth century, following the rapid developments in various branches of physical and natural science—the focal point of which was the Darwinian theory of biological evolution.[71] As Wilson points out we may with hindsight see that 'the confrontation of science and religion was . . . misunderstood . . . in the nineteenth century, and by fundamentalists until very recent times, and in some movements still'.[72] He convincingly argues that the 'real' danger to religion lay mainly in the increasing prestige of science. That this was the more salient factor is well illustrated by the rapid diffusion of various images of science well beyond the circles of intellectuals and the well-educated. The negative image of science was a major rallying point of fundamentalist movements in the late nineteenth and early twentieth centuries, especially in the U.S.A., where it was dramatized in the Scopes Trial of 1924.[73] The positive image has an equally widespread impact in middle-class and lower-middle-class circles, leading to the development of various para-religious and New Thought movements in Protestant societies, notably again the U.S.A. Christian Science is the best known of these. But spiritualism and theosophy were also important developments in this context. Spiritualism basically involved the idea of putting the problem of human survival and immortality of the soul to empirical, 'experimental test'.[74] Christian Scientists have attempted with no mean success to combine the 'scientific' and the religious roles, while on 'the other side of the fence' the rise of para-psychology has represented a scientific attempt to

preserve both a religious and scientific focus under the same intellectual umbrella. In the mid-twentieth century one of the most intriguing phenomena of this kind is manifested in the widespread, and
apparently increasing, subscription to astrological beliefs. Maître has
tried to account for the increasing vogue of the latter in France. The
'official' prestige of science and the claims made on its behalf have
not been (and probably cannot be) matched by the appropriate range
of scientific *knowledge*. Given this circumstance, plus the declining
significance and credibility of orthodox religion, many people have
turned to astrology as a form of speculation clothed in secular-
scientific form—in order 'to get answers to the vital questions left
open by science'.[75]

In the case of the minister-psychiatrist relationship we find a
similar case of mixing. Gradually a definite religio-psychiatric movement has developed, mainly in the U.S.A., during the past seventy-
five years or so, culminating in such bodies as the Religio-Psychiatric
Clinic in New York and the Academy of Religion and Mental
Health. The actual proportions of psychiatrists and ministers respectively who participate in the movement are small and the interchange
is 'riven with incompatible norms'.[76] But we note more generally
that the impact of psychiatry and psychoanalysis upon the minister's
role definition has been much greater than the focus on the specific
religio-psychiatric role would suggest. This second point leads us to
a different level of analysis—away from the straightforwardly
practitioner role to that of more general ideas concerning religious
orientations in relation to scientific ideas about the 'quality' of man.

We have already noted that much of modern psychology is
behaviourist and determinist in orientation and to that extent
basically incompatible with a religious orientation.[77] Moreover (non-
behaviourist) Freudian psychoanalysis is in its pristine form also
fundamentally antagonistic to religion.[78] But on the other hand there
have been meeting points between the role of the religious preacher
and the role of the psychologist, where the role of the psychologist
has been 'bent' in the direction of a popularized focus upon the
adjustability of individuals. Fromm has drawn a useful distinction
between psychoanalysis which aims primarily at *social adjustment*
and psychoanalysis which aims at *cure of the soul*.[79] The social adjust-

ment type of orientation has been extremely influential in various types of inspirational religious teaching and in the writings particularly of Norman Vincent Peale.[80] The basic theme in this type of instrumental approach to religion is that of the good which religion can do for the individual, the internal satisfactions derived from it in terms of functioning efficiently and successfully in the wider society. In contrast, psychoanalysis, in spite of its pristine antireligiosity, has fused with certain forms of religious prescription in the sense of 'caring for' the individual. In these terms the religious orientation shifts *away* from an explicit concern with a relationship to God, to a concern with the inner richness of human experience and the intrinsic worth of human relationships. Similarly, the psychoanalytic focus shifts in the direction of an explicit concern with man's humanity and sociality. The convergence is basically a *humanistic* one. Fromm notes in his approving comment on this convergence a statement of Abbé Pire: 'What matters is not the difference between believers and unbelievers, but between those who care and those who do not care.'[81]

Those religious practitioners, preachers and intellectuals who have subscribed to the social adjustment conception of religious fulfilment for the individual are offering a kind of challenge to sociology because they are taking the situations to which the religious individual can and should adjust as given, as unproblematic; whereas it is precisely those situations in which the sociologist is primarily interested. Many of the radical theologians, those often eschewing concern with the religious individual as such, have subscribed to the situational-ethical position—that view which maintains that individual behaviour should depend on social circumstances and that the guiding principle should be love for others.[82] *Most* sociologists would agree that no social system is viable in these simple terms, while the dividing line between the radical-theological advocacy of situational ethics can very easily shade into the type of instrumental religiosity so prominent in the writings of a Norman Vincent Peale. Indeed some have claimed that even Tillich's recommendation that the achievement of ultimacy is the peak religious experience and the concern with problems of ultimacy is the definitive religious orientation can be squared with Peale's emphasis upon inner satisfaction.

The Scientific Stance

We stated in the first chapter that scientific and religious orientations were in opposition and yet we have seen in the present chapter that religion has, admittedly at considerable cost to its integrity, managed to achieve a series of *modi vivendi* with scientific orientations, especially during the past one hundred years or so. These have either taken a para-scientific form, as with Christian Science, where the 'religious cost' is relatively low, or they have involved a more thoroughgoing accommodation amounting to rapprochement. In the para-scientific case the *modus vivendi* is achieved only in terms of vague scientific language and a focus upon the substance of certain branches of natural science. Norms of science, such as scepticism and disinterestedness in the outcome of inquiry and analysis, are necessarily eschewed, if a supernaturally oriented religiosity is to be maintained.[83] The more thoroughgoing type of accommodation is manifested only within the confines of the religious intelligentsia—reaching its extreme in the willingness to accept the 'theological negation of theology'. It is thus at the point where the norms of scientific endeavour come to be taken very seriously that the religious orientation is at considerable risk. Such norms may be embraced either by explicit intent—as with some of the most prominent Death-of-God theologians—or *by default*.[84] A good example of such encapsulation is provided by that stream of modern theology which stresses the need for de-mythologization of religious beliefs. The argument that conceptions of God as 'being out there' or 'in the sky' are inappropriate both to modern modes of expression and, particularly, to the structural and experiential circumstances of modern societies *should* logically lead the advocate into the arena of detached discussion of explaining why, for example, medieval Europe subscribed to such beliefs.[85]

Circumstantially, then, even in the absence of a self-declared attempt to cross into the scientific camp, the religious intellectual not only frequently comes to adopt a generally scientific style of discussion, he also increasingly encounters sociological problems. It would appear that it is the combination of the relatively detached scientific stance and the substantive concern with 'sociological' problems which therefore makes for the maximum degree of 'religious fragility'.[86] This observation obviously applies only to those who come to the problems in question from an initially religious position. There are others who appear to embark on the analysis of such issues from an initially detached position. In these cases 'religious' or 'sacred' can readily be applied philosophically to various aspects of the general socio-cultural condition.[87] This is the case with Luckmann's analysis. Eliade's procedure is similar: he argues that a sacred cosmos is continuously posited and revised on the basis of man's experience of worldly chaos. (We may fruitfully compare such positions with that of Parsons. When required to confront religious and sociological perspectives, Parsons argues that sociologists have discovered that empirically our socio-cultural situation *is* basically an *ordered* one. In one obvious sense this puts him at odds with Eliade; and yet for Parsons and many other sociologists order exists in the socio-cultural situation largely because of our normative conceptions of the way the system works.)

For sociology to arise in modern societies it was necessary that the recognition of man's capacity for self-reflection become fairly explicit. Sociology like any other activity is susceptible to the control effects of culture. It follows that cultural changes in Western societies increasingly placed a premium upon the reflectiveness of man in the period prior to the diffusion of sociological notions among groups of intellectuals. It may well be that it is the belief in man's capacity for reflection about his own circumstances which is the major long-term contribution of Christianity—a view which diverges somewhat from Weber's emphasis upon the Christian contribution as being the development of rationality. But just as Altizer can in effect speak of the theological analysis of theology— turning theology upon itself—so we have in this book talked a great deal in terms of the sociological analysis of the sociological perspective. Where such successive regressions of turning perspectives 'on to themselves' lead is obviously a question which cannot be answered. In principle, the fact that it cannot be answered will probably remain the ultimate defence of the religious perspective itself.

Notes to Chapter 7

1. In addition to previous citations, see Oliver R. Whitley, *Religious Behavior: Where Sociology and Religion Meet*, Englewood Cliffs, 1964.

2. Conflicts between the sociologist's definition of religion and those of religious adherents, practitioners and intellectuals raise again the thesis discussed at some length by Peter Winch, *The Idea of a Social Science*, op. cit. (See above, p. 77, n. 81.) Winch's argument that sociology as a science interested in objective laws and generalizations is illegitimate comes to a head in relation to the present analysis when he maintains that if an individual says an activity is religious the analytic observer must treat it as such (p. 87). The purposefulness, subjectivity and *rule-governed* nature of socio-cultural life make the search for causal regularities impossible, says Winch. His argument has been rebutted by sociologists on a number of occasions. But in one minor sense this book persistently acknowledges the significance of 'the Winch problem'. That is, we have paid a lot of attention to the norms and language of the religiously committed. But we also do the same with *sociologists*. Sociology is no less a socio-cultural activity than the phenomenal activity which the sociologist studies—nor is Winch's activity as a philosopher. As we shall argue a great deal rests in such a debate on the *reflective* attributes of human beings and to this extent all human beings are, as a matter of degree, sociologists. Thus the search for objective 'laws' is itself part and parcel of the socio-cultural condition. Sociology is in this respect merely an institutionalized and specialized concentration on something which is inherent in the human, but especially Christian condition. For reviews of Winch's thesis, see, *inter alia*, Lukes, 'Some Problems about Rationality', op. cit., and Alasdair MacIntyre, 'The Idea of a Social Science', *Aristotelian Society, Supplementary Volume*, LXI (1967), pp. 95-114. See the very effective criticisms in Ernest Gellner, 'The Entry of the Philosophers', *Times Literary Supplement*, April 4, 1968, pp. 347-9.

3. On societal values in relation to the practice of sociology, see Talcott Parsons, *Sociological Theory in Modern Society*, New York, 1967, chs. 3, 5 and 6. Cf. Charles Taylor, 'Neutrality in Political Science', in Peter Laslett and W. G. Runciman (eds.), *Philosophy, Politics and Society: Third Series*, Oxford, 1967, pp. 25-57.

4. For the cognitive structures of science and religion see Harold K.

Schilling, *Science and Religion*, London, New York, 1963. For a brief survey of the modern debate about the significance of cognition in religion and theology, see Jules Laurence Moreau, 'Theology and Language', in William A. Beardslee (ed.), *America and the Future of Theology*, Philadelphia, 1967, pp. 52–75. (One of the classic statements in an anthropological context is that of Malinowski, op. cit.) The following, highly instructive, discussion was published too late for consideration here: Ian G. Barbour, *Issues in Science and Religion*, London, 1968.

5. Martin, *Pacifism*, op. cit., p. 13. For the historical and analytic continuities between classical Christian and modern sociological accounts of social inequality, see Stanislaw Ossowski, *Class Structure in the Social Consciousness*, London, New York, 1963.

6. Martin, *Pacifism*, loc. cit.

7. A third and frequently more effective rivalry has to do with the greater *prestige* of science in modern industrial societies. See below, p. 219. Cf. Bryan Wilson, *Religion in Secular Society*, op. cit., pp. 47 ff.

8. For the intellectual changes within the history of Christianity which very gradually facilitated the crystallization of a definite sociological perspective, see, *inter alia*, J. B. Bury, *The Idea of Progress*, London, 1921. See also Harry Elmer Barnes and Howard Becker, *Social Thought from Lore to Science*, New York, London, 1952. For discussion of the crucial late eighteenth-century period see Carl Becker, *The Heavenly City of the Eighteenth Century Philosophers*, op. cit. Much more generally see Lovejoy, *The Great Chain of Being*, op. cit. For a good discussion of sacred and religious themes in the work of the classical sociologists, see Robert A. Nisbet, *The Sociological Tradition*, New York, 1966, pp. 174–220.

9. For Comte's emphatic insistence on the abstract status of the individual as opposed to the concreteness of society, see August Comte, *A Discourse on the Positive Spirit* (trans. Edward Spencer Beesley), London, 1903, pp. 117–18.

10. Dahrendorf, *Essays in the Theory of Society*, op. cit., p. 77.

11. This of course applied particularly to the early writings of Marx. See the somewhat exaggerated depiction of the 'religious Marx' in Robert Tucker, *Philosophy and Myth in Karl Marx*, Cambridge, 1961. See also the brilliant discussion of broader issues in Eugene Kamenka, *The Ethical Foundations of Marxism*, London, 1962.

12. Witness the recent upsurge in writings on the theme of alienation, notably amongst sociologists in France. The rapid diffusion of Marxist

Q

beliefs and values amongst French intellectuals in the immediate post-1945 period involved a significant convergence with left-wing Catholicism. See Jean Lacroix, *Marxism, existentialisme, personnalisme: presence de l'éternité dans le temps*, Paris, 1949. See more generally H. Stuart Hughes, *The Obstructed Path: French Social Thought in the Years of Desperation 1930–1960*, New York, 1967, *passim*, but esp. pp. 161–3. In Germany and America, the Frankfurt school of sociology, notably Herbert Marcuse, has focused particularly on the quality of man as such—through a selective synthesis of the writings of Marx and Freud. See, *inter alia*, Herbert Marcuse, *One Dimensional Man*, London, New York, 1964; *Eros and Civilization*, Boston, 1966 (new ed.).

13. So frequently is this asserted that the list would fill pages of this book. See in particular Tucker, op. cit. (Many have tried, like Tucker, to discredit Marx's general theory through a demonstration of its religious messianism, fervour and so on. There is something ironic about this view. Even more questionably, the attempt to discredit Marx or Marxism on the grounds of his or its religious underpinnings is a rather gross example of the commission of the *genetic fallacy*; i.e., that the truth or falsehood of a theory can be judged in terms of its psychological or social sources. This kind of perspective must be clearly distinguished from the dialogues between Christians and Marxists which have increased in popularity in the last few years. Here the ostensible intention is often to disclose common foci and interests of the two stances. For example, see the interchange between Roger Garaudy ('Christian-Marxist Dialogue') and Johann Baptist Metz ('The Controversy About the Future of Man') in *Journal of Ecumenical Studies*, 4 (Spring, 1967), pp. 207–22 and 223–34.) The Marxist, Lucien Goldmann, deliberately traces the Christian-religious origins of Marxist thought and stresses the act of faith (in the future, which men make for themselves in and through history): *The Hidden God* (trans. Philip Thody), op. cit.

14. Dahrendorf, op. cit., pp. 19–87.

15. See the excellent general discussion of scientific, including sociological, ideas in Robert K. Merton, *On Theoretical Sociology*, New York, 1967, pp. 1–37.

16. And of course one can go back to ancient philosophers for such views; although not in such clearly differentiated form. For example, Cornford describes Plato as having made 'the last and greatest attempt to formulate the mystical faith in rational terms'. F. M. Cornford, *From Religion to Philosophy*, p. 142. Quoted in Madge, *Society in the Mind*, op. cit., p. 43.

17. For a brief survey see Roland Robertson, 'Social System', in G. Duncan Mitchell (ed.), *A Dictionary of Sociology*, London, New York, 1968, pp. 191–3.

18. In this perspective the analogy of the theatrical role is taken to its ultimate extreme. In more recent work Goffman has supplemented this with an emphasis upon the colour of the individual being involved in a series of 'gambling', risk-taking and 'strategic' situations. Erving Goffman, *Interaction Ritual*, Garden City (New York), 1967, esp. pp. 149–270.

19. See especially, *The Social Construction of Reality*, op. cit. See also Peter Berger and Stanley Pullberg, 'Reification and the Sociological Critique of Consciousness', *History and Theory*, V (1965), pp. 198 ff.

19a. But cf. Berger, *A Rumor of Angels*, op. cit.

20. Thus notwithstanding its sympathy for Marxism and a tendency to speak in economic determinist terms, we must clearly separate this perspective from those which have attempted a more explicit fusion of Marxist and phenomenological thought, such as Sartre, whose work in some ways is very congruent with some of the substantive concerns of a Christian orientation. This is well-illustrated in his conceptions of *bad faith (mauvais foi)* and 'authenticity'. Authentic men choose on behalf of mankind, make choices for freedom. (See Jean-Paul Sartre, *Existentialism* (trans. Bernard Frechtman), New York, 1947.) Sartre's great emphasis upon human choice, upon consciousness being for itself (*pour soi*) and upon the 'projects' which give meaning to the life of individual men and women has led to a critical confrontation of the relationship between subjective orientations and actions and objective constraints on such orientations and actions. See in particular Jean-Paul Sartre, *The Problem of Method* (trans. Hazel Barnes), London, 1963. The concern to preserve at all costs the free creativity, the *praxis* of man, leads in effect to the denial of the validity of sociology as normally accepted. For an approach which emphasizes human praxis and the significance of individual and collective purposefulness over against objective constraints, yet remains within the fairly well-accepted domain of sociology, see Alain Touraine, *Sociologie de l'Action*, Paris, 1961. See also in different vein Alfred Schutz, *The Phenomenology of the Social World* (trans. George Walsh and Frederick Lehnert), Evanston, 1967. (For the notion of the authentic *society*, see Amitai Etzioni, *The Active Society*, Glencoe, 1968, ch. 21. Much of Etzioni's discussion complements the views put forward in this chapter.)

21. Dahrendorf, op. cit., p. 87.

22. Ibid., p. 95.

23. Ibid., p. 101.

24. For an outstanding discussion of role analysis and adjacent themes see S. F. Nadel, *Theory of Social Structure*, London, 1957.

25. William Kolb, 'Images of Man and the Sociology of Religion', *Journal for the Scientific Study of Religion*, 1 (October, 1961), pp. 5–22.

26. Talcott Parsons, 'Comment on William Kolb, "Images of Man and the Sociology of Religion"', *Journal for the Scientific Study of Religion*, 1 (October, 1961), pp. 22–9.

27. For a good general discussion of the institutionalization of religion, see Thomas F. O'Dea, 'Five Dilemmas in the Institutionalization of Religion', op. cit., pp. 30–9. For another critique of Parsons' general conception of religious phenomena, see Thomas F. O'Dea, 'The Sociology of Religion', *American Catholic Sociological Review*, 15 (1954), pp. 73–103. For a defence see P. L. Pemberton, 'An Examination of Some Criticism of Talcott Parsons' Sociology of Religion', *Journal of Religion*, 36 (1956), pp. 241–56.

28. 'Comment on William Kolb . . .', op. cit.

29. Aron, op. cit., p. 9. See particularly Émile Durkheim, *The Division of Labour* (trans. George Simpson), Glencoe, 1947.

30. The respective conceptions of what the division of labour consisted in also differed somewhat. For a useful comparison of Marx and Durkheim see Steven Lukes, 'Alienation and Anomie', in Laslett and Runciman (eds.) 1967, op. cit., pp. 134–56.

31. To this extent there is an overlap here with the views of Marx, Sartre and others. But the conception of integral man and the task of sociology advanced here says nothing about economic determinism or the primacy of economic factors in the operation of society. Nor does it rest on or imply a general philosophy of history. Emphatically it does proclaim the moral viability of scientific sociology. But on the other hand it implies nothing of the Comtean kind of prescription—i.e., that sociology itself becomes an ethical system. It merely sees sociology as having an inherent capacity to promote human freedom, but at the same time fully acknowledging that sociology or a general sociological orientation may disclose limits on human action which many may find uncomfortable. As I see it this is one of the major themes in Gouldner's excellent discussion of the *raison d'être* of social theory. Alvin W. Gouldner, *Enter Plato: Classical Greece and the Origins of Social Theory*, op. cit.

32. See particularly Peter Berger, 'Towards a Sociological understanding of Psychoanalysis', *Social Research*, 32 (Spring, 1965), pp. 26ff. See also Philip Rieff, *The Triumph of the Therapeutic*, London, New York, 1966. See also below, p. 221.

33. The most extreme warning against such a procedure is supplied by the militant anti-intellectualism of fundamentalist Protestants in the U.S.A. In the 1920s anti-intellectualism and anti-German sentiment fused into radical criticism of German Biblical scholarship and theology. Richard Hofstadter, *Anti-Intellectualism in American Life*, op. cit., p. 133.

34. We have concentrated very much here on conceptions of individual man and man in general. But there is, of course, also the collective, societal aspect of the problem to which some modern theologians have directed their attention, as have religious intellectuals. The 'political' aspect of religiosity is stressed in Harvey Cox, *The Secular City*, op. cit., and *On Not Leaving it to the Snake*, New York, 1967. (Cox has been critical of the Death-of-God theologians.) For a provocative discussion of the sociologist's capacity to improve the quality of societies as such, see Nathan Glazer, 'The Ideological Uses of Sociology', in Paul F. Lazarsfeld *et al.* (eds.), *The Uses of Sociology*, New York, 1967, pp. 63–77. See Etzioni, *The Active Society*, op. cit.

35. Weber, *The Sociology of Religion*, op. cit., p. 124.

36. Ibid., pp. 124–5.

37. Ibid., p. 125.

38. It is worth noting here that in England the drop in the proportion of clergymen who have had a university education in theology has been accompanied by an increase in the number of lay people who have obtained theological degrees. See T. O. Ling, 'Religion, Society and the Teacher', *Modern Churchman*, X (1967), pp. 142–51.

39. Thomas J. J. Altizer, 'Creative Negation in Theology', *Christian Century*, July 7, 1965, p. 864.

40. As is apparent in, for example, Altizer and Hamilton, *Radical Theology and the Death of God*, op. cit. More generally see the recent Thomas J. J. Altizer (ed.), *Toward a New Christianity*, New York, 1968.

41. Berger, 'The Sacred Canopy', op. cit.

42. See, *inter alia*, Gerald H. Anderson (ed.), *The Theology of the Christian Mission*, New York, 1961; Charles W. Form (ed.), *Christianity in the Non-Western World*, Englewood Cliffs, 1967.

43. Much work has been done in England in the *philosophy* of religion. Jewish theology unfortunately gets little or no attention here. It must be emphasized again that what follows is not intended in any way to deal with theologians in terms of their theological excellence, but rather their sociological significance.

44. Hughes, *The Obstructed Path*, op. cit., p. 252. This is a representation of views expressed in Stephen Toulmin, 'On Teilhard de Chardin', *Commentary*,

XXXIX (March, 1965), pp. 53-4. See also Thomas Kuhn, *The Copernican Revolution*, New York, 1962 (Paperback edition). For a brief discussion and presentation of Maritain's work, see Will Herberg (ed.), *Four Existentialist Theologians*, Garden City, New York, 1958, pp. 27-96.

45. (It must be emphasized that this book was completed before the recent controversy within the Catholic Church over birth control methods.) For the U.S.A. see Hofstadter, op. cit., pp. 136-41. In the last few years some American Catholic priests and those of other nationalities, most notably Dutch priests, have adopted deviant doctrinal positions, while Spanish priests have been prominent in the articulation of protest against the Franco regime. See also Ivan Vallier, 'Religious Elites: Differentiations and Developments in Roman Catholicism', in S. M. Lipset and Aldo Solari (eds.), *Elites in Latin America*, pp. 190-232.

46. Of course it is not simply French existentialism which has been important here. Other European sources have been of probably greater importance —notably the work of Kierkegaard. See Herberg (ed.), ibid., *passim*.

47. See Glock and Stark, *Religion and Society in Tension*, op. cit., ch. 5; Charles Y. Glock *et al.*, *To Comfort or to Challenge*, Berkeley, 1967.

48. See, *inter alia*, Robert Lee, *The Social Sources of Church Unity*, New York, 1960; and Peter Berger, 'A Market Model for the Analysis of Ecumenity', *Social Research*, 30 (Spring, 1963), pp. 77-93.

49. Berger, *The Sacred Canopy*, p. 159. See also V. A. Demant, *Religion and the Decline of Capitalism*, London, 1952.

50. Berger, op. cit., p. 162.

51. Ibid.

52. The Consultation on Church Union includes branches of Methodism (including Negro branches) and Presbyterians and Episcopalians, Disciples of Christ, Unitarians and members of the United Church of Christ. It should be noted that the Church of South India, often held up as a model of church unification, was established in response to the exigencies of the missionary situation. See B. G. M. Sundkler, *The Church of South India*, London, 1954.

53. For some important aspects and concrete examples of ecumenicism, see Nils Ehrenstrom and Walter G. Muelder (eds.), *Institutionalism and Church Unity*, London, New York, 1963.

54. Dietrich Bonhoeffer, *Prisoner for God* (ed. Eberhard Bethge, trans. Reginald H. Fuller), New York, 1953. See also Martin Marty (ed.), *The Place of Bonhoeffer*, New York, London, 1962.

55. Or to argue that this is a post-Christian age, Christianity being synonymous with (undesirable) religiosity. Gabriel Vahanian, *The Death of God*, New York, 1961, pp. 49-51.

56. Larry Shiner, 'Toward a Theology of Secularization', *Journal of Religion*, LXV (October, 1965), pp. 219–95. See also Shiner, *The Secularization of History*, Nashville, 1966.

57. For the thought of Paul Tillich see especially *Systematic Theology*, Vols. 1–3, Chicago, 1951–63; and *The Courage to Be*, New Haven, 1952, London, 1962.

58. See Paul van Buren, *The Secular Meaning of the Gospel*, New York, 1963, London, 1965.

59. Berger, *The Sacred Canopy*, op. cit., p. 27. See Eliade, *Cosmos and History*, op. cit.

60. The Christological emphasis is particularly strong in the works of Hamilton. As we have noted, Altizer takes the idea of God literally being dead most seriously. Christian argues that for Hamilton 'the death of God is not taken with ultimate seriousness'. (C. W. Christian, 'The New Optimism and the Death of God', in Christian and Wittig (eds.), op. cit., p. 98.) He argues that even in the case of Altizer a 'hidden God' is detectable. (Ibid., p. 97.) See also more generally Bryan R. Wilson, 'God in Retirement?', *Twentieth Century* (Autumn, 1961), pp. 19–27.

61. Thomas J. J. Altizer, *Mircea Eliade and the Dialectic of the Sacred*, Philadelphia, 1963.

62. Thomas J. J. Altizer, 'Theology and the Contemporary Sensibility', in Beardslee (ed.), op. cit., p. 15. (Cf. the classic H. R. Niebuhr, *The Kingdom of God in America*, Hamden (Connecticut), 1956.) In locating Altizer as having an historical conception of God and Christianity, it should be noted that his eschatological diagnosis is that the 'sacred becomes incarnate in the profane . . . Christian dialectical understanding of the sacred must finally look forward to the resurrection of the profane in a transfigured and thus finally sacred form'. Altizer in Altizer and Hamilton, op. cit., p. 155. There is a more explicitly 'hopeful' theology developing among both Protestant and Catholic theologians in Europe, partly based on Marxist ideas. See, *inter alia*, Jurgen Moltmann, *The Theology of Hope*, New York, 1967.

63. Robert Bellah, 'Civil Religion in America', op. cit. See also Herberg, *Protestant, Catholic, Jew*, op. cit. For another sociologist keen to stress the sacred quality of societies see Edward Shils, 'Charisma, Order, and Status', *American Sociological Review* XXX (April, 1965), pp. 199–213. (We would reserve the term civil religion for such cases as Shintoism—where the religious component is definitely present and refers explicitly to a political entity. State Shintoism was abolished in Japan in 1945.) Long has excellently indicated some of the societal constraints at work in

this area of thinking. Writing in connection with Altizer he says: 'From a religious point of view, the American experience expresses what Rudolph Otto described as *mysterium fascinosum*. Otto describes by this term the quality of the religious object which attracts and evokes the desire for comfort, unification, and identification with the religious object. The contrasting attitude, *mysterium tremendum*, that quality which describes the distance of the object of religion from the worshipper, has been relegated to a residual category in the American experience. The deistic orientation of the founding fathers already presents us with a *deus otiosus*, a god who has removed himself from the center of this new world.' Charles H. Long, 'The Ambiguities of Innocence', in Beardslee (ed.), op. cit., p. 42. It is this, above all, which underlies the so-called 'secularity of American religion'.

64. Talcott Parsons, 'Social Science and Theology', in Beardslee (ed.), ibid., p. 155. Cf. Wilson's comment that 'once an artistic tradition has freed itself from the particulars of a given religion, it then becomes much more completely a rival to religion than science is ever likely to do'. Wilson, *Religion in Secular Society*, op. cit., p. 43. For the significance of Parsons' emphasis upon 'order' in relation to Eliade's notion of chaos, see below, p. 223.

65. See, *inter alia*, Reinhard Bendix, 'Tradition and Modernity Reconsidered', *Comparative Studies in Society and History*, 9 (1966-7), p. 324.

66. For a good exploration of the unfolding and preformist character of structural-functional theory, see Amitai Etzioni, *The Active Society*, op. cit. (The early and concluding parts of this book converge very much with the points we make in this chapter.) See also Nettl and Robertson, *International Systems and the Modernization of Societies*, op. cit., Pt. I. Structural-functionalism has in such respects some affinity to writers like Adam Smith and Hegel who used such terms as 'the invisible hand' and 'the cunning of reason'.

67. Vahanian, *The Death of God*, op. cit., pp. 199-201.

68. Samuel Z. Klausner, *Psychiatry and Religion*, New York, 1964.

69. Ibid., p. 3.

70. Ibid., pp. 3-4.

71. For a history of disputes between religion and science, see A. D. White, *A History of the Warfare of Science with Theology*, London, 1896 (2 vols.).

72. Wilson, *Religion in Secular Society*, op. cit., p. 46.

73. John Scopes was tried for using an evolutionist textbook in Tennessee. See Ray Ginger, *Six Days or Forever?*, Boston, 1958.

74. On this and related matters see Mircea Eliade, 'The Quest for the "Origins" of Religion', *History of Religions*, 4 (Summer, 1964), pp. 154–69. For brief discussions of the para-scientific and adjacent themes, see John Hick, *Philosophy of Religion*, Englewood Cliffs, 1963, chs. 3 and 4.

75. Jacques Maître, 'The Consumption of Astrology in Contemporary Society', *Diogenes*, 53 (Spring, 1966), p. 83.

76. Klausner, op. cit., p. 265 and *passim*.

77. So-called depth psychology *is* frequently held to be particularly compatible with religious interests and motivations.

78. See the excellent discussion in Philip Rieff, *Freud: The Mind of the Moralist*, loc. cit.

79. Erich Fromm, *Psychoanalysis and Religion*, New Haven, 1967 (originally published in 1950), p. 64. (For a comparison of the thoughts of Tillich and Fromm, see Guyton Hammond, *Man in Estrangement*, Nashville, 1965.)

80. For instrumental religiosity, see Louis Schneider and Sanford Dornbusch, *Popular Religion*, Chicago, 1958. On the therapeutic significance of religious ritual generally, see Wallace, *Religion: An Anthropological View*, op. cit., *passim*.

81. Fromm, op. cit., p. viii. Cf. David Bakan, *The Duality of Human Existence*, Chicago, 1966.

82. For brief surveys see the chapters entitled 'The New Ethics: "Love Alone"' and 'The New Sex Code: "Permissiveness with Affection"', in Henlee H. Barnette, *The New Theology and Morality*, Philadelphia, 1967, pp. 31–71. See also John A. T. Robinson, *Honest to God*, London, 1963; David L. Edwards (ed.), *The Honest to God Debate*, London, 1963; Joseph Fletcher, *Situation Ethics: The New Morality*, Philadelphia, 1966; John A. T. Robinson, *Christian Morals Today*, Philadelphia, 1964. For some pertinent philosophical criticisms of the situationist position, emphasizing the disconnection between religious beliefs and moral commitments in the modern historical period, see Alasdair MacIntyre, *Secularization and Moral Change*, Oxford, 1967, pp. 70 ff. and *passim*.

83. On sociological treatments of scientific norms see Norman W. Storer, *The Social System of Science*, New York, 1966.

84. They have undoubtedly been embraced most thoroughly and conscientiously by Tillich.

85. See above, p. 154. For a sociological engagement with theological issues in these terms, see Peter L. Berger, 'A Sociological View of the Secularization of Theology', *Journal for the Scientific Study of*

Religion, VI (Spring, 1967), pp. 3–16. See Robert Bellah's comment on *Honest to God*, in *Christianity and Crisis*, XXIII (November 11, 1963), pp. 200–1.

86. To speak of 'religious fragility' does not necessarily mean that modern radical theology is on the point of collapsing. In our discussion of religious sectarianism we considered the social circumstances which were productive of the maintenance of an 'epistemic community'. It is interesting to note the social mechanisms through which the epistemic community of 'non-religious theology' is maintained. Crucial in this respect have been the number of outlets available to the theologians, particularly books and periodicals. *Playboy* magazine for example has 'legitimated' Death-of-God theology, and the general discussion of morality in the past few years through the various media of communication has enabled radical theologians to occupy an interstitial area between religious institutions and discussion in the mass media of the state of society. (One suspects however that a precondition for public survival is theological novelty and sensation.)

87. See above on culture and religion, p. 94.

8

Epilogue: Secularization

Much has been written on the theme of secularization in recent years; and we have often confronted it in the present essay. However, rather than discussing the debate in elaborate detail we have chosen to focus briefly on one major aspect of the problem, in terms of the framework established in chapter three.

In addition to a distinction between cultural and social-structural dimensions of the secularization process we need to distinguish also between processes of secularization which are in the main internal to the religious sphere and those which are principally external to it.[1]* It will be seen that this is little more than a translation of the distinction in chapter two between religious and non-religious spheres.[2] Thus there are four potential sources of secularization. But since we have in one way or another at least touched upon all of these factors it is more pressing for us to point to a very much neglected aspect of the secularization theme, namely the *directions* which secularization may take. Many sociologists talk only of the secularized condition in negative terms; i.e., religion no longer exerts social or cultural control.[3] On the basis of our previous substantive discussions and the empirical evidence which we have about religious change in the modern world, presentation of the schema shown overleaf may fruitfully illuminate the main tendencies towards secularization at the *cultural* level.

The horizontal axis of this typology indicates the relationship which the believers have to religious culture. *Rentention of frame-work* means that significant tenets of religious culture are adhered to, but that a definite shift away from fully-fledged religiosity has occurred. Thus within this category are orientations which concern the 'secularization of religion' theme. *Neutralization* refers to a con-dition in which beliefs and values often implicated in religious

* Notes for this chapter begin on page 241.

culture are subscribed to, but on a non-religious basis. There is no 'otherness' with respect to a non-empirical reality. *Abandonment* is self-explanatory. The distinction between *intellectual* and *practical* bases of culture has to do with the degree to which cognitive

RELIGIOUS BELIEFS, VALUES AND SYMBOLS

	Retention of framework	Neutralization of framework	Abandonment of framework
Intellectual emphasis	(a) Rational religion	(c) Immanentism	(e) Positive atheism
Practical emphasis	(b) Instrumental religion	(d) Supernatural-ism	(f) Areligiosity

activity is valued for its own sake, an emphasis upon 'thinking things through' (intellectualism), or, on the other hand, the degree to which considerations of practical contingency are emphasized and intrinsically satisfying cognitive activity regarded as an unnecessary luxury (practicalism).[4]

(*a*) *Rational religion:* Underlying this pattern is the theme of rationalization of religious culture as adumbrated by Weber. Probably the major example of this type of secularization has been Unitarianism and its offshoots. More generally, some branches of American Puritanism have historically been extremely sceptical about many aspects of Christian belief. In the modern period Methodism and Congregationalism manifest a great deal of rational religiosity.[5] Basically rational religious commitment is one involving an inbuilt tendency to search into and justify logically the grounds for religious belief.

(*b*) *Instrumental religion:* The major manifestation of instrumental religiosity is so-called inspirational religion—religious commitment which inspires the believer to achieve 'great things'.[6] Religion is viewed as a therapy and as a tool at the individual level. More generally and macroscopically, instrumental religion is to be seen in the political deployment of religious symbols.[7] Thus secularization has proceeded distinctively in this direction at two levels, the individual and the collective. The latter is historically the older. In the modern period its definite crystallization may be seen in the political view that social discontent in England in the first half of the nineteenth century could and should be alleviated by 'more religion'.[8]

(c) *Immanentism:* Immanentist beliefs are a form of secularization, *in so far* as it is claimed that social life *in and of itself* manifests 'extra-special' qualities. The immanentism of which we speak in reference to the modern period is therefore a much diluted form of spiritual immanentism in which it is literally believed that there is what Swanson calls 'an intimate influencing of one spirit by another, the influence occurring through the actual transfer of a power from one spirit to another'.[9] The most clear-cut case of immanentist secularization is where there occurs a manifest and explicit transference of commitment from a spiritual conception within a religious tradition to a non-spiritual commitment within the historical framework of that tradition.[10] Many of today's radical theologians and religious teachers in mainline religious collectivities subscribe to non-spiritual immanentism.[11]

(d) *Supernaturalism:* The term 'supernaturalism' is employed very advisedly and tentatively. What we have in mind is in fact a rather crucial aspect of the current religious situation. It is a form of secularization which one would expect to emerge particularly from within a Catholic traditional-religious context, but not exclusively so. Supernaturalism is taken here to refer to a set of phenomena which is extremely broad in scope. It embraces astrology, alchemy, demonology, spirit fetishes and witchcraft, as well as mere superstition. The basic organizing theme is that of occultism. The extent of such phenomena cannot be estimated with anything approaching even a confident approximation, mainly because of the 'principled' secretiveness, not to speak of the illegality, which characterizes subscription to some of them. Historically, of course, many of these practices have been very significant and some have been contained within Christianity itself, notably witchcraft and belief in evil spirits. (The exorcizing of demons and spirits is still in fact carried out by some Church of England clergymen.) The multiplicity of phenomena included within this category suggests the need for greater analytic refinement, such that we could differentiate between the varieties of supernaturalism and their determinants. We have already seen that astrological beliefs may spread on the basis of a break in the plausibility of traditional religious beliefs and an internalization of the efficacy-of-science ideal coming into a dissonant relationship with scientific ignorance.[12]

In sum, supernaturalism is characterized simply by a belief in the operation of extra-human and extra-physio-chemical forces. Within this category various degrees of significance may be attached to this belief, ranging from the minimum exhibited in superstition to the maximum entailed in astrology. It is distinguished minimally from religion, including rational and instrumental religion, by its implicit denial of a moral dimension. Sometimes as in the case of demonology and satanic cults it may be explicitly immoral.

(e) *Positive atheism:* By positive atheism we mean a cultural circumstance in which the constructive virtues for the human and socio-cultural condition of an anti-religious stance are upheld. The adjective 'positive' is appropriate here also because it highlights the secularization theme. *Positive* atheism shares many of the concrete concerns of orthodox religious belief systems. Its major manifestations are in humanist movements and organizations and the academic intelligentsia.[13]

(f) *Areligiosity:* This is fairly self-explanatory. As we have seen, Weber diagnosed that industrial societies were characterized to a large extent by areligiosity—by a condition of disenchantment and lack of concern about basic problems of meaning and human significance. The industrial working class according to Weber is a major bearer of this orientation to religion. The suggestion here is that the areligious form of secularization is not by any means as significant as is implied by Weber's thesis. Certainly we have evidence of areligiosity (or negative agnosticism) being fairly widespread (as opposed to positive agnosticism, which in terms of our typology shades into positive atheism); but on the, admittedly impressionistic, evidence areligiosity in Western societies is not significantly more common than some of the other secular tendencies we have mentioned here. Areligiosity in the present sense is characterized by an acceptance of everyday realities, a reluctance to impose any kind of systematic coherence or sense of meaning to them other than their purely intrinsic qualities.

A tendency towards a greater intellectualization of modern societies would reduce the ongoing significance of instrumental religion, supernaturalism and areligiosity; conversely anti-intellectualism and popularization involve a shift from rational religion, immanentism and positive atheism to the other three types. As befits a genuinely typological formulation our six secular types are only *tendencies*. Many concrete belief systems in fact cut across our types. Frequently a basically areligious posture coexists in the same sub-culture with elements of superstition. The well-publicized subscription of certain popular singers and film stars to the teachings of an Indian *guru* combines elements of immanentism and instrumental religion. Jung's conception of the collective unconscious includes both immanentist and supernaturalist elements. Some gnostic sects combine rational religion and instrumental religion. The examples are manifold.[14]

So much for the cultural dimension of the secularization process.[15] At the *social-structural* level, the main criterion of secularization is the degree of detachment of the collective vehicles of ostensible religious commitment from that commitment.[16] Thus concern with organizational preservation *per se* is a major manifestation of secularization in social terms. It may emerge from two, often coalescing, factors: first, a diffuse commitment to the rational efficacy of the organization; and, second, a concern with the preservation or enhancement of the status of officials within the collectivity—or even simply a motivation to preserve the social standing of 'religiosity', as opposed to its implementation. (Resistance to secularization may subjectively take the form of attempts to rationalize the organization —to help the latter withstand diagnosed processes of secularization in the cultural sphere.[17])

In this note on secularization we have drawn almost exclusively on Christian examples—primarily because secularization is most easily applicable to that context. But it is possible to see many of the same processes at work in other contexts. Hinduism would appear to be particularly susceptible to the whole range of cultural directions of secularization discussed here, with Islam and Buddhism not far behind.[18] Furthermore we may see in the phenomenon which Apter describes as political religion in the newly independent societies of Africa various manifestations of instrumental religion and immanentism—and to a lesser extent rational religion;[19] while there are enough historical continuities to demonstrate that communism was an immanentist form of secularization, tending now, perhaps, outside Chinese Communism, towards the positive atheist form.

That we have said so much, especially in this and the preceding chapter, about secularization and non-religious aspects of modern social science and theology should in no way divert attention from the fact that religious phenomena are still vital topics of study in the modern world. While we have leaned heavily upon an exclusive definition of religion, and to that extent limited the range of religious themes available for analysis, we have on the other hand tried to highlight the continuities between strictly defined 'religion' and other cultural patterns in the modern world. Moreover, if the analysis is accurate in pinning down a firm, inexorable series of secularization processes and showing how sociology itself may be contributing to these, we must still be extremely wary about attributing too much significance to the present. *Presentism*, that posture which tends to claim the uniqueness of the modern period, clouds our judgment as to the long-drawn-out historical unfolding of changes we diagnose in the modern world, and also persuades us that the changes we see are inevitably coming to some early point of termination or fruition. This book should not be interpreted in such terms. Undoubtedly the past was less religious than it is often made out to be. The prevalence of the arrested forms of secularization which we have discussed seem to indicate that the mainly secular world is certainly not immediately at hand; while there remain powerful social factors making for the continuation of religious commitment in sectarian form.[20] In spite of standardization of educational systems and mass-media output, the actual range of social experiences to which industrial man is exposed is probably getting *larger*. The sociologist would be unwise not to acknowledge the possibility of new religious forms arising as a consequence of this; not to speak of confusions and tensions arising from the meeting of new cultural forms.

Although it has not been a central theme of this book, it will probably be apparent that much of the discussion has pointed to the need for a fundamental reconsideration of the type of work which is done by sociologists in the field of religion. Sociologists of religion sometimes complain that theirs is an underprivileged or deprived sub-discipline. In making this complaint they tend to speak as if it were merely a matter of persuading others to take the study of religion seriously—as if religion were a subject demanding close sociological attention, but that their colleagues with other interests did not realize this. The sociology of religion has been neglected because many have regarded it as a 'soft' subject, irrelevant to the real forces shaping modern societies and engaged in by those who have intellectual and emotional commitments outside sociology. The reassertion of 'hard' themes such as the operation of force and the significance of coercion in modern life may well accelerate this trend, notwithstanding the institutional provisions which sociologists of religion have made for themselves recently—new journals, yearbooks, conferences and so on. But on the other hand, there are important, relatively new, growth-points in the social sciences with which those interested in religion could readily relate their work: the study of communication, culture and symbols, not to speak of older preoccupations such as the analysis of identity-formation and the sociology of knowledge. 'Religion' as such is relatively neglected by those concerned with the major aspects of modern societies because in large part this neglect reflects 'real' life. But a great deal needs to be done by sociologists of religion in joining with those interested in the broader cultural themes discussed at numerous points in this book. This may well mean that in the long run the sub-discipline as such will disappear. But many of the features of human societies which have usually been connected most closely with religious phenomena will remain paramountly important.

R

Notes to Chapter 8

1. Cf. Wilson, *Religion in Secular Society*, op. cit., pp. 36ff.

2. Above, pp. 65–7.

3. In contrast to the wholehearted embracing of the secular condition by Harvey Cox. Consider the statement by Cox in which he suggests a synthesis of the work of Barth and Parsons. See John Watts Montgomery (ed.), *The 'Is God Dead?' Controversy*, Grand Rapids, 1966. For a useful survey of meanings of secularization see Larry Shiner, 'The Concept of Secularization in Empirical Research', *Journal for the Scientific Study of Religion*, VI (Fall, 1967), pp. 207–20.

4. It must be stressed that although we speak here of directions of secularization, that is shifts at the cultural level from a religious towards a less religious or non-religious condition, this does not imply that individuals as such always reach such a cultural position from a religious one. They may move between two or more of the six patterns, never having been in a religious condition at all. It is not suggested that there has been a recent historical shift from a religious cultural pattern to these six patterns. As a matter of degree, each of the six patterns can be discerned as extending far back in history.

5. In the U.S.A. the members of these denominations are much less likely to believe in the existence of the Devil, life after death, the divinity of Christ, and so on, in comparison to those of Lutheran, Baptist and Presbyterian bodies, not to speak of the sects. See Glock and Stark, *Religion and Society in Tension*, op. cit., pp. 86–122. See also Charles Y. Glock and Rodney Stark, *Christian Beliefs and Anti-Semitism*, New York, 1966, pp. 3–40.

6. See Schneider and Dornbusch, op. cit. See also A. Roy Eckhardt, *The Surge of Piety in America*, New York, 1958; and Martin Marty, *The New Shape of American Religion*, New York, 1959.

7. For American evidence see particularly Herberg, *Protestant, Catholic, Jew*, op. cit. For the political significance of religion in historical perspective, see Werner Stark, *The Sociology of Religion: Established Religion*, London, New York, 1966. See also Reinhard Bendix, *Nation-building and Citizenship*, New York, London, Sydney, 1964, ch. 3, esp. p. 68.

8. This was a position stated many times by members of political and economic elites during the period of early nineteenth-century industrialization in Britain, culminating in the first and only official census on the religious 'quality' of the nation in 1851. See K. S. Inglis, *Churches*

and the Working Classes in Victorian England, London, Toronto, 1963. See also more generally Reinhard Bendix, *Work and Authority in Industry*, New York, 1956. We should not exaggerate the modernity of this phenomenon of political manipulation of religious culture. Cf. Eisenstadt, 'Religious Organizations and Political Process in Centralized Empires', op. cit.

9. Swanson, *Religion and Regime*, op. cit., p. 5.

10. More general beliefs in the inherent spiritual qualities of a society are good examples of immanentist beliefs. Stark traces the significance of these in French, British, Russian and other societies. He sees them as clear-cut examples of religiosity as such, not examples of secularization. See Werner Stark, op. cit.

11. We have already noted strong immanentist tendencies within the work of some sociologists of religion. It should also be pointed out that the Marxist notion of dialectical processes is also strongly immanentist in tone. Another good example of a kind of immanentism is provided by the work of Marshall McLuhan. See particularly *Understanding Media*, New York, London, 1964. One of McLuhan's claims is that modern means of communication, notably television and film, with their use of tactile and visual forms of expression and their non-linear mode of statement make it possible for man 'to participate in the Body of Christ' for the first time in human history. For a useful overview see Gerald Emanuel Stearn (ed.), *McLuhan: Hot and Cool*, New York, 1967.

12. Above, p. 220. Speculatively, it seems that many people engaging self-consciously in various forms of magic do so in a purely instrumental, even tongue-in-cheek manner. That is, they do not actually 'mean' what they say and do. They may not believe it is effective and may do it simply 'for kicks'. See, for one example, the graphic description of demonstrators exorcizing evil spirits from the Pentagon in Norman Mailer, 'The Steps of the Pentagon', *Harper's Magazine* (March, 1968), pp. 94–102.

13. e.g. Huxley's 'religion' of evolutionism.

14. Troeltsch's view that mysticism would be the dominant religious form among the highly educated during the twentieth century is relevant here. The basic ingredient in Troeltsch's conception of mysticism is, as Demerath points out, the inviduation of religious experience, which embraces the atheist as well as the spiritualist. (Demerath, *Social Class in American Protestantism*, op. cit., pp. 38–9.) This conception is of a rather different order than the six directions of secularization posited here, as it cuts across all three of our intellectualist patterns. What is particularly

interesting about some intellectual beliefs at the present time is their much closer alignment to Eastern religious forms. It may be speculated that Christianity has so to speak 'done its work' in the Western world, and that the problem of motivating men to engage in economic processes in a highly activist fashion is much less significant than the problem of 'making sense' out of a situation of affluence, leisure and mobility. Hence the attractions of more passive and personal religious forms. The attractions which Zen Buddhism has had for some Western intellectuals would appear to lie particularly in what Watts describes as its emphasis upon 'feeling life instead of feeling something *about* life'. Alan W. Watts, *The Spirit of Zen*, New York, 1958 (third edition), London, 1959, p. 18.

15. For a brief attempt to bring the cultural and social dimensions together, see Robertson, 'Factors Conditioning Religious Belief', op. cit.

16. The fact that the social-structural and the individual-commitment aspects of secularization have been explored so thoroughly in other works is why we have said very little about them in this note. Previous discussions in this book have focused on some aspect of these problems. See above, pp. 138 ff. Among the many contributions which have surveyed the problem are Gibson Winter, *The Suburban Captivity of the Churches*, New York, 1961, and *The New Creation as Metropolis*, New York, 1963; Peter L. Berger, *The Precarious Vision*, op. cit., and *The Noise of Solemn Assemblies*, op. cit. For England, see Leslie Paul, *The Deployment and Payment of the Clergy*, London, 1964; Bryan R. Wilson, 'The Paul Report Examined', *Theology*, LXVIII (1965), pp. 89–103, and *Religion in Secular Society*, op. cit., *passim*. In general theoretical terms, see O'Dea, 'Five Dilemmas in the Institutionalization of Religion', op. cit. At the individual-commitment level, see, *inter alia*, Luckmann, *The Invisible Religion*, op. cit., pp. 28–40; Argyle, op. cit.; Wilson, op. cit.; and Martin, *A Sociology of English Religion*, op. cit.

17. For example, Leslie Paul, 'The Church as an Institution—Necessities and Dangers', *Journal of Ecumenical Studies*, 4 (Spring, 1967), pp. 268–79.

18. Hinduism is particularly interesting since the social-structural dimension is so crucial to secularization. The very intimate connection of *caste* and Hinduism has meant that absorption into the caste system has been the most salient form of Hinduistic conversion. This identification of Hinduism with caste structure means that attenuation of caste distinctions effectively erodes Hindu culture generally. See M. N. Srinivas, *Religion and Society among the Coorgs of South India*, Oxford, 1952.

19. Apter, *The Politics of Modernization*, op. cit.

20. Both in the sense of religious sects as such and the possible 'sectarian retreat' of churches and denominations. Witness, for example, the 'hardliners' in the Catholic hierarchy; or, in different vein, the development of Pentecostal tendencies in the Church of England—and even in some American Catholic congregations. Other aspects of religious persistence have been discussed, in *very* different terms, by David Martin. See Martin, 'Towards Eliminating the Concept of Secularization', in Julius Gould (ed.), *Penguin Survey of the Social Sciences*, London, 1965, pp. 169–82. 'Some Utopian Elements in the Concept of Secularization', *International Yearbook for the Sociology of Religion*, 1965, pp. 87–96; 'Sociologist fallen among Secular Theologians, *The Listener*, April 25, 1968, pp. 528–9.

Name Index

Subject Index